CHOICES & CHANCES

SOCIOLOGY FOR EVERDAY LIFE

CHOICES & CHANCES

SOCIOLOGY FOR EVERDAY LIFE

LORNE TEPPERMAN
UNIVERSITY OF TORONTO

ANGELA DJAO
DE ANZA COLLEGE

HBJ

Harcourt Brace Jovanovich, Publishers
San Diego   New York   Chicago   Austin   Washington, D. C.
London   Sydney   Tokyo   Toronto

Our only guides are our interests, viewed in the largest possible sense; our interests made as self-aware as possible, since it is unlikely we can attain what we do not want, and impossible to want what is not conceived as attainable.

JACQUES BARZUN*

Darwin, Marx, Wagner: Critique of a Heritage (2nd edition). Garden City, NY: Doubleday Anchor Books, 1958.

PREFACE

This book urges you to examine your goals and opportunities, then consider the chances that you will get what you want from your education, career, marriage, parenthood, and other parts of your life. It argues that we ought to live with our eyes open, gather evidence about the world, choose in our own best interests (broadly defined), and behave rationally.

People's lives are intertwined with and limited by what sociologists call *social structure*. Our life choices are shaped and limited by the choices and actions of people around us: this is sociology's most central insight. Dominant or popular ideology teaches that people generally get what they want from life, if they want it enough and acquire the right skills and credentials. Supposedly, they alone are to blame if they fail to get what they want. Yet research shows that most people do *not* get what they want, but settle for what they can get. How can we explain this fact, and what does it teach us?

Sociology—the systematic study of social relations—emerged in the nineteenth century as an attempt to understand the enormous social changes caused by the Industrial Revolution and the French Revolution. Even today sociology is, at its core, a prolonged debate about the human ability to improve social life through reason and organized action.

Sociology does not claim that people are entirely rational, or even that sociologists must be, or can be, entirely rational. But it does argue that we must all try to distinguish between beliefs and feelings on the one hand and facts and reason on the other. That is what I am urging you to do when you read this book.

None of us thinks about life in a completely rational way. Often we find it hard, almost impossible, to change the way we make life choices. We feel almost imprisoned by our fears, passions, and unexamined certainties. We may prefer to consult our feelings on major decisions, do what family and friends advise, go with hunches, or take a shot in the dark. Sometimes we even rely on luck to get us through. Yet deep down we all know that there must be a better way of making important choices.

I cannot claim that the "advice" this book offers is complete or foolproof. It is only a first approximation, and I have found it helpful in organizing my own thinking. Ideally, this book will make you wonder whether some of the things you feel sure about are really so, and it may get you thinking about the ways you make your own life choices. I assume, simply, that whatever your particular life goals may be, you are aiming to get as much satisfaction out of life—that is, *life satisfaction*—as you possibly can. All the analyses that follow are aimed toward that goal.

Research on life satisfaction has developed quite intriguingly in the past decade or two. It now offers sociology rich information about who is most satisfied with life (and various parts of life—work, marriage, and so on), under what conditions, and why.

You may choose to doubt or ignore the conclusions this book has drawn. After all, a sociological conclusion about a category of people to which you belong will not inevitably apply to you. No one knows which characteristics—alone or in combination—will guide or predict a given person's behaviour. But if we get you to analyse the way you live your life, and the choices you are making, in a different way, the book will have succeeded, whatever you decide to do.

HOW THIS BOOK RELATES TO YOUR TEXTBOOK

This book was written to supplement, not replace, the large multitopic textbook you are probably using in your introductory course. How do the two books connect?

First, your textbook may discuss sociological topics in an abstract, general way that you may have trouble relating to your own daily life. You may not see how the theories it discusses—especially those theories attributed to Marx, Weber, and Durkheim (sociology's founders)—bear on life today. This problem has led some students to believe that theorizing is something people used to do but don't do any more; or that only geniuses can make theories.

Actually, all sociologists make and test theories. Even you make theories about society. This book uses theories that can be related to those written about in your textbook. But it does not make the connection with those theories obvious; that is something your instructor may want to do in discussing this book with you. As you learn new things from this book, try connecting them to things you heard in lectures or tutorials, or read in the textbook. Everything should connect.

But theorists may not always agree. Sociology thrives on theoretical debates fueled by different assumptions about reality, findings that conflict with one another, and disagreements about the quality of certain evidence. Lively debates are the evidence of a living discipline, so do not be frustrated or annoyed if a point made in this book fails to match a point made elsewhere. Ask your instructor about the disagreement; talk about it; and think of ways to resolve it. That is how sociological research begins.

Another way that this book differs from your textbook is that it offers advice, while your textbook does not. You should not take the advice without thinking, but rather use it to sharpen your own investigation of personal goals, opportunities, and experiences. This book simply takes the sociological knowledge found in your textbook and asks, If this theory is true, what should follow? How does this affect me? Nothing will make you take a theory more seriously than if you consider whether to risk your future on its being true. So this book encourages you to think of sociological theories as predictions with important consequences for your life.

What you read in your textbook about education is agumented by what you read here about educational decisions you must make; what you read in your textbook about work, by what you read here about career choices; what you read about families in your textbook, by what you read here about marriage and parenthood; and so on. You will find a considerable overlap between this book and your textbook.

This book will make your understanding of the course textbook richer and more personal. By showing how theories can apply to your own life, this book will show the ways sociology—a living, growing discipline— can shed light on issues of immense personal and social importance.

Lorne Tepperman
Angela Djao

ACKNOWLEDGMENTS

This book was originally written for Canadian students, using Canadian data. The process of revising it for American students has proved interesting and, surprisingly enough, fairly easy; for American students have most of the same concerns as Canadian ones, and American society is, in a great many ways, very much like Canadian society. This serves to remind us that the world is becoming more and more like the "global village" Marshall McLuhan called it several decades ago.

Bringing out this American version of the book has also been eased by the excellent guidance from Harcourt Brace Jovanovich's main office in San Diego—especially from Marc Boggs, the acquisitions editor; and Julia Ross, our manuscript editor; as well as Eleanor Garner, permissions editor; Suzanne Montazer, designer; and Mandy Van Dusen, production manager. We thank them for their kindness and consummate professionalism.

We also want to thank, once again, Jack Veugelers—now a graduate student in sociology at Princeton University—for the excellent research assistance he provided while still an undergraduate at the University of Toronto, and all our colleagues who offered advice on earlier versions of the book. Finally, we are grateful to Elizabeth Clifford for creating an index for this edition.

As before, we dedicate this book to our families, who provided so much understanding support, and to our students, whose ideas and concerns were the starting point for this book.

CONTENTS

CHAPTER ONE

PATTERNS OF DESIRE:
Why You Want What You Want

INTRODUCTION

Life in a modern society is full of choices. People seem to like having choices, but choosing well is difficult and burdensome. The consequences of a wrong choice can be costly or painful. Taking responsibility for our choices is often unpleasant. We can close our eyes to choice and try to believe that there is only one way to live, but few of us these days can believe that for very long. Evidence of different kinds of lives surrounds us. The more we learn about the world, the more variety we can see, and the more things we learn to desire. We find that we can choose for or against things in a great many situations.

On the other hand, none of our choices is free. Every choice has a consequence. Every choice has a cost, if only the cost of foregoing another choice we might have made. Moreover, every choice is limited by what we know about the situation, who we are in society, what we have to trade for the thing we want. In those respects some people have more choice than others, a better choice of possible lives. But no one has unlimited choice, and no choice is cost-free. That is a condition of living.

Moreover, many major experiences in life are not chosen at all. They may include unwanted pregnancies, marriage breakdowns, forced unemployment, disabling accidents, abusive parents, betrayal by friends, the outbreak of war, and economic depression. They may also include passionate infatuation, lucky winnings, devoted friends and family, inborn skills and aptitudes, peace, and prosperity. You are not to blame for the first category of experiences, nor to be praised for the second. These are simply contexts within which you are fortunate or unfortunate enough to live your life.

Within this human condition, we all work out our life's desires. This fact never changes, only situations and desires change. So a book about life choices in America today must look at America as it exists today and ask, What do people want out of life? What satisfies them? What are people's main concerns? What kinds of people are most satisfied with their lives, and how do they get that way?

These are the kinds of questions this chapter hopes to answer. Philosophers have been discussing these questions, in one form or another, for thousands of years; the answers are important and hard to discover. We hope to begin answering these questions in a different way—a sociological way—using evidence collected from the people around us.

Answering these questions will take the whole book. In relation to life satisfaction, this chapter introduces the questions in their most general form. This chapter will discuss the kinds of people who are most satisfied.

The chapters that follow will examine particular aspects of life, and things that contribute to satisfaction in each of those "domains." Finally, we shall examine two theories that attempt to account for what people want and how satisfied they are with what they get.

People are more than a mere sum of social characteristics and psychological drives. They embody a complex mix of motives that defies easy summation. Moreover, people provide exceptions to every rule social science can devise. It is this delicacy and complexity of everyday life that makes social science challenging. But like natural scientists, historians, and novelists, sociologists seek the underlying order in apparent chaos—the laws that govern and predict tomorrow's universe. Let us begin by showing that this goal is at least approachable.

What You Want

Most of us are fairly self-centered. By that we do not mean "selfish," always putting our own interests before anyone else's. We mean we are wrapped up in our own ideas, plans, and values. We rarely take the time to think about other people's thinking. This lets us imagine that our own thoughts are unique, unlike anyone else's. We believe that the things we want to get or do, the choices we plan to make in life, and even the ways we spend our time and money are uniquely our own. We may also feel that we have unlimited opportunity to get what we want, and that with enough luck and planning, we will get it.

So, if we asked you about your own life and what the future is likely to hold, after reflecting on the particulars of your life you might tell me something like this:

> Overall, my life is going pretty well. I feel that things are going my way. I am generally pleased about having accomplished something I intended to do. Of course, sometimes I feel restless or bored or depressed. But I see my current life as close to the best life imaginable. In fact, I feel pretty certain that my life tomorrow is going to be far better than it is today.

This is what the average American adult thinks, according to surveys and studies of the quality of life in America (see Campbell, 1981). But we do not mean to suggest that everyone is the same, with the same ideas, desires, and plans. People vary a lot in all these respects, and survey data show this very clearly. With social surveys, researchers in the late 1950s began assessing people's sense of well-being. They found that a sense of well-being comes from people's perceptions of their quality of life. It comprises two central components: happiness and life satisfaction. Happiness is a spontaneous feeling reflecting the pleasant and unpleasant experiences of a person's life. Satisfaction is the judgment a person makes of his or her present compared with some appropriate standard. When people are asked questions about their sense of well-being on a national basis, survey results have consistently shown that in general Americans feel positively about their life experiences and are mostly satisfied with their life situations. The majority would say that they have had all the happiness they are entitled to.

The quality-of-life surveys also ask people to rate their lives—past, present, and future—against the worst life and the best life they could imagine. Results show that most people think they deserve a life close to the best imaginable. Moreover, the best life they can ever expect to have is also very close to the best life they can imagine.

Americans are unabashedly upbeat. Most people rate their lives—past and present—in the top half of the rating "ladder"—closer to the best life than to the worst life they can imagine. They do the same when they rate their expected future lives, believing that they will come close to the best lives they can imagine (Cantril, 1965; Cantril & Roll, 1971; Watts & Free, 1974).

In fact, Americans are among the most optimistic people in the world. A review of Gallup polls conducted in 30 countries during the 1980s reveals that most people in the world are *not* optimists (Michalos, forthcoming). Asked "So far as you are concerned, do you think that [next year] will be better or worse than [the year just ending]?" about two respondents in three indicate that they think next year will be no better, and possibly worse, than last year. By this measure, the world's greatest optimists can be found in the United States, Argentina, Greece, and Korea—where more than half of the respondents regularly expect that next year will be better than this one. By contrast, only 35 to 39 percent of Canadians, Chileans, and South African whites say that next year will be better, and they are still twice as likely to express optimism as Germans, Austrians, and Belgians.

Some people are less optimistic and more satisfied with life than others. In fact, the two sentiments are connected. What makes people vary in this way? What patterns their views?

We are tempted to say things like "Who knows why? People are just funny that way!" or "Everybody's different. There's no accounting for people's views." But to say this is to fall into the trap of being self-centered—claiming that everyone is unique and that the variation among people is infinitely great and unexplainable. We have already noted that people assess their lives in similar ways. This uniformity puts the lie to some people's belief that human behavior is beyond explaining. When people's desires and concerns differ or vary, they do so in patterned, predictable ways. It is on this fact of "patterned variation" that all social science—sociology, psychology, anthropology, and other related disciplines—rests.

Because the issue is so basic, this chapter will devote a great deal of time to showing that people's views about life vary in patterned, predictable ways. Later chapters follow the same theme through particular domains of life—education, career, marriage, child-rearing, and so on. By the end of this book, we will have discovered that people's lives really can be understood better with the help of social science concepts and measurements.

Not only are life satisfactions patterned but so are life concerns—the things that people hope to get out of life. What, then, are the most important life goals of average young Americans? What are they hoping to get out of life?

Although Americans are sometimes described as materialistic and acquisitive, no single concern—whether with financial well-being or with marital happiness—dominates their desires (Atkinson & Murray, 1982). Quality-of-life surveys (Campbell et al., 1976; Campbell, 1981; Andrews & Withey, 1976) have found that Americans are quite diverse in their goal orientations. Four areas—family life, financial situation, work, and leisure—all prove to be of great importance to Americans; none is more significant than any other in the general population's perceptions of life quality. Nor have researchers been able to find major value differences among population subgroups. It would seem, therefore, that most Americans are more or less equally concerned with these four areas of life, and not primarily concerned with materialistic goals.

A life goal that is becoming increasingly important for the adult population is self-fulfillment (Yankelovich, 1982). Many Americans are rugged individualists who are deeply committed to developing their own individual personality and potential. For them, "creativity is a life style." These Americans spend a lot of time and money in the search for excitement, sensation, new experiences, self-discovery, and self-improvement. They focus their lives on themselves. About one American in six is strongly committed to this kind of personal gratification and self-fulfillment. A majority of Americans (63 percent) pursue similar goals more moderately; another 20 percent pursue completely different, more traditional life goals (Atkinson & Murray, 1982).

Survey data from 1952 to 1986 have shown an unmistakable increase towards this modern individualism of self-fulfillment or "me-first" mentality. According to some writers (Bellah et al., 1985; Glen, 1987), modern individualism has been strong in the United States from the very beginning. Until the midtwentieth century it coexisted with a strong commitment to civic duty and political participation (classical republicanism), and biblical religion; then, it began to eclipse these goals. As a result, ever greater numbers of Americans have shifted from emphasizing moral and religious obligations to emphasizing autonomy and freedom of the individual. Guided by the principle that one's most basic obligation is to oneself, the individual withdraws allegiance from social groups and societal institutions. In this way, modern individualism as self-fulfillment threatens the family, the community, the economy, traditional religions, and the society.

Summing up this point, Americans tend to hold similar views of their past, present, and future lives. They are on the whole satisfied with their lives, and they are among the most optimistic people in the world. Among young people, life concerns center on having a good family life and being successful in their work. Americans generally are also very individualistic, and appear to be increasingly so in the last four decades.

Patterns of Variation

The rest of this chapter will explore the ways desires and satisfactions vary, and theories about that variation. This exploration has two main purposes. The first is to understand better why certain Americans want what they do out of life, and why some feel more or less satisfied than average. Bear in mind that the present chapter does not answer these questions fully. Later chapters will answer similar questions about particular domains of life in greater detail. A second and more important purpose is to demonstrate that people's desires and life concerns are *patterned*: they vary in predictable, largely understandable ways among different segments of the population.

Variations in Time   People's satisfaction with life, and their particular desires and concerns, vary over time. That is why we cannot understand what it was to live in another historical period unless we understand fully the values people held, goals they set for themselves, and satisfaction they felt with social conditions that might not satisfy us today.

These variations are easiest to see when we compare large chunks of time—for example, the Middle Ages and today. An ambitious work of early American sociology studied how people had changed their values over thousands of years (Sorokin, 1941). Data collected from a variety of civilizations showed that, historically, major civilizations of the world had gone through cycles of value change, returning repeatedly to certain key concerns.

People's values change slowly and repeatedly over long periods of time, often returning to earlier concerns and ways of thinking. So historical context is all-important if we want to understand why people want what they do out of life, and how they feel about their lives at any given moment in time.

However, values and perceptions about the quality of life also vary over periods shorter than millennia. Comparing years closer to the present also allows us to use standard, well-understood instruments to measure changes. For example, between 1957 and 1972—a turbulent period marked by conflict in American society over the Vietnam war, civil rights, and rising crime rates—there was a perceptible decline in the number of people saying they were very happy. This was followed by a modest rise in measured happiness from 1972 to 1978 (Campbell, 1981).

A declining sense of well-being was most noticeable among the young. In 1957, 40 percent of people aged 20 to 29 described themselves very happy; but in 1972 only 26 percent of Americans the same age were very happy; and in 1978, only 29 percent were.

Young people in the 1970s were not particularly happy, nor were they very satisfied with life. Except in the domain of health, people under 30 were less satisfied than older people in respect to their family life and friendships, education and work, housing and neighborhood—even in respect to the country as a whole.

Also, in 1978 young people were less positive about their experiences than older people, even though in the 1960s they had been more positive than their elders (Campbell, 1981). In short, Americans under 30 in the 1970s had a lower sense of well-being than people the same age a decade earlier.

One explanation of this dissatisfaction is demographic—that is, due to population changes. A new birth group, or *cohort*, born between 1948 and 1957, entered adulthood during the 1970s. These younger Americans are part of the "baby-boom" generation, born at a time of high birth rates. Much research suggests that this group is passing through life more frustrated and unhappy than earlier cohorts (Jones, 1980; Easterlin, 1980). People born at a time of high birth rates must compete more intensely for spaces in colleges and universities, scholarships, entry-level jobs, higher career positions, housing, and other rewards throughout life. By contrast, people born between 1939 and 1948—who were teenagers in the 1950s and young adults in the 1960s—had it much easier. Since they were relatively fewer in number, they enjoyed smaller school classes, expanding educational opportunities, and more job possibilities when they entered the work force.

But even this relatively small cohort grew less happy in the 1970s, as they passed into their thirties. The explanation lies in something that happened to people during that decade—an economic slowdown or recession that started around 1974 and produced its worst effects in the early 1980s. Throughout this period, employment and career opportunities worsened for everyone but especially for younger people. Young adults' diminished sense of well-being in 1978 partly reflects frustration and disappointment with this state of affairs.

With a return to economic growth, everyone's life satisfaction should increase. However, some cohorts, especially the baby-boomers, may feel relatively dissatisfied throughout their lives. Their expectations about life—based on the experience of earlier cohorts who had entered adulthood during periods of economic growth, or were visibly prosperous when the baby-boomers were growing up—are high. Under intensely competitive economic conditions, baby-boomers will have to lower their expectations if they are to feel more satisfied with life. And, to some degree, this will happen through aging alone. Data show that aging generally increases life satisfaction by lowering standards, reducing needs, and moderating desires.

Young people born after the baby boom—in the late 1960s and the years since—already show the change of desires that one might expect from people living in a period of economic difficulty. Research from many countries shows that high school and college students today have much more practical goals than baby-boomers did in the 1960s and early 1970s.

For example, annual surveys conducted by the American Council of Higher Education and the Higher Education Research Institute at UCLA show that almost three-quarters of college freshmen in 1987 and 1988 saw making more money as a very important goal and a main reason for going to college (*San Francisco Examiner*, January 10, 1989; and *The Chronicle of Higher Education*, January 11, 1989). Fewer than two in every five freshmen attach the same importance to developing a meaningful philosophy of life. Moreover, data collected continuously since 1966 demonstrate that these views are part of a long-term trend—a growing materialism and declining concern with a "meaningful philosophy." Indeed, the two concerns have completely reversed their degree of importance for freshmen in the last 20 years.

Given this growing concern with financial well-being, it should come as no surprise to find that young people's life satisfaction declined during the recessionary 1970s.

What, then, do we know about the way satisfaction changes over time? Satisfaction changes for a variety of reasons. Basic conceptions of life may take generations and even centuries to change. In the course of a single lifetime, the average sense of well-being in a society will be affected by relative numbers of old and young (since older people are more satisfied); the sizes of cohorts (since very much larger-than-average cohorts are less satisfied); the economic conditions of the period (since periods of growth are more satisfying periods); and the length of time people have had to adjust their expectations to an economic decline or other social difficulty.

However, economic and demographic factors are far from the only influences on people's life satisfaction. In fact, they may be among the less-important influences. This fact becomes clearer when we examine other variations in satisfaction—for example, variations by country at a given point in time.

Variations from Country to Country Do people around the world all share the same basic concerns and feel the same amount of satisfaction with life; and if not, why not? Research since the 1960s provides ample evidence that people in different parts of the world do not feel the same amount of satisfaction with life; there is a great deal of variation in life satisfaction and happiness from one society to another. However, evidence is mixed on whether the cross-national differences in subjective well-being are related to differences in the level of national socioeconomic development.

At any given time, people living in different societies will differ in their life satisfaction. One study shows that Canadians, despite having the highest gross domestic product per capita (standard of living), are only fourth-ranked among nine nations where the majority of people surveyed say they are very satisfied with life (Atkinson, 1979). Denmark ranks first in overall satisfaction, despite a third-ranking standard of living. Ireland, with nearly the lowest standard of living among the countries studied, has the second-highest proportion of people indicating great satisfaction with their lives.

Income and standard of living are only weakly connected with life satisfaction; people can be poor but satisfied, a point we shall consider later. Satisfaction is largely determined by people's expectations. The greater the gap between what people have and what they expect to have, the more dissatisfied they will be. Accordingly, the less optimistic Danes and Irish average much higher levels of satisfaction than the more optimistic Canadians. High hopes are more likely to lead to great disappointments, hence less satisfaction with life.

Asking the same questions of 14 international samples, Cantril (1965) found that the people living on Israeli kibbutzim are the most satisfied of all with their present lives. Next most satisfied are respondents in the United States and Cuba. Least satisfied with their lives are respondents in Poland, India, and the Dominican Republic. Using an index of socioeconomic development (that is, modernity) that comprises 11 items—including gross national product per capita; number of doctors per 10 000 people; percentage living in cities with populations over 100 000; and percentage of literate people—Cantril found that average life satisfaction is only weakly related to the level of development.

Socioeconomic development, or modernization, does not necessarily make people more satisfied with life: it also creates new desires, hopes, and fears. In modernizing countries, people have to adjust their expectations of life to take into account new possibilities. Failure to satisfy these new expectations and desires is dissatisfying.

On the other hand, Inkeles and Diamond (1980), after examining over 20 cross-national studies, concluded that there is a strong and positive relationship between the level of socioeconomic development of a nation, and the sense of well-being or personal satisfaction of the population. People living in the more-developed countries have a greater sense of personal satisfaction and competence. The strongest evidence of this comes from the first global survey of public opinion: "The nations with the highest per capita income almost invariably top every test of psychological well-being and satisfaction in major aspects of life" (Gallup, 1977: 461, quoted in Inkeles & Diamond, 1980).

Inkeles and Diamond, nevertheless, found some "countertendencies" in the advanced stages of socioeconomic development. Although *present* personal satisfaction rises with an increase in the gross national product per capita, expectations for improvement in the *future*, both personal and national, tend to fall. In other words, the highest stages of economic development bring a loss of optimism about further personal and national improvement.

More recently, Inglehart and Rabier (1986) found astonishingly large differences in the levels of subjective well-being reported in 10 Western societies of the European Community. These differences changed little over the period from 1973 to 1983. People in Denmark and the Netherlands consistently ranked among the highest on life satisfaction and happiness. The Irish (both North and South) also ranked high on both overall life satisfaction and happiness. By contrast, Italians and Greeks ranked lowest on both satisfaction and happiness, while people living in France and West Germany ranked next above them on both. Interestingly, nationality is by far the strongest predictor of life satisfaction and happiness, far surpassing such other predictors as recent changes in one's own financial situation, family income, marital status, education, age, occupation, and religion.

Very few of these cross-national differences can be traced to long-term differences in economic development or recent changes in the economic environment of the 10 Western societies studied. Moreover, those 10 nations are otherwise quite similar to one another geographically, culturally, and politically. Inglehart and Rabier argue that different societies have different cultural baselines concerning the public expression of personal happiness and life satisfaction. In some societies, people tend to rate life much more positively, and enthusiastically, than in others.

As to life concerns, Cantril (1965) allowed people to speak freely about their hopes and fears, then coded the answers they gave into categories—including "personal economic situation," "family references," "health," "personal values and character," "job or work situation," and "social values." People answer in such different ways in different countries that it is difficult to summarize and compare concerns. But personal economic aspirations are mentioned by more people than any other; they outnumber all other concerns in the poorest countries—the Dominican Republic, Brazil, India—and even in some prosperous countries, like West Germany, by a considerable margin. Next in frequency of mention are family references: these are more common than, or almost as common as, personal economic concerns in the kibbutzim, Israel generally, Nigeria, Yugoslavia, and the Philippines. References to personal values are extremely common in rapidly developing places (the kibbutzim, Nigeria, Cuba, and Egypt) but less common in countries where modernization has been stifled (India, the Dominican Republic, and the Philippines) or completed (the United States and West Germany).

Health concerns are mentioned somewhat more often than social values, and are voiced most often in the rapidly developing or developed countries. Almost no one mentions health aspirations in India or the Philippines. Jobs and work are the last category of hopes mentioned by large numbers of people. No simple pattern can be detected in the percentages raising this concern: it is no more common in developing or developed, socialist or capitalist countries. On the contrary, if we take into account the fact that respondents in some countries express many hopes while those in other countries express relatively few, the percentage expressing hopes about jobs and work is reasonably constant. About 5 to 15 percent in every country express hopes concerning this issue.

What, then, do we learn about people's desires from such an ambitious comparison of nations? Do people all share the same basic concerns and feel the same amount of satisfaction with life? In short, the answer is no. Except at a very general level, people do not share the same life concerns around the world.

We learn most about national differences by comparing countries that are alike in many ways. Such comparisons are most like controlled experiments, the preferred method of research in physical science. By comparing similar societies, we are in effect "holding constant" a great many factors while only one or two possible explanatory factors vary. The few varying factors are, logically, the only possible cause of differences in the thing to be explained.

Atkinson and Murray (1982) compared Canadian data on life satisfaction with similar American data collected by Campbell, Converse, and Rogers (1976). Despite a remarkable similarity between the two peoples, certain key differences in the kinds of satisfactions that best predict overall life satisfaction do emerge.

The most important difference is, as noted above, that Americans "can be described as more diverse in their value orientations" than Canadians. Canadians are rather single-minded. They place much more importance on romance and marriage than Americans do. In fact, their satisfaction with life overall is primarily determined by these relationships. When these relationships are going well, they feel that life as a whole is going well. Further, in Canada "marital concerns would more often take precedence over material considerations" than in the United States. Among other things, work has much more influence on life satisfaction in the United States than in Canada; but apparently, this is not due to a greater American concern with monetary reward.

The very high value Canadians put on love and marriage supports the claim that Canadians are more "collectively oriented," or attached to groups, than Americans. On the other hand, the greater significance of work for Americans demonstrates that a greater value is placed on achievement, or accomplishment, in the United States. Atkinson and Murray (1982: 29) conclude that "the greater value of social relationships in Canada, and of achievement in the United States, reflect long-standing societal differences which will persist in the future."

To summarize, people's satisfaction and life concerns vary among societies in complex ways. Material factors like standard of living are not enough to explain these differences. Even such similar countries as the United States and Canada show different patterns, suggesting long-standing, deep-rooted cultural values that defy easy explanation.

Variation across Ages People living in different periods and nations differ, but they are not the only ones. People of different ages also vary in their life satisfaction, with older people being generally more satisfied than younger ones. People's life concerns also change as they get older.

As they age, people pass through a life cycle—a sequence of typical, important stages. At each stage, certain concerns become paramount and others trivial. That is because, as people age, they enter and leave social roles (Nicholson, 1980).

In our early lives we are most concerned about relations with our parents. Our childhood home is the culture and society we know best, and we measure everything else—including our wishes, hopes, and self-esteem—against what we have learned there. As we age, all this changes radically. We become acquainted with a much larger world at school. Our peers (and their values) are much more varied than our parents and siblings. Moral certainties are thrown into doubt by the evidence of acceptable variation in the world. In adolescence, needs for peer acceptance increase at the same time as we are searching for an identity and purpose of our very own. We feel torn between the often conflicting goals of finding our own true selves and gaining social acceptance as "one of the crowd."

In a national survey of students in their early adolescence, the majority of respondents chose "to get a good job when I am older" (84 percent) and "to have a happy family life" (82 percent) as very important life goals. These goals are also very important to American adults, as we saw earlier. What is interesting is that between the fifth and ninth grade, goals such as autonomy ("to make my own decisions"), future ("to do something important with my life"), and friendship become increasingly important. At the same time, worry about peer relationships also increases with age. Values that decrease in importance through the middle and junior high school years include God, church, and concern for people and the world (Benson, Williams, & Johnson, 1987).

Annual nationwide surveys of seniors in high schools since 1976 reveal a consistent pattern in what young people hope to get out of life (Bach-

TABLE 1.1 "Important things in life": percentage rating "extremely important" by high school seniors 1976–1984. (Source: Bachman, Johnston, & O'Malley, 1986, p. 217, Table 8.1.)

	1976	1977	1978	1979	1980	1981	1982	1983	1984
Males									
A good marriage and family life	66	69	70	73	70	71	69	69	67
Finding steady work	66	65	67	68	68	69	73	74	73
Being successful in my work	53	55	58	56	55	58	61	60	59
Strong friendships	57	58	63	62	59	60	62	60	61
Finding purpose and meaning in my life	54	53	57	55	54	52	51	52	48
Females									
A good marriage and family life	80	78	80	82	82	82	83	82	79
Finding steady work	61	58	62	63	62	65	70	73	71
Being successful in my work	52	53	54	57	55	57	60	61	59
Strong friendships	60	62	65	65	67	65	66	65	64
Finding purpose and meaning in my life	75	72	74	73	68	72	71	72	67

man, Johnston, & O'Malley, 1986). Table 1.1 shows the five life goals given the highest rating in a list of fourteen for the years 1976–84. It would seem that people in their late teens continue to hold the same goals they had held in early adolescence. Male and female seniors in high school generally agree on the important things in life, with some exceptions. They differ most in regard to the life goal "Finding purpose and meaning in my life." This goal is consistently rated extremely important by 15 to 20 percent *more* of the female seniors than the male seniors. Female students are also more likely to rate "a good marriage and family life" as important.

Teenagers are in the process of asserting their individual identity. They want to be loved but not limited; hence, not only do they value a happy family life but they also put increasing emphasis on autonomy and friendship in their attempt to separate themselves from the nuclear family life.

The high ratings high school seniors give to "Finding steady work" and "Being successful in my work" reflect the two dominant values of "achievement and success" and "activity and work" in American society (see Williams, 1970). But the desire for success and work may mean different things to high school seniors and adults. To adults, work and material success are means of attaining family security. To teenagers, these are means of freeing themselves from family constraints and proof that they have achieved full membership in adult society.

With the passage from adolescence into adulthood, people assume new roles and become engrossed in different interests. Work and financial security are important concerns for those under 30, married or single. Marital and family concerns dominate the child-raising period between ages 25 and 45 when a majority of Americans get married and raise a family. Leisure activities begin to occupy the time of married people with an empty nest: they are usually over 45 with the youngest child over 17. Health becomes a very salient issue for people over 65, many of whom may also have to cope with widowhood (Campbell, 1981).

This all makes sense. People create and raise families in their thirties and forties, so family life *should* typically be most important at this time. At this age, health is not yet a problem, and leisure is limited by career and family duties in a way that it will not be 10 years later, when all the children have left home. Finally, work and financial considerations are less important at that age because by age 35, a career path has largely been established and financial conditions improve slowly and gradually after that point, if at all.

Not only life concerns change with age, so does overall life satisfaction. Life satisfaction generally increases with age (Campbell et al., 1976; Campbell, 1981; Mookherjee, 1987). This is a pattern we shall see repeated time and again in this book.

Changes in life satisfaction are somewhat different for men and women as they pass through their life cycles. Both sexes experience an eroding sense of well-being in early parenthood, and then an improvement in later adulthood. But the age-based change is more profound for males than females. Married, childless women under 30 are more satisfied with life than anyone else—male or female. Among men, the most satisfied are fathers still living with their wives, whose grown-up children have left home (Campbell, 1981). As this suggests, male and female lives are quite different, even today in America. Young women start out more satisfied than men and end up in old age less satisfied than men. Old age is a lonelier and more economically distressed time for women (who are more likely to have lost their spouse) than it is for men.

The rest of the book will deal with these issues more thoroughly. At this point, note only that life satisfaction and life concerns vary considerably by age and stage in the life cycle. To know a person's outlook, it is not enough to know his or her age, but age and life-cycle stage certainly make a great difference.

Variations across Status and Income Groups   Social position also influences people's life concerns. Common sense says that it is better to be rich than poor, famous than unknown, and powerful than powerless. Are rich people really more satisfied with life, as lay wisdom tells us?

In an effort to answer this question, Diener, Horowitz, and Emmons (1985) sampled people from *Forbes* business magazine's list of the wealthiest Americans, and compared them with people selected randomly from telephone directories. Those agreeing to participate completed a questionnaire about life concerns.

Wealthy respondents prove to be happy a higher percentage of the time, score significantly higher on two different life satisfaction scales, and report significantly lower levels of "negative affect"—that is, unhappiness. Not all the wealthy are happy, of course; in fact, some are just as unhappy as the unhappiest ordinary person sampled. Further, few respondents, whether wealthy or ordinary, believe that money is a major source of happiness. However, this denial may simply reflect the notion, common in our culture, that "money can't buy happiness."

Wealthy and ordinary people also differ in what satisfies them. Wealthy respondents more often mention self-esteem and self-actualization as sources of their satisfaction, while ordinary people more often mention physiological (food, shelter, and other basic human needs) and safety concerns as sources of satisfaction.

But bear in mind that Diener et al. were comparing ordinary people with some of the wealthiest people in the world. What if we compare the poorer 99 percent of the population with one another: does income still make a difference? No; your income makes only a small difference in your overall life satisfaction. Income influences people's satisfaction with their financial situation; not surprisingly, people with high income are more satisfied financially (with income, standard of living, and savings) but not necessarily more satisfied in other areas such as interpersonal relationships and self-development (Campbell, 1981).

While there is only a modest relationship between levels of income and overall life satisfaction, your income quartile (that is, the fourth of income distribution you are located in) has a greater influence on measurements of happiness (see Table 1.2, Campbell, 1981: 241). Those with high incomes are more likely to describe themselves as "very happy" than low-income people, although over the years, the happiness gap between the high- and low-income groups has narrowed. So, in the United States, a large income can buy the average person some life satisfaction and a fair amount of happiness (Campbell, 1981).

However, life concerns do vary with socioeconomic status. (Socio-economic status, or SES, is a combined measure of education, income, and job prestige.) People with higher SES rate "social values" such as love, marriage, family life, and friendship significantly higher than people with low SES; conversely, they rate "material values" like prosperity and economic stability lower. And, just as Diener et al. (1985) discovered in comparing the wealthy with ordinary people, higher-status people place significantly more value than lower-status people on the "need for being," such as achievement, self-development, control over one's own life, and excitement (Robertson, 1987).

Variations across Racial and Gender Groups   As America is a multi-racial society, do people of different racial origins differ in their life concerns and satisfaction? There is little research evidence indicating that racial minorities differ from the majority of whites in their life goals and desires. Blacks and other minorities pursue essentially the same American dream and are preoccupied with the same concerns as the general American population—family life, financial situation, work, leisure, and self-development.

However, data on Americans' perceived quality of life collected since the early 1970s have shown that being black has a negative influence on the sense of well-being which is independent of socioeconomic status. Within all income groups, blacks are more dissatisfied than whites. Blacks with high incomes are more positive about their lives than blacks with low incomes, but less positive than whites with similar incomes (Campbell et al., 1976; Campbell, 1981). Blacks also score significantly lower on measures of life satisfaction, general happiness, marital happiness, trust in people, and self-rated physical health than whites regardless of SES, marital status, or age (Thomas & Hughes, 1986).

As with the general population, SES variables such as income and education have little impact on the overall life satisfaction of blacks (Jackson, Chatters, & Neighbors, 1986). Legal, social, and economic changes since the Second World War have improved material conditions for black

Americans. However, during the same period, income and educational levels of the whites have also risen, leaving the gap between the two racial groups unchanged. Meanwhile, the civil rights movements of the 1960s may have heightened expectations among the blacks. As their rising expectations go unfulfilled and they continue to experience systemic discrimination and blocked opportunities, blacks experience little psychological benefit from conditions that are actually improving. Thus the disparity between rising expectations and opportunities provides an explanation for the lower levels of well-being experienced by the blacks (Thomas & Hughes, 1986; Schaefer, 1987).

Very little is known about the differences in life satisfaction, if any, between the majority group and other racial minorities—Hispanic, Asian, and American Indian. However, Ortiz and Arce (1986) found that Mexican Americans, like blacks, report lower levels of perceived quality of life than the general American population.

We have already noted some of the differences between men and women in their life satisfaction and concerns. Are there other differences between males and females in their sense of well-being? After all, sex differences are obvious in every society. In the United States, despite recent changes in gender roles and gender relations intended to diminish sex differences, men and women still live different lives. They are socialized with different values, learn different norms and roles, and develop different expectations. Yet measurement of several aspects of well-being has led to one important finding: men and women differ very little in their life satisfaction and feeling of happiness. This is all the more interesting in view of the many inequities that women do experience in American society (Campbell et al., 1976; Campbell, 1981).

While American men and women in the general population do not differ very much in their satisfaction with life as a whole, Campbell et al. (1976) found that black women are less satisfied with life than black men. Data collected in the 1980s reveal that black women are also less satisfied with their lives than white women (Mookherjee, 1987).

Ortiz and Arce (1986) also found gender differences in the perception of quality of life among Mexican Americans. Among higher-status Chicanos, women report the same or an even higher quality of life than men do; but among lower-status Chicanos, women report a lower quality of life than men. Ortiz and Arce do not think that these gender differences are due to the practices and beliefs of Chicano culture. Rather, they see a structural explanation.

Poverty and low educational levels reduce the satisfaction of most lower-status Mexican Americans, but women are hit hardest. A large number have only recently entered the paid labor force. Like other women who work for pay, employed lower-status Mexican American women end up working a longer day than their husbands or boyfriends, who avoid regular housework. (We discuss domestic sharing of work further in Chapters 5 and 6.) This workload, and the difficulty adjusting to it, has a worse effect on them than it does on women of other racial groups whose participation in paid employment increased more gradually.

How can we explain the variations in life satisfaction and concerns we have observed so far? Two main theoretical approaches are considered below—Maslow's theory of a need hierarchy and Michalos's theory of multiple discrepancies.

Two Theories of Satisfaction

Maslow's Need Hierarchy   Psychologist Abraham Maslow put forward a central theory in the study of life satisfactions. It holds that every human being longs and strives for self-actualization, the complete fulfilment of his or her unique potentiality. Attaining such fulfilment is the ultimate and supposedly essential human need. Such fulfilment will bring any person the greatest possible satisfaction.

Maslow's theory is not original. His "essentialism"—which looks for the essential, basic, or universal qualities of human nature—may originate in the thinking of Plato and Aristotle. Moreover, Karl Marx offers sociologists a related, more refined approach. Marx's *Early Philosophical Manuscripts* (1844/1985) discusses "alienation" as stifled self-fulfilment under capitalism. According to this theory, psychological well-being must grow out of social and economic well-being. Individual satisfaction must be achieved through societal change.

According to Marx, alienation results from economic exploitation, most advanced under capitalism, which deprives people of control over their labour and the fruits of their labour. People seek to fulfil their creative impulses in work. But the need to sell their labour for wages denies these impulses and estranges people from their work, their true selves, and others similarly forced to work for wages (see Rinehart, 1987, for a good summary of this theory).

The essentialist theories of Marx and Maslow differ in important ways. For Marx, the end of exploitive wage labour brings self-fulfilment, since it ends alienation. Self-actualization is impossible under capitalism but virtually assured under socialism. Social impulses will be liberated by the ending of capitalist exploitation alone. Presumably, belonging and acceptance will follow easily once people are no longer alienated from themselves and others.

On the other hand, Maslow appears to believe that self-actualization is possible under a variety of social and political conditions. However, the attainment of belonging and acceptance is always problematic: it cannot be assured, any more than the attainment of food, shelter, and physical safety can be assured. These are all goals people have to attain on their way to self-actualization.

The most distinctive feature of Maslow's theory—the one that makes it most *unlike* Marx's (let alone Plato's or Aristotle's) and most *like* theories in developmental psychology—is that it is a "stage theory." It proposes that people must pass through successive stages of fulfilment—survival, security, belonging, esteem—before being able to reach, or even want, total fulfilment or "self-actualization." The failure to complete one stage prevents a person from successfully proceeding to the next stage.

Thus, for example, a person who has not attained physical security cannot hope to attain belonging, and may not even want it yet. A person who has not attained belonging cannot (and will not) hope to attain esteem. The stages must be passed through in order, and all lower-level needs must be satisfied before self-actualization is possible. Even for people who have passed through all the lower stages of fulfilment, self-actualization is not guaranteed: it is merely a possibility.

Few have attempted to test Maslow's stage theory with representative survey data. One exception is a study by Atkinson and Murray (1982), using Canadian survey data. Like Maslow, the researchers find it useful to distinguish between "sustenance values and needs" and higher-level values such as belonging, esteem, achievement, and actualization. The failure to satisfy sustenance needs—needs for physical well-being and economic security—results in a partial fixation on these concerns, while satisfaction reduces their importance, just as Maslow would predict. People with a low income (or poor health) are particularly likely to focus their desires on income (or health) improvement, while other Canadians are not.

Yet even here, the evidence supporting Maslow's theory is weak. Even among people failing to fulfil these basic needs—poor people and sick people—health and economic security are far from dominant concerns and have only a weak influence on overall life satisfaction.

The survey evidence supports Maslow's theory even less when we consider people who *have* satisfied their "basic needs." "Values of belonging, esteem, achievement and actualization . . . do not appear to be stratified as Maslow suggests," say Atkinson and Murray (1982: 31). People failing to fulfil any of these secondary needs do not fixate on the unfulfilled need, inflating its importance in their lives. They do the very opposite, and substitute other domains as sources of gratification. Thus, unmarried people with good jobs and high incomes place more than average value on their work, while unmarried people with lower incomes place more than average value on leisure, because other aspects of their lives are not rewarding enough.

Stage-one and -two values operate by different rules and have different potentials for influencing the general quality of a person's life. For example, poverty and poor health can reduce the quality of a person's life, but "high incomes and good physical condition seem to have limited potential for increasing well-being, at least directly." On the other hand, stage-two domains—for example, work, family, and leisure stisfactions—"carry the potential to make life genuinely enjoyable as well as miserable" (Atkinson & Murray, 1982: 33).

The researchers conclude that "the substitutability of second-stage values offers some relief from frustrations encountered in particular domains," if optional sources of reward are available.

At least in our society, survival and security needs must be satisfied before people can look to other domains for fuller satisfaction. Incomplete fulfilment of sustenance needs leads to fixation, and starving people cannot substitute love and esteem for a good dinner. In this sense, objective reality sets limits on how people will seek and achieve satisfaction.

Yet for the majority—whose sustenance needs *are* met—higher-level needs can be satisfied in a variety of ways. In general, people make do with what they have at hand. They do not pine after the impossible. Objective reality does not set problems that must be dealt with in a single way.

This means that the young, single person beginning his or her adult life can find satisfaction in a variety of ways. One will find it in a career, another in marriage, and a third in leisure activities or friendship. Even the greater emphasis on fulfilment through family and romance in Canada than elsewhere is no more than a tendency, not an ironclad law. In practice, people will set their goals to capitalize on real opportunities for satisfaction, *given* their personal values.

To summarize, Maslow and other essentialists would argue that your satisfaction in life depends on the size of the gap between what you have attained and what you want to attain. In turn, what you want to attain— whether you know it or not—is a hierarchy of goals culminating in self-fulfilment. According to this theory, everyone wants the same things— call them essential or universal wants—and must attain them in the same sequence if they are to achieve maximum life satisfaction.

Data fail to support this theory. Principally, we have strong reason to doubt that everyone wants the same things. Evidence shows that wants (concerns, hopes, and desires) vary by age, period, country, and social class; they even vary in other ways we have not yet considered. Second, evidence shows that frustrated desires are remedied by the substitution of one satisfaction for another. As a result, researchers find little connection between people's sense of satisfaction with life and their actual material or social well-being, measured objectively. Once people have satisfied the most basic needs for food and shelter, their life satisfaction can be raised by a wide variety of material, social, and cultural "goods."

In conclusion, we find little evidence of a single, essential, and universal set of needs—no one path to life satisfaction.

Multiple Discrepancies Theory   People's needs and desires are not patterned in any simple or rigid way. Rather, they vary according to personal background and present opportunity. Our backgrounds and personal histories present us with images of the "good life." We grow up hoping for a certain kind of future. Often our hoped-for futures are strikingly similar to the adult lives we witnessed as children in the parental home. Sometimes they are strikingly different, as among people who vow they will never turn out like their parents did. What is remarkable is the strength of relationship—whether positive or negative—between what we learn as children and what we become as adults.

Our hopes—what we want and expect—are not only shaped by parents and siblings. They are also influenced by other significant people we encounter in growing up: role models, mentors, idols, good friends, enemies, and so on. We are also influenced by the groups we belong to and by the outlooks, norms, and behaviours they teach us. Finally, there are a number of institutions and groups in our society whose purpose is to influence or manage our wants: the media, advertising agencies, politicians, interest groups, and churches are among them.

Consider the role of the mass media. Young people spend enormous numbers of hours beside their radio and television sets. The media show us imaginary characters being rewarded for certain qualities, behaviours, or values. By identifying with these characters, we receive *vicarious*, or second-hand rewards. The fact that these rewards are vicarious does not seem to lessen their influence on how we think and behave.

So our personal background and the future it has taught us to expect have been shaped by family, friends, and people we "meet" only through the media. Other influences at work or school—agents of "adult socialization"—continue to mold us throughout life. It is the general thrust of Alex Michalos's "multiple discrepancies" theory that our satisfaction with life will be determined by discrepancies between life as it is and life as we thought it should or would be. The more our real life departs from the life we compare it with, the more dissatisfied we will be.

To state the theory of multiple discrepancies more formally, people's life satisfaction is determined by the size of the gap or discrepancy between what they have attained and what they want. But unlike Maslow, Michalos does not argue that everyone wants the same things. Rather, his theory holds that what you want is determined by the sum of six perceived discrepancies: discrepancies between what you have today and (1) what relevant others appear to have; (2) the best you had in the past; (3) what, three years ago, you expected you would have today; (4) what you expect to have five years from now; (5) what you think you deserve; and (6) what you think you need.

All these perceived discrepancies are, in turn, affected by objectively measurable discrepancies. That is, the gaps we perceive have some basis in reality, although no one-to-one relationship exists. "All discrepancies, satisfactions and actions are directly and indirectly affected by age, sex, education, ethnicity, income, self-esteem, and social support" (Michalos, 1985: 348). These social characteristics, which influence our opportunities for getting what we want out of life, also influence our perceptions and our sense(s) of having, or not having, what we want.

Life satisfaction is determined as much by our bases of comparison—and the personal histories that shape them—as by objective reality, the opportunities and troubles that face us every day. According to this theory, people are drawn forward by a picture of the future, of life as it "should be" for them, and by a desire to close the gap between what they expect, want, and get.

Each person's picture of the future is the result of self-comparisons with "relevant others" and with his or her own past. It is also shaped by things we feel we need and deserve—undoubtedly all originating in earlier experience but difficult to track to their sources. So for the most part, we are not driven forward by objective need, but drawn forward by the discrepancy between what we have and what we want. (In turn, what we want is, largely, what we had expected to have.)

Typically, the discrepancy between what we have and what we want is measurable: we do not simply fantasize these things. Some men who want to look like Robert Redford but believe they do not are probably right, and dispassionate observers would agree with their assessment of a gap between desire and reality. Sociologists can reliably and validly measure what people do and do not have, and even point to objective, real factors that create the shortcomings. As noted, age, gender, education, ethnicity, income, self-esteem, and social support are factors that influence what we do and do not really have. This list is far from exhaustive, but offers a good starting place.

The factors that influence our opportunities to get what we want also influence or pattern our desires. Traditionally, females have been taught not to want the same things as men, for example. This kind of training lowers dissatisfaction when opportunities really are limited. When aspirations and expectations rise more rapidly than opportunities (generally, or for particular groups such as women, racial minorities, old people, and so on), dissatisfaction rises rapidly even if opportunities are actually increasing. What is key is the relationship between rates of change in opportunities and desires. When opportunities grow more slowly, discrepancies increase and so does dissatisfaction.

We noted earlier that few people in our society are very dissatisfied with life: most are moderately satisfied. The rarity of dissatisfaction testifies to two facts. First, people lower their expectations and aspirations as they confront limited opportunities; and they substitute attainable desires for unattainable ones. Second, the images of the future that fuel our desires are often remembrances of an even more limiting past.

This theory helps us explain the absence of radical political sentiment among the unemployed and otherwise seriously disadvantaged. In part, some would argue, political inaction results from obstacles to political mobilization. Others would say that it lies in "false consciousness," meaning a false perception of how the world really operates. While both explanations may be right to some degree, multiple discrepancy theory implies a third explanation: namely, people form their visions of the future in a backward-looking, conformist, and moderate way. We do not compare ourselves with millionaires, then strive to narrow the discrepancy between what we want and what we have, any more than we compare ourselves with movie stars, then try to close the gap. The actual—our everyday experience—forms the basis for our assessment of the possible. Usually, what people want is what they can get, and this becomes ever truer as people age.

The result is social conservatism, especially among adults. It is important to counter this conservatism with a progressive vision and well-founded information about *possible* comparison groups (Michalos, 1987: 44–46). People tend to know most about people a lot like themselves; therefore, they set low standards for their own futures. More and better information about others with whom they might *reasonably* compare themselves will help them strive, personally and collectively, for a better life. This is movement out of a Fool's Paradise (characterized by satisfaction based on poorly founded information) into a Real Paradise (characterized by satisfaction based on well-founded information). Better information about the present and a commitment to a better future are necessary conditions for self-improvement and social change.

How can we judge what is truly possible for human beings to achieve? Seeking the truly *impossible* is ridiculous and sometimes hazardous. Failing to seek the truly *possible*, when it is desired and known to be possible, is slothful. But people's failure to seek the possible because it is not known to be possible, though desired, is the problem Michalos seeks to solve.

Consider this analogy. An excellent runner has just run a four-minute mile and has to decide whether to shoot for a three-minute mile. Is that truly possible—a worthwhile goal—or truly impossible—a ridiculous and possibly dangerous goal? Without more information, the runner can make no sensible decision. Available information confirms that no one has ever run a three-minute mile. On the other hand, evidence shows that people have been running ever faster miles. Therefore, a three-minute mile may be possible for some runner, some day. The question has now changed form. It is now, Can *this* runner, given his or her particular abilities, hope to run a three-minute mile in his or her lifetime?

Social conservatism is supported by a common failure to investigate the limits of the possible, due to limited information, misinformation, and backward- rather than forward-looking images of the future. In a "Real Paradise," well-informed people journey to the boundaries of the truly possible, then accept the result. Knowing what is truly possible is no easy matter, nor is accepting a less than ideal result. But if multiple discrepancy theory is valid, this is the only sensible and ultimately satisfying life strategy.

Does the theory actually work? If it does, measurable multiple discrepancies should predict people's life satisfaction better than any other variables we can think of and measure. In an early study, Michalos (1985) asked nearly 700 university undergraduates to answer questions about their lives, and measured the strength of relationships between discrepancies and satisfaction.

Multiple discrepancies "explained . . . 53% [of the variance] in global S[atisfaction] and 50% or more in 7 out of 12 domain S[atisfaction] scores." The model was particularly successful in accounting for people's satisfaction and financial security, paid employment, leisure activity, religion, and self-esteem. We conclude that the theory performed very well indeed. Roughly half of all the variation in people's satisfaction—overall as well as in particular domains of life—was "explained" by the variables in the model, leaving another half to be explained by other factors. By conventional standards, this is a very strong finding.

The finding has now been replicated—and, if anything, strength-ened—by data collected from over 6000 university students around the world (Michalos, 1987). As researchers' data-sets become larger and more varied, multiple discrepancy theory appears to make even more success-ful predictions.

The impact of discrepancy variables on satisfaction is indirect. Dis-crepancies such as the gap between what relevant others appear to have and what you have influence the discrepancy between what you have and what you want. In turn, this discrepancy influences your satisfaction. From this fact Michalos concludes that "the idea of *managing* satisfaction and happiness is plausible. . . . The very same processes that make it possible to rightly persuade people of things that are true, good and beau-tiful, also make it possible to wrongly persuade people of their opposites, falsehoods, evil, and ugliness" (Michalos, 1985: 393).

So, for example, people's satisfaction can be increased by downward comparison with less fortunate others. Moreover, we could inflate peo-ple's satisfaction in a number of other ways: by making them want less, misremember the past, and expect little (or less) from the future. This dangerous potential for pacifying discontent is a matter we shall consider further, toward the end of the book.

For Michalos (1987), the solution is a theory of value and a moral theory that will help people identify "good management." As well, "there is a fundamental role to be played by all [informal and formal] educa-tional institutions. People's satisfaction and happiness can be more or less cognitively well-founded, and reasonable people will want to be sure that they are essentially well-founded."

In a nutshell, "cognitive well-foundedness" is the goal behind this book. We want to explore patterns of desire and opportunity in real life, so that we know better what we are pursuing in life, as well as how and why we are doing so. It is only in the context of good information that a rea-sonable life can be lived. Sociology as well as philosophy has a role to play in that endeavour.

CONCLUDING REMARKS

Within our culture today, people share similar life goals and life satisfac-tions. Most people want what most other people of their own age, gender, and class want, allowing for subcultural variations of certain kinds. How-ever, people's goals and satisfactions are not universal. They vary over time and place. They vary over millenia, and they vary less dramatically over decades. They vary from one civilization to another, one country to another, and even (as we shall see in Chapter 7) one region of North America to another. That is why we must know the social and cultural context in order to understand people's satisfaction with conditions *we* might not find satisfying.

The effect of socioeconomic development on national goals is very much like the effect of maturation on individual goals. Both tend to increase information about choices and raise expectations, thereby diminishing satisfaction; and both tend to increase the potential for real achievement, thereby increasing satisfaction. The two influences tend to offset each other.

Different countries are about as variable as different people in their goals. In a very abstract sense, everyone wants the same things: family, security, peace, a job, and so on. This gives support to Maslow's theory of a need hierarchy, which we discussed at length. Yet countries and individuals order their concerns in different ways. Individuals within a given country are more like others living in the same country than they are like people living in other countries. It may simply not be useful to talk about "essential" or "universal" needs and concerns beyond food, shelter, and physical safety.

A major variable shaping life concerns and life satisfactions is *age*, and we shall return to it time and again. People of different ages see life differently: they have different concerns. As well, aging significantly affects satisfaction, increasing it in most cases. This fact is best proven by longitudinal data—data collected by following the same people as they age over time—not cross-sectional data—data which merely compare people of different ages at the same point in time. Unfortunately, social scientists have drawn most of their inferences about aging from cross-sectional data. So we must recognize that their conclusions are particularly liable to disproof in future.

But most of the findings point in a similar direction, the one we have taken. The reasons for greater satisfaction through aging are numerous and complex, but multiple discrepancies theory helps to identify them. Aging seems to produce low and diminishing expectations, narrower bases for comparison, less (and often worse) information about the truly possible, an increasing tendency to look backward rather than forward, and (for various reasons) an increasing aversion to risk. But older people may also possess a better sense of the truly possible than younger people. They may have learned from life.

People in different income groups also see life differently. Like people in wealthier countries, wealthier people have different concerns from poorer people: more concerns about self-actualization, for example, and fewer concerns about food and shelter. But unlike older people, they are not necessarily more satisfied. Rich people—who have a lot of information, high expectations, and a great opportunity for high achievement—run the greatest risks of disappointment. Paradoxically, the poor—who expect less, know less about what they do not have, and know that they have little chance to get it anyway—sometimes find it easier to achieve satisfaction than rich people.

Above the level of bare subsistence, not only are people's needs, concerns, and satisfactions culture-specific, they are subculture-specific. Our satisfaction is shaped by comparisons with people around us. Further, we are able and willing to substitute attainable for unattainable goals to maximize satisfaction. Where all else fails, we scale down our aspirations to increase our satisfaction. Whether good or bad, a Fool's Paradise or a Real Paradise, it is what people typically do. We want what we can get.

The next chapter discusses patterns of opportunity—why you get what you get.

REFERENCES

ATKINSON, T. H. (1979). *Trends in life satisfaction among Canadians, 1968–1977.* (Occasional Paper N. 7). Montreal: Institute for Research on Public Policy.

ATKINSON, T. H., & MURRAY, M. A. (1982). *Values, domains and the perceived quality of life: Canada and the United States.* Toronto: York University, Institute for Behavioural Research.

BACHMAN, J. G., JOHNSTON, L. D., & O'MALLEY, P. M. (1986). Recent findings from monitoring the future: A continuing study of the lifestyles and values of youth. In F. M. Andrews (Ed.), *Research on the quality of life* (pp. 215–34). Ann Arbor, Mich.: Survey Research Center.

BELLAH, R. N., MADSEN, R., SULLIVAN, W. N., SWIDLER, A., & TIPTON, S. M. (1985). *Habits of the heart: Individualism and commitment in American life.* Berkeley: University of California Press.

BENSON, P., WILLIAMS, D., & JOHNSON, A. (1987). *The quicksilver years: The hopes and fears of early adolescence.* San Francisco: Harper & Row.

CAMPBELL, A. (1981). *The sense of well-being in America: Recent patterns and trends.* New York: McGraw-Hill Co.

CAMPBELL, A., CONVERSE, P. E., & ROGERS, W. R. (1976). *The quality of American life: Perceptions, evaluations and satisfactions.* New York: Russell Sage Foundation.

CANTRIL, H. (1965). *The pattern of human concerns.* New Brunswick, N.J.: Rutgers University Press.

CANTRIL, H., & ROLL, C. W., JR. (1971). *Hopes and fears of the American people.* New York: Universe Books.

DIENER, E., HOROWITZ, J., & EMMONS, R. A. (1985). Happiness of the very wealthy. *Social Indicators Research, 16,* 263–74.

EASTERLIN, R. A. (1980). *Birth and fortune: The impact of numbers on personal welfare.* New York: Basic Books.

GLENN, N. A. (1987). Social trends in the United States: Evidence from sample surveys. *Public Opinion Quarterly, 51,* 4(2): S109–S126.

INGLEHART, R., & RABIER, J. R. (1986). Aspirations adapt to situations—but why are the Belgians so much happier than the French? In R. M. Andrews (Ed.), *Research on the quality of life* (pp. 1–56). Ann Arbor, Mich.: Survey Research Center.

INKELES, A., & DIAMOND, L. (1980). Personal development and national development: A cross-national perspective. In A. Szalai and F. M. Andrews (Eds.), *The quality of life: Comparative studies* (pp. 73–109). Beverly Hills, Calif.: Sage Publications.

JACKSON, J. S., CHATTERS, L. M., & NEIGHBORS, H. W. (1986). The subjective life quality of black Americans. In F. M. Andrews (Ed.), *Research on the quality of life* (pp. 193–213). Ann Arbor, Mich.: Survey Research Center.

JONES, L. Y. (1980). *Great expectations: America and the baby boom generation.* New York: Ballantine Books.

MARX, K. (1985). *Early philosophical manuscripts.* Harmondsworth: Penguin. (Original work published 1844.)

MICHALOS, A. C. (1985). Multiple discrepancies theory (MDT). *Social Indicators Research, 16,* 347–413.

MOOKHERJEE, H. N. (1987). Perception of life satisfaction in the United States: A summary. *Perceptual and Motor Skills, 65,* 218.

NICHOLSON, J. (1980). *Seven ages.* London: Fontana Paperbacks.

ORTIZ, V., & ARCE, C. H. (1986). Quality of life among persons of Mexican descent. In F. M. Andrews (Ed.), *Research on the quality of life* (pp. 171–91). Ann Arbor, Mich.: Survey Research Center.

ROBERTSON, I. (1987). *Sociology.* 3rd ed. New York: Worth.

SCHAEFER, R. T. (1987). *Racial and ethnic groups.* (3rd ed.). Glenview, Ill.: Scott, Foresman & Co.

SOROKIN, P. A. (1941). *The crisis of our age: The social and cultural outlook.* New York: E. P. Dutton.

THOMAS, M. E., & HUGHES, M. (1986). The continuing significance of race: A study of race, class and quality of life in America. *American Sociological Review, 51,* 830–41.

WATTS, W., & FREE, L. A. *State of the nation 1974.* Washington, D.C.: Potomac Associates.

WILLIAMS, R. M., JR. (1970). *American society: A sociological interpretation.* (3rd ed.). New York: Knopf.

YANKELOVICH, D. (1982). *New rules: Searching for self-fulfillment in a world turned upside down.* New York: Bantam Books.

CHAPTER TWO

PATTERNS OF OPPORTUNITY:
Why You Get What You Get

INTRODUCTION

Some of the things that will happen to you in life, or have already happened, have little to do with social inequality or your social class. A good friend dies, your mate falls out of love with you, you lose interest in your work: these things happen to people of every social class. They have happened in every society throughout history. In our society, the risks of these occurrences may vary slightly by social class, but other factors besides class also influence them.

However, many important things that will happen to you in life, or have already happened, are results of social inequality and social class. Poor people risk unemployment, poverty, illness, and a host of other unpleasant experiences. The rich and powerful can look forward to comfort, income security, and better-than-average health. Moreover, social inequality will not only influence what happens to you by chance, it will also influence your range of choices and the kind of choices you actually make.

Social inequality is any inequality between people that arises out of social relationships. For example, the inequalities in job recruitment, earnings, and chance of promotion for men and women are social inequalities. They arise out of social patterns of discrimination, not biological differences per se.

Likewise, the inequalities between people who hold different kinds of jobs—for example, factory workers and top managers—are social. They include inequalities of income, job security, working conditions, authority, and deference; and they arise out of different relationships to the means of production. One person controls the hiring and firing of workers; the other is controlled. One has only his or her labor to sell for wages; the other will often own a block of stock in the company.

Social inequalities fall into two main categories: inequalities of condition and inequalities of opportunity. Inequalities of *condition* include differences of wealth, authority, and prestige that translate directly into differences of physical and material well-being—food, shelter, physical security, good health, and so on. Indirectly, they translate into differences of mental health and happiness, as we shall see later in this chapter when we discuss "incapacitation."

Inequalities of *opportunity* are differences in the chance that people (or their children) will get to enjoy a different social condition—more wealth, authority, prestige, and so on. Some people, groups, and classes are more "socially mobile" than others, meaning that they have more opportunity to improve their social position. Some people will have a greater chance to get what they want out of life than others will.

Inequalities of condition and opportunity are not randomly distributed among members of society; rather, they are distributed among people primarily by social class. A *social class* is a relatively stable grouping whose members share common conditions and opportunities because of their common relationship to the means of production. Class boundaries remain from one generation to the next, separating a "working class" from a "capitalist class." The membership of social classes is also fairly stable. Although many people are socially mobile—moving out of their class of birth into another in adulthood—for many others class position is inherited—passed from parent to child over generations. As generations pass, certain families remain in the working class and other families remain in the capitalist class.

Most people know *something* about social classes and social inequality; they view these as problems with which American society must deal. Social inequality is so important to people that the constitutions of many nations specifically refer to opportunities that society owes its citizens. One of the earliest written constitutions, the American Constitution of 1787, pledges the government to ensure citizens the opportunity for "life, liberty, and the pursuit of happiness." Happiness is viewed as a natural, universal goal that the state must help its citizens attain more easily.

Two general assumptions guide the analysis that follows. The first is that the processes creating inequality are similar whether we consider individuals, groups, or nations. The same kinds of factors limit opportunity between groups or nations as between pairs of people.

Second, the two kinds of inequality discussed in this chapter—inequality of condition and inequality of opportunity—are connected. People cannot have an equal opportunity to get what they want if they start out with vastly unequal wealth, power, and respect. People who start out with more wealth, power, and respect *always*—in our society and every other—find it easier to get even more wealth, power, and respect. This is because wealth, power, and prestige can be exchanged for one another and "invested" for further gains. Thus, a society cannot equalize opportunity without greatly reducing the range of unequal starting points. If everyone were born with the same wealth, social position, and social connections, a great many people would have much more chance of getting what they want out of life than they do today.

The connection between types of inequality has two more implications. First, getting the most out of your own opportunities in life may mean taking part in collective action to reduce the range of inequality in our society. You can achieve only so much by yourself. Your own life chances are tied up with those of other Americans. Accordingly, this chapter will discuss collective as well as individual remedies to limited opportunity.

Second, we all live in the short run. In the long run, society may offer everyone more equal opportunity than it does today. But as the British economist John Maynard Keynes said, in the long run, we are all dead. So we must pay attention to the short run as well. Getting as much as you can out of life will mean more than collective action: it will also mean making sensible life choices within the context of unequal starting points and unequal opportunities.

Four Limits on Opportunity

Four processes limit people's opportunities to get what they want out of life, or to get an equal return on their investments of effort and talent—closure, incapacitation, decoupling, and scarcity.

Closure is the ability of certain groups to control access to certain rewards or opportunities. For example, closure can be exercised by a group of large organizations within an industry; an ethnic group within an occupation; a social class; or even, in small communities, by key individuals or families. It prevents people from entering contests they might win, or rewards people unequally for equal performances.

Through *incapacitation*, certain categories of people are persuaded not to compete for widely desired rewards. Our society's dominant ideology, or world view, teaches us that everyone has an equal chance, but in practice many kinds of people are discouraged from thinking themselves equal and competitive. Women, the poor, the old, the physically disabled, and young people have all been taught that certain kinds of behavior are inappropriate—unladylike, undignified, hopeless, and so on—or cannot succeed. The incapacitated "choose" not to compete.

Decoupling disconnects certain groups from rewards and key institutions. This lack of connection leads to a lack of information about available opportunities and ways of taking advantage of them. It also keeps people from first-hand acquaintanceship with others who could support or recommend them for rewards. People who are decoupled are not forced out of competition, nor do they eliminate themselves: they simply do not "know the ropes" or "have the contacts."

Scarcity is a shortage of desired goods or opportunities. While a shortage does not determine who will get the available opportunities, it does affect how many opportunities will be shared out in total. Often, people confuse scarcity with a poor distribution of desired goods due to closure, incapacitation, or decoupling. *True* scarcity can be reduced by producing more of the desired goods. Most often, scarcity makes itself felt in declining returns on investments; an example is "underemployment" of recent postsecondary graduates. We will discuss this problem at length in the next chapter.

Closure

What we commonly call "power" is exercised by certain groups who create rules—for instance, laws and structures of authority—that allocate desirable goods within society (Murphy, 1982). Research on American society by Mills (1956), Hunter (1959), Domhoff (1967, 1983), and Dye (1986) reveals that a person's social class largely determines his or her access to the most powerful (or "elite") positions in the economy and government. People born into the higher social classes are more likely to enter elite positions than people born into the middle class. Almost no members of America's economic and political elite come from a working-class background. This class-based difference in access is due partly to the decoupling of working-class people, as we will see shortly, and partly to closure. The upper class has traditionally closed its ranks to outsiders. Moreover, access to high-paying jobs in industrial societies has increasingly required a credential, often in the form of an educational degree, showing that the possessor has qualified for selection. Degrees from medical schools are particularly valuable credentials: virtually no doctors are unemployed or poorly paid. Who determines how these scarce degrees will be handed out: who will get them, and in return for what sacrifices?

Without a degree in medicine, no one is permitted to practice medicine. This limitation protects doctors by preventing competent nurses, paramedics, and other health professionals from breaking the medical monopoly on certain practices that generate high incomes. How did doctors achieve this unusual degree of closure over health care? This question interests many who study the professions and *professionalization*.

Closure and Professionalization   We see closure at work in the continuing battles over health care—debates about who shall pay and who is entitled to receive how much; and the exclusion of such competitors as chiropractors, homeopaths, and midwives from public recognition and coverage under public health plans. We also see lower-status educated groups—for example, social workers and psychologists—trying to "professionalize" themselves in hopes of higher status and better pay.

In some ways, we learn most about professionalization from the attempts that have failed. Mitford (1963) tells about the attempts undertakers have made to upgrade their status. Not content with being viewed (and paid) as technicians or businesspeople, undertakers seek greater credibility as "funeral directors" or "grief management consultants." So far their attempts have largely failed to persuade the public.

In America, professionalization has been part of the general rise of the middle class through its own efforts. The notion of "career" is a relatively new idea tied to the growth of a new middle class, the expansion of higher education, and the spread of a new demand for more credentials for more people (Bledstein, 1976). Professionalization has fed the American hunger for stable sources of authority in a rootless democratic society.

In other countries—France, Germany, Russia, and Italy among them—professions were brought into being by the state. For example, Napoleon instituted national schools of engineering as breeding grounds for higher-level civil servants (Larson, 1977). In these countries, the state, not an autonomous middle class, brought about modernization of the society. There, the professions—their training, credentials, and career paths—were shaped from the top down, not created by practitioners and sold to the state and public. In the older European societies professionalization was part of national economic and political planning.

This difference in origins may help to explain why, in America, the professions are neither part of an overall social plan nor easily ruled by any state authority. American professionals largely set their own income and social status in the absence of imposed controls.

In many respects, professional associations are little different from trade unions—both aim to protect and promote the economic interests of their members. They differ in only two important respects. First, professional associations help middle-class people protect middle-class incomes, while unions help working-class people protect working-class incomes. Because of the higher social origins of professions, people more willingly believe that professional associations really act in the public interest rather than in the private interest of their members.

Yet the public health movement in America has *not* been championed by leaders of medical associations. The reduction of illness and mortality in our society has historically owed more to public works, sewage and garbage management, clean water, and so on, than to the work of practicing physicians. Even today, medical associations show little interest in workplace safety, environmental pollution, antismoking campaigns, or any other fights against major causes of illness and death. Instead, American medicine increasingly addresses itself to high-tech, high-cost remedies that benefit only the very few—for example, the recipients of organ transplants.

Second, professional associations and unions, as movements, have used different means to protect their members. Unions typically threaten or use strikes to increase workers' incomes, employing collective means to pursue collective guarantees for their members. Professional associations occasionally do this. Mainly, they rely on political lobbying and the manipulation of public sentiment through the mass media to control the public "image" of their members. They aim to protect their members from political interference and personal liability in dealings with the public. Associations help their members earn whatever the market will bear in private dealings with customers. Professionalization provides some protection, but far from the amount the public believes it is receiving.

Medicine may be an exceptional illustration of the professionalization process. Because of the nature of the service provided—a matter of life and death—medicine has an almost unlimited market. Also, the scientific basis seems to produce desired results. The general lesson we learn from professionalization is that closure—in this case, control over public and private spending on specialized services—arises under certain kinds of historical, political, and economic conditions. It is a form of collective upward mobility that perpetuates and redistributes inequality. Professionalization advances primarily private interests by capitalizing on our fear of harm, belief in education, and inability to evaluate and control the people who serve us.

Closure and Structural/Cultural Pluralism   Another kind of closure is based on ethnic or racial origin. The job recruitment of people with similar ethnic backgrounds can be found in many workplaces. As a result, people of the same ethnic origins control specific organizations and even entire industries. When an ethnic group captures and monopolizes an economic activity, allowing access to that activity only or primarily on the basis of ethnic background, it is practicing closure.

Ethnic communities differ as much from one another as they do from the dominant Anglo-Saxon community. Structural and cultural pluralism is the main condition making ethnic closure possible (Gordon, 1964; Walzer, 1980; see also Breton, 1964). Pluralism refers to many subsocieties existing within one large society. It reflects the degree to which an ethnic group has created a set of social, cultural, and economic institutions sufficiently complete to allow near-total isolation from the rest of society.

A community's degree of institutional completeness determines the proportion of individuals who conduct most of their personal relations within the ethnic group. Ethnic organizations such as schools, camps, churches, business associations, social clubs, and mutual-aid societies or credit unions provide a context within which community members can meet and do business with other community members. These organizations make people more conscious of their ethnic origins. Like professional associations and unions, these organizations press for group interests.

In the United States, the degree of structural and cultural pluralism maintained by an ethnic community is largely determined by the extent of problems immigrants face on arrival. Immigrants may not be able to speak English. They may be unaccustomed to urban, industrial life or lack relevant job skills and job contacts outside their own community. On the positive side, they can speak in their native tongue; often have social contacts brought from their homeland; and may use their friendship or kinship contacts to develop job and business relations. So immigrants create a community that plays to their strengths and downplays their weaknesses.

Certain groups also face serious discrimination on their arrival in America and for some time afterward. Living in a situation of structural and cultural pluralism can protect immigrants in an actively hostile social and economic environment. This self-protective strategy has been historically practiced by Jews and Chinese in America, both victims of serious discrimination.

However, an ethnic community tends to maintain such a structurally and culturally separate subsociety even after the discrimination that created it has diminished or disappeared. The ethnic community not only defends its members against discrimination and pressures towards assimilation but also sustains the ethnic group cohesion by creating institutions, gaining control of resources, and providing a variety of educational, cultural, and social services (Walzer, 1980). Institutions formed within an ethnic community generate a demand for the services they provide. Thus, the mere survival of ethnic communities does not prove ethnic discrimination is occurring. Structural and cultural pluralism may also be fed by continuing fears of discrimination. For example, memories of the Holocaust and Israel's ongoing problems have undoubtedly strengthened the American Jewish community.

Conversely, some discriminated-against groups have little opportunity to practice closure in their own interest, despite good reason to do so. For example, blacks by and large lack the degree of structural pluralism that would help them prosper as a community. The reasons are complex, but slavery is at the bottom of the exploited and disadvantaged position of the blacks.

As slaves, the Africans who were brought to America and their descendants were treated as property from birth and for life. The slaves were denied the right to form a family; marriage between slaves was not legally recognized, and a slave could not marry or even meet with a free black (Schaefer, 1987). Denied a family—the building block of the ethnic community—and freedom of association, blacks found it impossible to create the economic, political, educational, and other institutions necessary for structural pluralism.

Under the yoke of slavery, cultural traditions that the Africans brought with them could not survive. For example, African religions were forbidden, and in their place the blacks were introduced to a version of Christianity that taught the virtue of submitting to their white masters. Even after Emancipation, "Jim Crow laws" in the Southern states kept the blacks segregated and in an inferior position.

More significantly, during the centuries of bondage a "tradition-of-enterprise" (Frazier, 1957), so vital to the creation of the economic institutions required for structural pluralism, disappeared from black culture. Consider the absence of credit associations: Light (1972) found that rotating credit associations had flourished in China, Japan, and West Africa, and were used by immigrants from China and Japan to finance their small businesses in the United States. Among West Africans, the custom of the rotating credit associations survived in the West Indies. There, demographic and economic conditions differed from those found in the United States during slavery and the post-emancipation period. The West Indian blacks would later bring West African rotating credit associations to the United States and use them to finance business.

However, American-born blacks—outnumbered by the whites and more severely subdued in the American south—experienced a great deal of difficulty maintaining African traditions, both during slavery and after emancipation. As a result, the rotating credit association disappeared from American-born blacks' cultural legacy. To some degree, this cultural loss would account for the blacks' lack of business success and also their failure to develop institutions that could protect the black communities against exploitation and discrimination by other groups.

What we usually mean by the term "discrimination" is just closure practiced by the majority against a minority group. It was not until the civil rights movements of the 1960s that the blacks were able to break through white closure and, sometimes, form their own closure.

The Jews illustrate a different kind of closure. Given the average levels of education they have attained, Jews are underpaid in work organizations that other ethnic groups control. As a group, Jews have avoided such discrimination and moved ahead by working hard, getting educated, and establishing themselves in certain well-paid occupations, especially business and the professions. Yet in large part, they have achieved their success by isolating themselves from work situations that would make them vulnerable to discrimination by Anglo-Saxons.

Today, few white ethnic minorities and virtually no people of color have made it to the economic elite. Dye (1986) identified only 20 blacks in 7,314 positions of authority in top-ranked public and private organizations. But some minorities are doing well economically. As ethnic communities have prospered, so have ethnic individuals. Certain key institutions—for example, universities—appear to have broken traditional barriers of discrimination against ethnic and racial minorities, but others—such as the largest industrial corporations and the oldest financial institutions—remain firmly in the hands of WASP (White Anglo-Saxon Protestant) males.

Human rights legislation is aimed at preventing discrimination, but it has been far from successful to date. In Table 2.1 we compare the median income of white and black families, while holding constant the educational level of the householder. Even among householders with the same amount of formal education, there is an income gap of approximately 15 to 25 percent between black and white families.

The decision you make about your career should therefore take into account the strengths and weaknesses of your own ethnic, racial, or status group. If you choose a career within your own community, ethnic or class closure will work for you, not against you. Whether working within that community is likely to satisfy depends on your own skills and aspirations, and on the degree of closure your community is able to forge—the range and number of opportunities it offers. In the long run, more satisfactory solutions are needed; we will discuss those solutions in later chapters.

Incapacitation

As adults and children, we learn to live effectively in the real world. Socialization teaches us how and why to conform to cultural values and social norms. But socialization also teaches us how to *not* function in the real world. This crippling socialization, which we all receive, is incapacitation. For many people, it means learning ways of thinking about ourselves that make us less than what we might otherwise be. Incapacitation is any socialization that induces low self-esteem, a low sense of mas-

tery or control, and feelings of alienation and distrust. Generally, incapacitation makes people believe that they *cannot* and *should not* do what
they hope to do. This socialization leads people to lower aspirations, lack
of assertiveness, and even withdrawal from competition.

So, for example, youngsters are taught that there are a great many
things they cannot understand and discuss reasonably with their elders,
because they lack the necessary experience, wisdom, or insight. They are
told to wait until they are older; then, presumably, they will understand
and see that their elders were right. Age is held against youngsters; their
ability goes untested.

More often than not, old people are treated like children, as if they lack
common sense and insight. They are typically pampered or ignored, but
not treated as adult equals. From the moment of their forced retirement
from the work force, they are taught "We think you *can't!* We think you
can't!" For older Americans, too, age is held against them; ability goes
untested.

However, the old and young are not alone in their incapacitation.
Among adults, women make up the largest number of incapacitated people. Women are not only denied the chance to try a great many things but
are also taught that they cannot do them and should not want to. For

TABLE 2.1 Median Income of Black and White Families Holding
Householder's Education Constant, 1985. (Source: Bureau of the Census,
1986: 85).

	White Families	*Black Families*	*Ratio Black to White*
TOTAL	$37,290	$27,178	.73
Elementary	24,870	21,406	.86
High School			
1–3 years	27,845	22,334	.80
4 years	33,457	25,396	.76
College			
1–3 years	38,088	29,092	.76
4 years	47,912	38,258	.80
5 years or more	55,144	47,699	.86

NOTE: Figures are median income from all sources, including salaries, wages, commissions,
public-assistance payments, dividends, pension, unemployment compensation and so on,
but not capital gains. Householders are 25 years of age or older and are year-round, full-time
workers.

example, until the enactment of Title IX (Educational Amendment Act of 1972) which prohibits sex discrimination in school sports and mandates schools to provide equal facilities and experiences for male and female students, many potential female athletes were not encouraged to participate in sports. Even today, Title IX has not been fully enforced and women's athletic programs are still inadequately funded. Moreover, sexist attitudes still discourage women from engaging in supposedly male sports such as football, basketball, baseball, weightlifting, wrestling, and long-distance running. One study (Snyder & Spreitzer, 1983) found that only 44 percent of female basketball players, as compared to 70 percent of women gymnasts, perceived themselves as being "very feminine." Traditional notions of "feminine" behavior are as limiting to women as the bustles and other ridiculously encumbering clothes they used to wear in the name of fashion.

However, we must avoid the error of "exceptionalism" when studying the incapacitation of young people, old people, women and the poor (see, for example, Lewis, 1966; Sennett & Cobb, 1973), the unemployed (Schlozman & Verba, 1979), and the stigmatized (Goffman, 1963; Lemert, 1972). As Mills (1943) pointed out, these social problems (and others) are connected by a common thread, and we cannot understand the individual case without understanding that common element. The unifying element in cases of incapacitation is our society's dominant ideology. This ideology teaches people who are victimized—by the class structure and otherwise—to blame themselves (Ryan, 1976).

What do average Americans think about their opportunities? Research evidence suggests that Americans have mixed views. According to Campbell and his associates (1976), people slowly but surely adjust their aspirations to their circumstances. In the course of one's lifetime, the gap between aspirations and achievements narrows, partly because some goals have been achieved and partly because expectations have fallen to more realistic levels (Campbell, 1981). Mickelson (1989) argues that young people can accurately assess their future opportunities and the returns they can expect on their occupational achievements. In keeping with the future they foresee, they put more or less effort into academic achievement. Like others, they are largely resigned to the limits on their opportunity. This is what Mann (1970) has called a "pragmatic acceptance" of the facts of social inequality.

On the other hand, many Americans feel that people should set goals that are hard to achieve, and that what one gets out of life is one's own doing, not the result of luck or chance. In a study conducted in Boston and Kansas City by Coleman, Rainwater, and McClelland (1978), 60 percent of adults reported upward social mobility: that is, their socioeconomic status was higher than that of their parents. Respondents attributed their upward social mobility to personal achievement and the availability of great opportunities in this country. They felt that the key to gaining high status is putting out the greatest effort. Such views suggest a belief that nothing can stop a committed person.

However, these views—on the one hand, resigned, on the other hand, committed—are not the views of two distinct groups. Rather, a large proportion of Americans are ambivalent or confused about their opportunities for life satisfaction. In a sense, everyone knows about such constraints as closure, decoupling, and scarcity. But people rarely confront such knowledge consciously and rationally, and take appropriate action. Our thinking is largely "ideological," and ideology is primarily a system of beliefs—untestable by reality—and only partly a system of ideas and knowledge.

Moreover, the idea that people can make the lives they want is rooted in an old philosophical outlook that political theorist C. B. Macpherson (1962) has called "possessive individualism." Macpherson summarizes this outlook—which developed out of seventeenth-century English political debates—in seven propositions:

1. What makes a person human is freedom from dependence on the wills of others.
2. Freedom from dependence on others means freedom from any relations with others, except those relations which the individual enters voluntarily with a view to his own interest.
3. The individual is essentially the proprietor of his own person and capacities, for which he owes nothing to society.
4. Although the individual cannot alienate the whole of his property in his own person, he may alienate his capacity to labor.
5. Human society consists of a series of market relations.
6. Since freedom from the wills of others is what makes a man human, each individual's freedom can rightfully be limited only by such obligations and rules as are necessary to secure the same freedom for others.
7. Political society is a human contrivance for the protection of the individual's property in his person and goods, and [therefore] for the maintenance of orderly relations of exchange between individuals regarded as proprietors of themselves. (pp. 263–264)

What Macpherson has called "possessive individualism" is at the root of what others have called "laissez-faire capitalism," "liberal democracy," or the "liberal ideology." It emphasizes the rights of individuals against government interference, and protects people's rights to carry out economic exchange any way they want to, so long as they do not break laws.

Liberal democracy rests on free choice, free competition and, as a result of the other two, a free market in labor, goods, and ideas (Macpherson, 1962). These freedoms are usually found in societies with a capitalist economy, universal suffrage, and two or more political parties. But given social inequality—unequal starting points—freedom comes into conflict with fairness. That is because liberal democracy holds people responsible for protecting their own interests in exchange with others. It denies that any collective interests may be more important than individual interests: for example, environmental protection and world peace, as against unlimited resource use or weapon-selling. It also forgets that some people are less able than others to protect their own interests.

The assumption that people can protect their own interest and that no one else—including government—needs to do so, is completely unfounded. Even during the heyday of laissez-faire capitalism (the nineteenth century), governments regularly interceded on behalf of business and hereditary wealth (Polanyi, 1944). Increasingly, governments also came to realize that widespread poverty endangered the social order. This problem called for more and more comprehensive "poor laws" and, eventually, social welfare legislation after 1830.

During the worldwide Depression of the 1930s, governments learned to intercede more comprehensively. British economist John Maynard Keynes showed that capitalism could not survive without large-scale government intervention in the economy; government needed to "prime the pumps" and stabilize earning, spending, and saving.

Today, modern economies operate through an extremely complex mechanism of government legislation and assistance to both business and private citizens. Virtually no sphere of life goes unregulated today. In this sense, the assumptions of possessive individualism are quite unfounded.

However, our "institutions of information"—mass media, churches, and even schools—continue to promote the belief that people are free to make their lives whatever they want to. Hard work and merit are rewarded. Sloth and crime are punished. Moreover, government and other collective bodies—especially trade unions—interfere with people's right to choose. These kinds of ideas, trumpeted by leaders of business through the mass media they own or control, are attractive enough to survive year after year.

But we witness the falsity of these ideas much more often than we see their truth. People we know are often *not* rewarded for hard work and merit. Conversely, the upper classes inherit enormous wealth, generation after generation; this tells us that hard work and merit have little to do with rewards. Moreover, corporate crime, government patronage, and tax laws that favor the rich over the poor all prove that the cards are stacked against ordinary people.

What keeps our society together in the face of this systematic inequality and demonstrated untruth? Surveying studies of public opinion from several capitalist countries, Mann (1970) concludes there is little evidence that people generally agree with the beliefs and values of liberal democracy: there is neither consensus nor consistency in their views. To a large degree, it is this ambivalence that makes the system work. "Cohesion in liberal democracy depends on the lack of consistent commitment to general values of any sort and on the 'pragmatic acceptance' by subordinate classes of their limited roles in society" (Mann, 1970: 423).

But Mann also finds evidence of *false consciousness*; this too may produce order and social cohesion. False consciousness is a perception of society that incorrectly describes everyday reality to disadvantaged people. For example, it holds the disadvantaged person responsible for circumstances beyond his or her control, and in that way incapacitates.

So, for example, a person who is laid off or unable to find work will be led by false consciousness to focus attention on personal failings as the explanation, rather than on a high unemployment rate, discrimination, business mismanagement, or bad government handling of the economy. A two-earner family that is struggling unsuccessfully to meet all its financial, occupational, spousal, and parental obligations may turn its aggression inward—spouse against spouse, parent against child (and vice versa)—in this way destroying the family, rather than blame exploitive or inflexible employers, inadequate legislation, and uncontrolled prices.

Mann (1970) finds evidence that false consciousness does exist, incapacitating workers. Workers are indoctrinated—by the mass media and in other ways—to subscribe to vague political philosophies that contradict their everyday experience and support the status quo. (Appeals to patriotism, tradition, harmony, and national greatness are among the stated goals of such philosophies). In this way, workers are incapacitated by the inconsistency of their beliefs.

They are further incapacitated by failed attempts to alter their circumstances. Consider the case of unemployment. Hartman and Erskine (1988) found no evidence of unemployment leading to a perceived need to change the form of government among the jobless (see also Schlozman & Verba, 1979).

In some situations, incapacitation is due less to false consciousness or a sense of personal fault than to a feeling of powerlessness that is rooted in reality. But often the origins are more pervasive, harder to see, and harder to change. For example, Baldus and Tribe (1978) studied perceptions of inequality among schoolchildren. By Grade 6, a high proportion have learned to consistently match social class indicators such as clothing, type of housing, and quality of car with one another: fancy clothes, a nice house, a new car, and so on "go together." Moreover, people with good clothes, houses, and cars are believed to care more about their appearance, to be trying harder. Finally, and most worrisome, the richer people are supposedly nicer and "better" people—more honest, better behaved, and harder working.

Children from poorer families are just as likely as children from wealthier families to make these assessments. Moreover, these beliefs grow stronger and more consistent with age. The result is what Sennett and Cobb (1973) have called "hidden injuries of class." Ordinary people who are not rich, not powerful, and not respected cannot easily live with such negative images of themselves, so they find ways of salvaging their dignity and sense of personal worth.

One way is by dominating others who are even less powerful—poor whites dominating blacks, native people, or other minorities; poor men dominating their wives and children; children tormenting other children or pets. Another way is by imagining that the poor are morally superior to the rich. Both ways are documented in a landmark study of the "authoritarian personality" (Adorno, Frenkel-Brunswik, Levinson, & Sanford, 1969).

According to Sennett and Cobb (1973), people also employ "dreams and defences" to heal these hidden injuries. People who feel worthless dream of becoming "worthwhile" through their own (or their children's) upward mobility, winning a lottery, or some other stroke of good fortune. Women's romance books and magazines are about just this—Cinderellas who (as nurses, secretaries, or other male-helpers) meet and marry their Prince Charming through a combination of good luck, virtue, and wile.

Defenses against incapacitation by feelings of worthlessness include splitting the "real person" from the "performing person." People try to avoid feeling like they belong to the despised or menial role they play. They think, "In reality, I am someone else—not Clark Kent, but Superman. I possess enormous hidden powers that I will reveal at the right moment, winning deserved admiration." This theme of the dual, split, or hidden personality runs throughout mass entertainment because, for so many, it is a necessary escape from daily indignity.

This defense offers most people a (temporarily) constructive adaptation to a destructive social order—"constructive" because it allows people to continue functioning; temporary because it fails to solve the problem. "It stills pain in the short run, but does not remove the conditions that made a defense necessary in the first place" (Sennett & Cobb, 1973: 219).

Decoupling

Often without knowing it, even people who are not victimized by closure and incapacitation will suffer restricted opportunity if they are *decoupled* from major sources of opportunity and power in society.

The word "decoupling" suggests a disconnected railway or subway car that has been left unused on a side track. Like train cars, people are connected to one another and often pull one another forward or back. Contrary to the dominant ideology that holds each of us personally responsible for our own fate, much of what happens in life actually results from the actions of others, many unknown and distantly connected to us.

Consider how the careers of church ministers are shaped by very distant events. The job vacancy created by a minister's death or retirement often sets off a chain reaction resulting in the upward movement of dozens of other ministers (White, 1970). For this reason, social mobility is as much the result of "vacancy chains" as the accomplishment of individuals.

Under varying economic conditions, an initial move may produce longer or shorter chains of reaction. Retirement or death may not always lead to a long chain reaction of replacements. Sometimes the departed person's job is eliminated, taken on by someone holding a second job, or filled by a newcomer brought in from outside. These kinds of reactions are probably most common in organizations "downsizing" in response to economic difficulty.

Yet even when a vacancy chain fails to operate, our opportunities are still tied to formal and informal contacts with other people. This fact is compellingly demonstrated by studies of the American upper class (for example, Domhoff, 1967, 1974; Dye, 1986; Kolko, 1962). Members of the upper class are tied to one another by a variety of common associations and experiences—marriage; kinship; attendance at the same private schools, summer camps, and universities; membership in the same social clubs; and service on the same boards of directors. Upper-class people are much better acquainted with others in their class than middle-class or working-class people are.

The size of a group affects mutual acquaintanceship. The upper class is small, which makes knowing most other members easier. Another factor is structural pluralism: upper-class institutions and activities are just as exclusive as ethnic institutions, and for the same reasons. Upper-class people have property interests to protect against encroachment by the government and by the lower classes. Class-based institutions and shared experiences produce mutual acquaintanceship, a basis upon which closure can be exercised against outsiders. Similarly, wide contacts among upper-class people form the basis for job recruitment into elite positions.

Social contacts are also important in the middle class. A survey of managers showed that people typically find good jobs through personal contacts (Granovetter, 1974). Yet most people believe that others *do not* find jobs in that way. Most of us are swayed by the ideology that people succeed or fail through their own efforts, so that we think our own experiences are unusual when they are not.

When an employer has a position to fill, many people have suitable qualifications. If the job opening is advertised, many applicants will have to be screened or interviewed. Investigating every applicant to find the best would be very expensive. So employers often ask their personal contacts—people they know and trust—to recommend someone good enough for the job. In this way, the employer can find someone with the right qualifications at relatively little cost. That person may not be the single most qualified individual in the whole country, but will be qualified enough to do the job. Employers want a satisfactory, not an optimal, solution to their problem.

This method of hiring also gives the employer information about a candidate that is unlikely to surface in a resume. The candidate recommended by a trusted friend or acquaintance probably has the right attitude as well as credentials.

People find jobs in the same way as employers find job candidates. Job-seekers want to know if the job is a good one, the boss a good boss, the prospects for advancement good, and so on. They will find out more by talking to an acquaintance with first-hand knowledge of the organization, the job, and the boss than in any other way. Impersonal sources of information (for example, organizational brochures and formal interviews) are unlikely to reveal as much about these matters.

So on both sides of the job market—among people who are hiring and people who want to be hired—"networks of personal contact" provide the best information about jobs or candidates. As a result, many jobs find people, or people find jobs, through networks of personal contact. In fact, the best-paying jobs are filled in this way.

Granovetter found that valuable job information is most often passed on by acquaintances, not close friends or relatives. "Acquaintances" are people you can call by their first name, but are not (emotionally) close friends. We have a great many more acquaintances than close friends, so the likelihood is simply greater that we will get useful information from an acquaintance. Beyond that, close friends tend to have the same information about jobs. Their total information is limited because it is duplicated. By contrast, a person's acquaintances are less likely than his or her friends to know one another, and conversely, they are more likely to know many other people. Acquaintance networks can become very large indeed, numbering hundreds or even, in some cases, thousands of people.

Job referral chains could, therefore, be enormously long, but in practice they are not. People do not trust information that comes from someone at five removes from the job or candidate any more than they would trust information a stranger provided. This is because we live in a "small world," as psychologist Stanley Milgram's studies of social networks have shown (Travers & Milgram, 1969). Most people have thousands or tens of thousands of "acquaintances" at five removes; at ten or fifteen removes, every pair of people in the country is likely to have *someone* in common. Therefore, in practice, only acquaintances or acquaintances of acquaintances are likely to pass on valuable job information.

Each acquaintance brings you information and connections that other acquaintances are unlikely to duplicate. So acquaintanceships prove enormously valuable in getting a job. Your chances of hearing about a job or having an employer hear about you are best if you have many acquaintances. But how can a person maximize these chances? Granovetter does not believe that people ought to purposefully "network" in order to increase the number and variety of their acquaintanceships. Few people respond favorably to that kind of overture. They quickly see it for what it is—crass opportunism.

However, one strategy *is* likely to increase opportunities. People who have changed organizations the most times will have the most acquaintances. Beyond a certain point, of course, job-changing becomes counter-productive. If you changed organizations every day, no one would learn what you can do. But a person changing jobs three or four times over 15 years might end up knowing people in 30 or 40 different companies, since usually his or her acquaintances are also changing companies. People with an average job tenure of three to five years seem to do best.

Further, people who begin moving between organizations early in their careers seem to benefit most. This process creates a "snowballing" of career opportunities. People who remain with the same organization for much of their working life have a lot of trouble finding another job when forced to do so.

How far to generalize these findings is hard to say. At least in higher-status jobs, making many contacts, then moving on to another organization, seems to pay the greatest dividends. You get the maximum benefit from this process when your entire network is expanding through your acquaintances' actions as well as your own actions.

This implies that maximum career benefits are to be gained by investing your time in acquaintanceship, not friendship, kinship, or other relationships. However, research on closure suggests that this strategy will work better for some people than for others. First, some organizations consider stability and loyalty very important, and view with suspicion people who have moved every three to five years. Second, for people seeking careers within ethnic communities, involvement with old friends and kin may be much more beneficial than acquaintanceships.

The value of acquaintanceships for finding good jobs *within* ethnic communities will vary according to the kinds of jobs the ethnic community controls. For example, acquaintanceship will be much more likely to uncover a good job in the prosperous and economically diverse Jewish or Italian communities than in the more limited Pakistani or Portuguese communities.

The process Granovetter describes may also be more characteristic of middle-class than working-class jobs. Working-class people are far more likely to find their first job through friends and relatives in a similar line of work; later in life, they start finding jobs by answering advertisements and other formal means. Middle-class people do the opposite: namely, they use their educational credentials to find a first job, then they find later jobs through people they have met at work.

This process works against groups that are underrepresented in better jobs or socially decoupled from the dominant group. For example, whites more often make the acquaintance of other whites, and men the acquaintance of other men. When asked to recommend people for jobs, whites will accordingly tend to recommend other whites, men other men. Even without intending to discriminate, the process produces a discriminatory outcome, in that the organization remains racially or sexually unbalanced.

The process is hard to change by appealing to employers' finer instincts. Acting otherwise would be costly for the individual employer. For example, hiring a qualified black or woman could mean instituting a time-consuming and costly employee search; the employer will avoid doing this unless obliged to by affirmative action laws. Such laws, therefore, will be important in forcing all employers to bear the costs of a wider than usual employee search.

Higher-status people tend to have much larger, more varied, and more valuable networks of contact than lower-status people. Higher-status people have more time and money to travel, meet people, and interact socially: this helps in forming acquaintanceships. Second, because they have higher status and more access to scarce resources, higher-status people are likely to receive more of other people's attention. Lower-status people will seek them out for advice, encouragement, and help. This will give the higher-status people a great many contacts even without making an effort. Finally, as noted earlier, elite and upper-class institutions bring higher-status people together on a regular basis.

At least in the beginning of their careers, people can do little to attain high status and thereby receive many helpful contacts. But people *can* make the best possible use of their network of acquaintances. People should keep up their contacts, even if it means taking time away from other activities they value. If you are looking for a job, let your acquaintances know it.

Further, people should not be incapacitated by the ideology that teaches us that applicants get the best jobs because they are the most qualified. Skills and credentials are certainly important to get you into the race. But after that, the competition for jobs and rewards has a lot to do with interpersonal relations. Unless you are among the ablest in your age group, hundreds and perhaps thousands of other potential job candidates share your qualifications. To the stranger filling a position, you look the same on paper as many others do. So do not ignore the opportunities that can come through your personal network if you use it wisely. (For reasons of space, we shall leave questions of how to use your network wisely to the many recent popular books on "networking.")

On the other hand, do not blame yourself if you fail to get the job you want when you want it. Remember that the job may have gone to someone who is no more deserving but who had the good fortune to link into the organization. Your lack of connection has deprived you of valuable information about available opportunities, ways of taking advantage of them, and first-hand acquaintances who could advance your interests. You were "decoupled."

Scarcity

A fourth reason people often give to explain limited opportunity is that there is not enough to go around: the desired good is in short supply, or *scarce*. Scarcity varies with the ratio of competitors to desired goods. Scarcity can be reduced by eliminating competitors (through closure, incapacitation, or decoupling) or by increasing the supply of goods.

We see scarcity all around us. But not only the poor suffer from scarcity. The middle class is increasingly victimized by scarcity, as witnessed by the growing inability of its young adults to own homes as their parents had done. The down payment of those who are able to buy their first home is often provided by "G.I. Financing"—the gifts and loans of "Generous In-laws" (San Francisco Sunday Examiner and Chronicle, April 2, 1989). A gap is widening between the rich and everyone else, so as the rich get even richer, the rest get poorer and the traditional middle ground disappears.

Beyond this material deprivation—which, presumably, could be remedied by economic growth and redistribution—we find "social limits to growth" (Hirsch, 1978). Increasingly, people value rare or scarce items— the unique vacation, the unusual home, designer clothing, and so on— *because* they are scarce. People want something that is all their own in a society of growing uniformity. Yet the sheer growth in our numbers makes this goal ever harder to attain.

Often we adapt by giving up something that we have long valued or even loved. We give up going to a beach that was once secluded, a perfect refuge, and is now packed with huge radios. We give up going back home, to the small town where everyone once knew everyone else now that it is a bedroom suburb for strangers. We give up a restaurant that used to have wonderful food; today, it is full of plastic, junk food, and Walt Disney decor. Can we find a way to replace these lost pleasures?

It is becoming ever more difficult and expensive to enjoy the truly scarce—good craftsmanship, privacy, and politeness, for example. This loss is largely due to the rapid growth of population and increased social and geographic mobility which, along with consumerism and rampant self-interest, have broken traditional standards and restraints. We cannot bring the old things back, and only if we have a lot of money can we replace them. So, like the employers discussed in the last section, we must seek satisfactory, not optimal solutions. This may mean looking at our choices in a new way and giving new value to things we had not valued before. Consider the problem in scarcity some demographers (or population experts) have called the "marriage squeeze."

Between 1945 and 1957 more babies were born each year than in the year before. Of these, roughly half were male and half were female. But women tend to marry men who are a few years older. A woman about thirty years old in 1987 would find a shortage, or scarcity, of men thirty-three or thirty-five years old. Men of this age would have been born in 1952–54, and many fewer men were born in each of these years than were born in each of the years 1955–57, when the woman in question was born. This is the "marriage squeeze" from the standpoint of single women about thirty years old.

As you might imagine, the situation reverses itself after a certain point. Women about twenty-five years old in 1987 would find no shortage of men several years older, since more men were still being born in each of the years 1959–61 than women in 1962–64. Now there is a shortage of brides, a marriage squeeze for single men twenty-five to thirty years old. What creative strategies do people use to deal with this situation of scarcity?

In response to these marriage squeezes, many traditional constraints on mate selection are disappearing. First and most obvious, people are marrying mates who, in the past, might have been considered too old or too young. Others are marrying outside their own racial and ethnic groups. More often than before people are marrying previously married people. Others are marrying across class lines.

Many who do not choose, or are not able, to solve the mating problem in these ways find alternative solutions: unmarried motherhood and sequential cohabitation, as examples. Still others adjust to a single life by shifting their concerns to work, leisure, and friendship. Singles today are less stigmatized than they were in the past. Our culture no longer thinks of marriage as the natural and inevitable condition of life.

The adjustments in this case are both personal and cultural—a new conception of adult life, family, and marriage, created partly in response to the marriage squeeze. Similar adaptations have been made at other times in history and in other countries, where one sex or the other has been in short supply due to war, migration, or another demographic quirk.

The same principle applies to all situations of scarcity. Scarcity is a normal state of affairs for many reasons, not only demographic. More often, it is due to closure—the monopolization of desired goods by people powerful enough to control access to them. The powerful are able to get far more than their share of what everyone wants—money, good housing, respect, and so on. Moreover, as Marx and Engels (Meek, 1954) argued against prevailing beliefs in "overpopulation," capitalism itself tends to produce scarcity. Capitalists want a large "reserve army of the unemployed" to keep down wages, and a shortage of food and consumer products to keep up prices. Moreover, under capitalism the investment in technology rises continually and the capital invested in workers' wages falls. According to this theory, capitalism creates too few, indeed ever fewer, jobs; prices rise; and inequality increases steadily.

The best long-term answer to this problem is to break monopolies on production and prices, and a political revolution may be needed to do so. However, most North Americans reject this solution: they may believe that the monopolists deserve what they have, believe that needed changes can be made gradually through legislation, or fear the consequences of a revolution. Thinking that the institution of private property is as valuable to them as it is to monopolists, they may fear its loss through political upheaval.

While some people see revolution as a creative solution to the problem of scarcity, many others see increased productivity as a better solution. Typically, high rates of economic growth give most people more of what they want without breaking the existing monopolies. Such growth has no effect on the extent of social inequality, but it makes inequality less visible and less painful to the majority.

Often America's prosperity has been achieved by colonizing less-developed countries—that is, by making them the source of cheap resources and labor power. We have solved the problem of local scarcity by exporting it, worsening someone else's economic situation in order to improve our own.

Given current levels of malnutrition in the world, a collective priority in the face of scarcity is producing more of what people *need*. For many today, primary needs for food, shelter, and physical security are simply not being met. At best greater economic growth is only part of the solution. The Third World remains largely locked out of the benefits of overall economic growth. Beyond that, too much of the world's economic growth is siphoned into arms production and warmaking.

In our own society, a variety of social collectivities—professional associations, workers' unions, ethnic groups, and so on—use monopolization to their own advantage. While this is, in a certain sense, a creative adaptation to scarcity, in the long run it cannot succeed. If every collectivity in the world mobilizes to secure a greater advantage, inequality will persist in more aggressive forms. Compare the situation to a parade people have come to see. First a few people stand on their toes to see the parade better, then a few more, and so on. When everyone is standing on tiptoe, each one's ability to see the parade is as unequal as it was before, but everyone has sore toes.

Long-run solutions to the problem of unequal opportunity must be worldwide and cooperative. Anything less will work for only a short time, or will result in economic, political, and military warfare.

What the human race has working against it is greed, extreme and widening inequality, and rapid population growth. Working in its favour is a demonstrated capability to use knowledge and science creatively, adapt to new circumstances, and occasionally cooperate for mutual benefit.

CONCLUDING REMARKS

We started by asking why you will not get everything you want out of life, and why some people will get more of what they want than you will. The answer to both questions is the same—class structure. Class structure means unequal opportunity to get what you want. A few will enjoy enormous benefits and privilege, and the majority will not; that is how a class system works. So in a sense, your situation is not only unlike other people's, it is opposed to other people's. As they grow richer, you grow poorer; and vice versa. Yet this view is partly an illusion.

Your opportunities are actually tied up with everyone else's. You certainly share common problems with other people in your own social class. Personal, individual remedies have been discussed in this chapter, and they are important; but in what Canadian thinker Marshall McLuhan calls the "global village," planet earth, they have limited value. In both the short and long run, your opportunity is tied to almost everyone else's. The class structure must be changed to achieve maximum benefit.

We shall discuss remedies to your problem of unequal opportunities in the last chapter. They fall into two main categories—individual and collective. The collective remedies, as we shall see, tend to take longer but do a better job.

Why you get what you get is largely the result of an extremely complex set of arrangements sociologists call *social structure*. The processes of closure, incapacitation, decoupling, and scarcity we have discussed tend to maintain that social structure. They do so by limiting what you get, but also by limiting what you want. Moreover, they limit your ability to close the gap between what you want and what you get when such a gap develops.

Not only do these processes of domination limit your opportunity and your desires, they also limit your conception of the truly possible—your consciousness of reality past, present, and future. Most people feel that they are less than they should be or can accomplish less than they actually might. All around us, people blame themselves for forces beyond their control or (sometimes) understanding—the laid-off worker, the job applicant without connections, the politely excluded, the searcher for a scarce mate. People who solve the problem in an ideologically wrong way—the "unladylike" woman, or the person who finds a job through acquaintances, for example—are liable to think they are deviant and wonder if they deserve the rewards they get.

Social inequality structures the way we think about our problems. It makes most people believe their common problems are actually individual problems, for which they alone are to blame. In this context, we should not be surprised to find that people try to find individual, not collective solutions to their problems; hold themselves responsible for what they get out of life; and try to close the gap between what they want and what they get by wanting less.

In the rest of this book we shall examine the ways that social structure affects your aspirations and opportunities in a variety of everyday domains.

REFERENCES

BALDUS, B., & TRIBE, V. (1978). Perceptions of social inequality among public school children. *Canadian Review of Sociology and Anthropology, 15*(1), 50–60.

BLEDSTEIN, B. J. (1976). *The culture of professionalism: The middle class and the development of higher education in America.* New York: W. W. Norton.

BRETON, R. (1964). Institutional completeness of ethnic communities. *American Journal of Sociology, 20*(2), 193–205.

BUREAU OF THE CENSUS. (1986). *Money income of the households, families and persons in the United States: 1985.* Series P-60, No. 156.

CAMPBELL, A. (1981). *The sense of well-being in America: Recent patterns and trends.* New York: McGraw-Hill Co.

CAMPBELL, A., CONVERSE, P. E., & RODGERS, W. L. (1976). *The quality of American life: Perceptions, evaluations, and satisfactions.* New York: Russell Sage Foundation.

COLEMAN, R., RAINWATER, L., & MCCLELLAND, K. A. (1978). *Social standing in America: New dimensions of class.* New York: Basic Books.

DOMHOFF, G. W. (1967). *Who rules America?* Englewood Cliffs, N.J.: Prentice-Hall.

————. (1974). *The Bohemian Grove and other retreats.* New York: Harper & Row.

————. (1983). *Who rules America now? A view for the '80s.* Englewood Cliffs, N.J.: Prentice-Hall.

DYE, T. R. (1986). *Who's running America? The conservative years.* (4th ed.). Englewood Cliffs, N.J.: Prentice-Hall.

FRAZIER, E. F. (1957). *Black bourgeoisie.* New York: Free Press.

GOFFMAN, E. (1963). *Stigma: Notes on the management of spoiled identity.* Englewood Cliffs, N.J.: Prentice-Hall.

GORDON, M. M. (1962). *Assimilation in American life: The role of race, religion, and national origins.* New York: Oxford University Press.

HARTMAN, J. T., & ERSKINE, W. B. (1988). Breaking the ice: Unemployment and the transformation of political consciousness in recessionary times. Paper presented at the American Sociological Association Meeting, 1988.

HIRSCH, F. (1978). *The social limits to growth.* Cambridge, Mass.: Harvard University Press.

HUNTER, F. (1959). *Top leadership, U.S.A.* Chapel Hill: University of North Carolina Press.

KOLKO, G. (1962). *Wealth and power in America.* New York: Praeger.

LARSON, M. S. (1977). *The rise of professionalism: A sociological analysis.* Berkeley, Calif.: University of California Press.

LEMERT, E. M. (1972). *Human deviance, social problems and social control.* (2nd ed.). Englewood Cliffs, N.J.: Prentice-Hall.

LEWIS, O. (1966). The culture of poverty. *Scientific American, 215* (4), 19–25.

LIGHT, I. H. (1972). *Ethnic enterprise in America: Business and welfare among Chinese, Japanese, and Blacks.* Berkeley, Calif.: University of California Press.

MACPHERSON, C. B. (1962). *The political theory of possessive individualism: Hobbes to Locke.* Oxford: Clarendon Press.

————. (1965). *The real world of democracy.* The Massey Lectures, (4th Series). Toronto: Canadian Broadcasting Corporation.

MANN, M. (1970). The social cohesion of liberal democracy. *American Sociological Review, 35*(3), 423–39.

MEEK, R. L. (ED.). (1954). *Marx and Engels on Malthus.* D. L. Meek & R. L. Meek (Trans.). New York: International Publishers.

MICKELSON, R. A. (1989). Why does Jan read and write so well? The anomaly of women's achievement. *Sociology of Education, 62,* 47–63.

MILLS, C. W. (1943). The professional ideology of social pathologists. *American Journal of Sociology, 49*(2), 165–80.

————. (1956). *The power elite.* New York: Oxford University Press.

————. (1959). *The sociological imagination.* New York: Oxford University Press.

MITFORD, J. (1963). *The American way of death.* New York: Oxford University Press.

MURPHY, R. (1982). The structure of closure: A critique and development of the theories of Weber, Collins and Parker. *British Journal of Sociology, 35*(4), 547–67.

POLANYI, K. (1944). *The great transformation.* New York: Farrar & Rinehart.

SCHAEFER, R. T. (1987). *Racial and ethnic groups.* (3rd ed.). Glenview, Ill.: Scott, Foresman and Co.

SCHLOZMAN, K. L., & VERBA, S. (1979). *Injury to insult: Unemployment, class and political response.* Cambridge, Mass.: Harvard University Press.

SENNETT, R., & COBB, J. (1973). *The hidden injuries of social class.* New York: Vintage.

SNYDER, E. E., & SPREITZER, E. A. (1983). *Social aspects of sport.* (2nd ed.). Englewood Cliffs, N.J.: Prentice-Hall.

TRAVERS, J., & MILGRAM, S. (1969). An experimental study of the small world problem. *Sociometry, 32,* 425–43.

WALZER, M. (1980). Pluralism: a political perspective. In Stephan Theernstrom, Ann Orlov, and Oscar Handlin (Eds.), *Harvard Encyclopedia of American Ethnic Groups* (pp. 781–87). Cambridge, Mass.: Harvard University Press.

WHITE, H. (1970). *Chains of opportunity: System models of mobility in organizations.* Cambridge, Mass.: Harvard University Press.

CHAPTER THREE

EDUCATION:
*What You Want and
What You Get*

INTRODUCTION

This chapter and others that follow examine specific areas—domains—of everyday life. There are four basic components to this and each analysis that follows: an examination of (1) the system of social institutions relevant to a domain; (2) demographic trends bearing on those institutions; (3) the choices people make in relation to that institutional structure, given their demographic characteristics; and (4) the impact of the choices they make, especially on life satisfaction. Each chapter will end by considering whether people typically get what they want in a particular domain, or grow to want what they get.

Later chapters will discuss careers, marriage, childraising, and other issues about which you will have to make choices as your life progresses. This chapter will discuss educational choices you are already making, and their likely consequences. Specifically, we will look at two educational issues that concern many students: How do people come to choose the education they get? and How do the choices they make affect their employability, job satisfaction, income, and social status?

Education benefits both individuals *and* society. The outcomes of educational decisions we will examine most closely—employability, job satisfaction, income, and social status—are not the only or even the most important benefits of a higher education; but students are keenly interested in questions of employment and pay following graduation. For this reason we focus mainly on these outcomes.

Some readers may want to skip this chapter. After all, they have already made their educational choices. In fact, older students may already be on their second set of educational choices, returning to school for new training and a new career. Moreover, many students may feel that whatever the reason for their choice and whatever the outcome, they will have to live with it, so the less said, the happier they will be. Others may think that they looked into their educational options well enough before making a choice, and do not expect to learn anything new here. These seem like good reasons for not reading any further.

On the other hand, Chapter 2 showed that people often think about their life choices in narrow or mistaken ways. Some readers may even want to reconsider their educational choices in the light of new information.

The Promise of Education

In North America we often hear claims about the benefits of education. Such promises are not new. British philosopher James Mill wrote in the nineteenth century that "if education cannot do everything, there is hardly anything it cannot do" (quoted in Michalos, 1981: 94). Today, many continue to believe in the promise of education. Many believe that education can help solve major social problems like crime and poverty. Others feel that combating ignorance through schooling will lead to social progress. For many Americans, education promises personal success: they consider schooling a ticket to greater opportunity, a better job, and a more enjoyable lifestyle than their parents had (Michalos, 1981: 95–96).

A modern bureaucratic society like ours uses schools to channel, train, and select young people for society's most important roles (Sorokin, 1957). This makes the effective functioning of the educational system— its openness to all, even-handed application of standards, reward for merit, and relevance to the society of which it is a part—central to the effective functioning of society. A good school system is important for the people who need educating, the labor market that employs their skills, and those whose prosperity and well-being ultimately depend on knowledge and expertise: in short, everyone. How far has our society moved toward an "effective" school system?

No one can deny that higher education changed radically in the United States since World War II. One reason was the launching of Sputnik by the USSR in 1957. This technical coup alerted the West to the need for more scientific research and training, if capitalist countries—particularly the United States and its closest allies—were to compete effectively for world power. Another was the baby boom, which resulted in the arrival of huge numbers of children at the primary and secondary schools in the 1950s and 1960s, and postsecondary schools in the 1960s and 1970s. A third factor was the civil rights movement of the 1960s, which opened the door of academia to minority groups that had been largely excluded from the mainstream of society. Lastly, the feminist movement of the last two decades has provided an impetus to women to attend and complete college. They are also entering, in unprecedented numbers, fields of study which are traditionally male-dominated—mathematics, physical sciences, engineering, medicine, law, and other professions. These factors largely account for the institutional changes that occurred in American education between 1960 and 1980.

The share of higher education in the GNP quadrupled from 2 percent during World War II to roughly 8 percent in 1980. A good indicator of the change is the growth in scientific and technical education. A new kind of postsecondary institution, the community college, was created to offer larger numbers of students technical and semiprofessional training in or near the students' home communities (Jones, 1980: 303). Some stu-

TABLE 3.1 Bachelor Degrees Awarded by Institutions of Higher Education in Life Sciences, Physical Sciences, Mathematics, and Engineering: United States, 1959–60 and 1985–86. (Source: Center for Education Statistics, 1988a; Bureau of the Census, 1969?).

Degrees Awarded		1959–60	1985–86	Percentage Change
Life Sciences:	Total	15,576	38,524	147
	Men	11,654	19,993	72
	Women	3,922	18,531	372
Physical Sciences:	Total	16,007	21,731	36
	Men	14,013	15,769	13
	Women	1,994	5,962	199
Mathematics:	Total	11,399	16,306	43
	Men	8,293	8,725	5
	Women	3,106	7,581	144
		1967–68	*1984–85*	
Engineering:	Total	37,368	96,105	157
	Men	37,159		
	Women	209		

dents take an inexpensive two-year program at a community college and transfer to a four-year college or university to complete a bachelor's degree. Community colleges grew in number from about 400 in 1958 to 1274 in 1980 (Jones, 1980; Horton & Hunt, 1984). By 1982, community colleges enrolled more than one-third of all students in higher education (12.3 million), and more than 40 percent of the entering freshmen (Center for Education Statistics, 1988; Cohen & Brawer, 1982). Led by the community college, universities and colleges across the nation are welcoming older students—those over the age of 25—to their campuses.

Within universities, technical and scientific programs have expanded with the help of more funding from the government. Table 3.1 shows the increases in the numbers of students graduating from American bachelor-degree programs in life sciences, physical sciences, and mathematics in 1959–60 and 1985–86. The number of students awarded engineering degrees in 1985 was more than two and a half times that awarded in 1968.

However, since the mid-1970s the number of bachelor's degrees conferred in the physical and life sciences—as well as in the humanities, social sciences, and education—has declined. At the same time, the number of technical and professional degrees (including business, computer, and information sciences) has increased, accounting for nearly two-thirds of all degrees awarded in 1984–85 (Center for Education Statistics, 1987). Such a shift in students receiving bachelor's degrees, from the traditional fields of arts and science, and education, to the technical/professional field, reflects the changing structure of employment opportunities in the 1970s and 1980s.

Since 1960, not only have women been entering universities and colleges in ever greater proportions but they are also breaking the traditional male monopoly on mathematics, the physical sciences, and engineering (MSE). According to Hilton and Lee (1988), the proportion of high school senior young women choosing MSE doubled to 40 percent from 1972 to 1982. And the relative loss in MSE for the young women between high school and first-year college was less than that for the young men. Table 3.1 also shows astonishing increases in the number of degrees women have earned in these fields.

Not only the numbers but also the "types" of students have changed; higher education has become more accessible to working and older students through an increase in the availability of part-time studies. In 1970, the typical college student was an undergraduate, male, between the ages of 18 and 24, and attending full-time. From 1970 to 1987, total enrollment in higher education increased substantially. The number of "typical" undergraduates grew, but proportionally greater gains were made by part-time students (an increase from 32 to about 42 percent), women students (41 to 53 percent), and students 25 years of age or older (28 percent in 1972 to 39 percent in 1986). Thus the typical college student today is a female undergraduate, most likely over 25 years of age and attending part-time (Center for Education Statistics, 1988b).

These trends are not unique to engineering, mathematics, and science. Indeed, all enrollments expanded, and programs and students became more varied throughout the postsecondary system. Moreover, students came to enjoy more freedom in putting together study programs. The traditional standardized university program of study was overhauled.

Not everyone was pleased by these changes. Even today, many feel that postsecondary education has been watered down. Some believe that universities neither enroll only the best students nor give their students the best possible education. Critics complain that recruitment and grading standards have fallen, and new kinds of disciplines and programs now offered for study (for example, Women's Studies, Ethnic Studies, Peace Studies, and other interdisciplinary courses) have no standards, intellectual tradition, or justification (Bloom, 1987).

Recent years have seen a slow return to more highly structured programs and stiffer grading in some postsecondary institutions. But as yet, little effort has been made to dismantle the interdisciplinary programs. Moreover, part-time and remedial programs have continued to expand, reaching out to ever larger numbers of previously excluded students. And women increasingly enter and graduate from programs leading to traditionally male-dominated professions. This institutional change has provided more-varied students with greater educational choice. Women, older students, and members of previously excluded ethnic and racial minorities are particular beneficiaries of these changes.

It is unlikely, then, that colleges and universities will return to limited course offerings, limited program choice, limited student recruitment, and domination of the postsecondary curriculum by the traditional humanities—languages, history, philosophy, and classics. Education *has* changed, but is it the change people had hoped for? Does postsecondary education in America today deliver on its promise of more opportunity for the traditionally disadvantaged? Does postsecondary education give people more opportunity and higher economic returns, the way reformers thought it would?

Who Gets a Postsecondary Education?

Even if postsecondary institutions admit applicants without bias, more students of some kinds will gain admission than others. They are just more likely to apply. This "self-selection" begins long before the end of high school, and it is based on gender, place of residence, social class and socioeconomic status (SES), and ethnicity, as well as ability. Let us examine each of these influences in turn.

Gender   Today, as in the past, more young women than young men graduate from high school. And, as we have seen, more women than ever before are enrolled in higher education. Not only do more women than men receive baccalaureate degrees but nationwide women now also outnumber men in master's degree programs (Mickelson, 1989). Only in the Ph.D. and professional programs are there more men than women. However, the gap between women and men is closing. The proportion of women receiving doctoral degrees from American universities increased from 25 percent in 1977 to 35 percent in 1987 (*Chronicle of Higher Education*, March 1, 1989: A 11).

The view of woman as an academic underachiever is nothing more than a myth; in fact, women's educational achievements equal and often surpass those of men (Mickelson, 1989). Yet women get lower returns on education both in terms of income and in occupational positions (to be discussed later in the chapter). One reason for the economic disparity between the sexes is that careers with the best pay, working conditions, benefits, and opportunities for advancement usually require strong backgrounds in mathematics and the so-called "hard sciences"—physical and biological sciences. In colleges and universities, these fields of study are still dominated by men; by contrast, the social sciences, humanities, and education are predominantly female fields.

Such gender differences in fields of specialization can be traced back to academic performances in lower levels of education. The overall high school grade-point averages for male and female students are comparable. However, boys outperform girls in visual-spatial and quantitative activities, while girls excel in verbal skills. While there are only slight gender differences in the enrollment in mandatory high school courses, boys are far more likely to elect higher-level mathematics, science, and computer courses. Girls in academic tracks are less likely to take additional mathematics and science courses beyond the minimum requirements necessary for college admission (Mickelson, 1989; West, Miller & Diodato, 1985).

The gender differences in fields of specialization may also be linked to structural factors such as curricular placement and counseling practices that even predate high school. Halliman and Sorensen (1987) found that among equally able boys and girls in elementary school, the former are more likely to be placed in high-ability mathematics groups.

While gender differences in the field of study are likely to continue for some time, there has been increasing similarity between women and men in the choice of majors in the last 25 years. In 1966, one-third of women were enrolled in education while only one out of every six (17 percent) were studying mathematics, science, or engineering. By 1974, approximately equal proportions of women were studying in education and the traditional male fields of MSE (21.6 and 20.1 percent respectively) (Heynes & Bird, 1982). Table 3.2 shows that gender differences in enrollment in the technical and professional fields have been narrowing in recent years.

Aside from the different fields of concentration, men and women college students differ in other aspects that may affect their future incomes and career opportunities. Although women are more likely to be enrolled for degree credit than men, they are more likely to attend a two-year institution rather than a four-year one. Women are also more likely to enroll in a public college or university, as opposed to a private institution (Heynes & Bird, 1982). Freshmen women are more concerned than

TABLE 3.2 Total enrollment in selected technical/professional major fields of study in four-year institutions of high education, by sex: Fall 1976, 1980, and 1986. (Source: Center for Education Statistics, 1988a, p. 167).

Major Fields of Study	1976	1980	1986
Architecture and Environmental Design	58,149	59,660	56,756
Men	76.0%	70.9%	65.0%
Women	24.0%	29.1%	35.0%
Business and Management	951,945	1,240,258	1,270,424
Men	71.4%	59.9%	54.4%
Women	28.6%	40.1%	45.6%
Dentistry	20,272	22,668	17,773
Men	89.0%	83.0%	72.7%
Women	11.0%	17.0%	27.3%
Engineering	374,815	503,960	486,180
Men	92.3%	87.7%	85.4%
Women	7.7%	12.3%	14.6%
Law	119,581	118,993	106,212
Men	74.2%	66.0%	59.2%
Women	25.8%	34.0%	40.8%
Medicine	58,085	74,132	65,711
Men	77.5%	74.3%	66.7%
Women	22.3%	25.7%	33.3%
Veterinary Medicine	6,126	8,164	8,849
Men	72.2%	61.0%	47.0%
Women	27.8%	39.0%	53.0%

men about financial factors related to college attendance, such as costs and grant-in-aid. Female students are concentrated in small, less-selective and less-affluent colleges. Men, on the other hand, are more likely to attend higher cost, larger, and more selective institutions. Men are even more likely than women to enroll in colleges that are far away from home (Rosenfeld & Hearn, 1982).

Lastly, men and women differ in what they consider as the most important reasons for going to college. Although equal proportions of both women and men consider "getting a better job" a very important reason, women are consistently more likely than men to give intrinsic educational objectives (for example, to gain a general education and an appreciation of ideas), and social reasons (for example, to meet new and interesting people) as important reasons. Men are more likely than women to consider "to be able to make more money" as an important reason for attending college (Hanson & Litten, 1982).

Location and Residence Like gender, location influences students' postsecondary educational plans. There is considerable variation among the states in the proportions of young people attending college. California, Utah, and Colorado have the highest percentages entering and graduating from college, while the Deep South and Appalachia have the lowest. Differences by state may reflect regional variations in economic prosperity. They may also reflect regional differences in value systems with less emphasis put on formal education in rural areas. On the other hand, some eastern states, such as New Jersey and New York, were traditionally more dependent on private institutions than the West, and did not emphasize public higher education until the past few decades (Havighurst & Levine, 1979).

Just as residence in some states or in rural areas reduces student postsecondary opportunity, so the size of the community also affects the chance of an individual to attend college. The larger the community, the more likely a high school graduate will be to attend a university. Students from small communities are more likely to stop studying altogether or enroll in a terminal community college program. Small-town and rural students are discouraged from studying past high school by the prospect of accumulating large debts and the possible scarcity of good summer jobs in their community. Further, young people from smaller communities have to leave home to get a postsecondary education. The cost and trouble of moving away increases the disadvantage of poorer small-town and rural youths.

On the other hand, the poverty of a region may influence educational plans more than its population density. Some rural areas contain a higher proportion of poor people, and children of the poor are less likely to get a higher education, however close to a postsecondary institution they may live.

Social Class and SES Educational choice is also heavily influenced by social class and socioeconomic status (SES). It is hard to tell which aspect of SES—parental income, occupational status, or educational background—makes the most difference to student plans (Jencks et al., 1972; 1979).

Parents influence educational attainments most by shaping the educational plans their children make, and in turn, how far they go in school. Of course, many students do not carry through their original plans. Students who have prepared to go to university sometimes decide not to go. These students can change their plans about education without delay or difficulty. However, students who have *not* prepared to go to university will find that decision a difficult one to change. Because of streaming, early decisions *not* to go to university are more likely to stick than early decisions to go.

The desire to attend college or university is related to both SES and gender, assuming the same level of ability. In a study of 10,000 high school seniors in Wisconsin (Sewell & Shah, 1967), of those with high IQ (intelligence quotient) scores, 91 percent of high SES boys, but only 52 percent of low SES boys entered college. The equivalent percentages for girls were 76 and 28 percent. On the other hand, among those of lowest mental ability, 6 percent of the low SES boys as compared to 39 percent of the high SES boys attended college. For the low-ability girls, those with low SES had only a 4 percent chance of going on to college but those from high SES families had a 33 percent chance.

Students with higher-status fathers (especially if they are boys) are most likely to receive encouragement and feel able to handle university. As a result, middle-class children are more likely than lower-class children to enter the high school program for students who are university bound.

By the time they enter high school, students have usually established a sense of their own ability, an inclination or disinclination to study, and a desire to take or avoid courses that can lead to postsecondary education. However, SES significantly influences the course-taking patterns of high school students. A national study of course selection in secondary schools (West et al., 1985) shows that high-SES students are more likely than other students to take college preparatory mathematics and science courses, whether as a concentrator or as a four-year college-bound student. Similarly, high-SES students are twice as likely as low-SES students to have taken computer science for credit.

By contrast, the low-SES students are overrepresented in vocational and general education courses. These vocational and general education students are also most likely to report going to work full-time immediately after graduating from high school; unlike the higher-SES graduates, they do not get to college.

Some parents may not understand the implications and long-term consequences of courses that their children take in the early years of high school. They would very likely acquiesce when their children decide to take undemanding courses. When parents fall down on the job, teachers and guidance counsellors must try to create and reinforce higher aspirations. The educators and social workers should provide a bridge between the family environment and the world of higher education and occupations, by explaining the opportunities that exist to students' families. Elementary school is not too soon to introduce children to the idea of a university education and its value both for the individual and society (Porter et al., 1982).

Socioeconomic barriers to higher education have lowered in the last few decades, but they are far from gone. Capable young people from less-privileged backgrounds are still more likely to enroll in terminal community college programs than in universities (Gilbert & Kahl, 1982). Such differences in access to postsecondary education, especially four-year college or university, reduce the chances that children will have substantially different jobs, incomes, or statuses than their parents. Postsecondary education still tends to transmit social status from one generation to the next.

Race and Ethnicity   American society includes many racial and ethnic groups. Access to postsecondary education in the United States varies as much by race and ethnicity as by gender, residence, and socioeconomic status. Although some minority groups have benefitted considerably from growing educational opportunities, others—especially Native Americans (Indians, Eskimos, and Aleuts), Chicanos and Puerto Ricans—have benefited far less.

Only 55 percent of Native Americans graduate from high school, a basic qualification for postsecondary education, as compared to 83% of the non-Hispanic white population (see Table 3.3). Among the Native American high school graduates, 17 percent enter college and 6 percent

TABLE 3.3 Higher education pipeline in the United States. (Source: Astin, 1982).

	Non-Hispanic Whites	Blacks	Chicanos	Puerto Ricans	Native Americans
Graduate from high school	83%	72%	55%	55%	55%
Enter college	38	29	22	25	17
Complete college	23	12	7	7	6
Enter graduate/professional school	14	8	4	4	4
Complete graduate/ professional school	8	4	2	2	2

complete college. The corresponding figures for the non-Hispanic whites are 38 and 23 percent.

In the past, Native American students had to leave reservations or their own communities to attend colleges in urban areas that were alien and alienating to them, both physically and culturally. Today, a few tribal-operated colleges, such as Standing Rock Community College, Little Hoop Community College, and Sinte Gleska College are located on or near Indian reservations (Garret, 1987).

The enrollment of Hispanic students in higher education institutions grew rapidly in the 1980s, increasing by 17 percent from 1984 to 1986. Despite the gains, Hispanics still are underrepresented in higher education. According to the American Council on Education, in 1986 Hispanics accounted for 5 percent of the total college enrollment, while they made up an estimated 7 percent of the United States population (San Francisco Examiner, January 16, 1989).

Like other minority groups, a high percentage of Hispanic students begin their higher education by attending a nearby two-year community college. However, Hispanics are the only group where a higher proportion is enrolled in the two-year colleges than in four-year institutions: 54 percent of Hispanic college students were found in two-year institutions, compared to 43 percent of blacks and 36 percent of whites.

The high concentration of Hispanic students in community colleges is criticized by some researchers as ill-serving these students (Nora & Rendon, 1988). Among the Hispanic students there is greater-than-average attrition from undergraduate colleges, particularly community colleges. Moreover, only a small number of Hispanic students transfer from a two- to four-year institution. Nationally, between 52 to 74 percent of community college students express the intention to get a baccalaureate degree, but only 5 to 25 percent of community students actually do so. However, this slippage in the educational pipeline is higher than average among Hispanic students.

For example, in California, which has the largest number of Hispanics in the largest system of community colleges in the country, community colleges experiencing the largest transfer losses are those with a very high proportion of Hispanic or black freshman students. Community colleges which have developed to provide access to higher education for ethnic minorities and students from low SES backgrounds, may inadvertently serve to perpetuate race and class inequalities in the United States. As a result, Hispanic students are underrepresented among the university graduates. In 1980, when Hispanics comprised more than 6 percent of the

United States population, they earned only 2.3 percent of bachelor's degrees, 2.2 percent of the master's degrees, 1.4 percent of the doctorates, and 2.2 percent of all the first professional degrees awarded.

Black rates of participation in higher education increased dramatically in the first half of the 1970s, from 16 percent (of all blacks aged 18 to 24) in 1970 to 23 percent in 1976. During the same period, the white participation rate was around 25 to 27 percent. Since 1976 black participation rates have edged downward, to 20 percent in 1985 (Center for Education Statistics, 1987).

The decline in college enrollment has occurred exclusively among black males. Blacks comprised an estimated 14 percent of the total United States population in 1986 (San Francisco Examiner, January 16, 1989). Yet black men accounted for only 3.5 percent of all college students in 1986, down from 4.3 percent in 1976. Black women, by contrast, maintained a steady share throughout the same period: 5.1 percent in 1976 and 5.2 percent in 1986.

Until the 1960s, most black college students attended the 110 or so predominantly black colleges or universities, reflecting the fact of segregation and discrimination at all levels of the educational system. Most of the so-called black colleges and universities were located in the South. Today, these traditionally black institutions still remain but they enroll only a fraction of the black student population. A high percentage of blacks now begin their college careers by attending a local community college. Some of the traditionally black colleges are no longer predominantly "black." However, other institutions, especially those in urban areas, are experiencing rapid growth in black enrollment in recent years, for example, University of the District of Columbia (Garret Press, 1987).

In an analysis of 1970 census data, Cheswick (1988) found that among the American ethnic groups, United States–born men from Chinese and Japanese backgrounds had higher levels of schooling than whites—13.1 years for Chinese and 12.7 years for Japanese, as compared to 11.9 years for whites. United States–born Jews had the highest level of schooling—14.0 years on average. The native-born Jewish, Chinese, and Japanese Americans also had higher earnings than the national average. In the past quarter-century, and especially since the late 1970s, there has been a sharp increase in immigration from Asia. Asian Americans, including the recent immigrants, account for a small but rapidly growing segment of postsecondary students today. They are overrepresented in higher education, accounting for 3 percent of the college students in 1980 although they made up only 2 percent of the total United States population.

Coming from diverse origins, Asian Americans have the highest participation rates in education. According to the 1980 census, among 20- to 24-year olds—the typical ages of college and graduate study—only 23 percent of whites were enrolled in school, compared to 48 percent of Japanese Americans; 60 percent of Chinese Americans; at least 40 percent of those with Korean, (Asian) Indian and Vietnamese ancestry; and 27 percent for those of Filipino background (Gardner, Robey, & Smith, 1985).

Like other racial minorities, Asian Americans are more likely to attend public than private colleges and universities. Eighty-three percent of Asians, 79 percent of blacks, and 77 percent of Native Americans attend public institutions, as compared to 77 percent of the whites. There are few (if any) distinctively "Asian American institutions." However, in regions where they are highly concentrated, as in California, Asian Americans are very visible on campus. For example, since the mid-1980s, Asian Americans have made up almost a quarter of each fall's incoming students at the University of California, in Berkeley.

The academic success of Asian Americans is not without its own problems. Some top universities in the nation have reportedly adopted unofficial admission quotas for Asian Americans, to limit their overrepresentation in higher education. In 1989, the Office of the United States Secretary of Education began investigating allegations of anti-Asian discrimination; the results are not yet known.

Is Education Becoming More Accessible?   Access to postsecondary education has slowly become more democratic. A young person's ethnic and socioeconomic background matters less today than in the past, and women now participate as much as men. Many changes occurred because large numbers of nonuniversity institutions—community colleges— were built, creating more postsecondary spaces. Community colleges are a major postsecondary alternative for lower social and economic strata.

However, massive government spending on higher education has not increased university access proportionally. Part of the reason may be found in Australia's experience. University tuition fees were abolished there in 1974, yet lower-class attendance did not increase significantly. In Canada, an examination of federal policy on postsecondary education came to this conclusion: "when a student is unsettled or lacks motivation, educational costs are often stated as the reason for dropping out after high school. . . . [However,] even if tuition fee levels fell to zero, the percentage of high school graduates who fail to go directly to college or university would not be affected substantially" (Standing Senate Committee, 1987: 47).

Cultural and motivational factors may better account for differences in educational choices. Parents' (and their children's) values, not their financial means, continue to determine educational achievement. Those students with higher-status, better-educated parents and those from ethnic groups that strongly value education develop with more of the motivation and know-how necessary for educational success. They are the children of "cultured classes" who are more familiar with the social structures and the cultural milieux of academe than those of working-class origins. They are more aware of the long-term consequences of their program and course choices, and are better prepared to face the social and academic demands of higher education. Accordingly, in order to increase participation by children from low-SES families or some ethnic minorities, financial support alone is not enough; rather, programs aimed at planning for postsecondary education would have to be established much earlier in their educational careers.

Children from the higher classes seem to have something extra, which Bourdieu (1977) calls "cultural capital." Its measurable traits include a knowledge of music and literature; frequent attendance at cultural events such as concerts, museums, and plays; interest in reading books and listening to music; and, equally important, the tendency to think of oneself as educated, artistic, or "cultured." Students with the most "cultural capital" are most likely to complete a postsecondary education and gain a high-status job, regardless of parental social status or education (DiMaggio & Mohr, 1985).

Despite student aid and reduced tuition, lower-income students continue to feel pressed to give up studying and contribute financially to the family, or to their own support. Lower-income students are more reluctant to take out student loans, fearing difficulty in repaying these loans. But however the economic and motivational issues are mixed, earlier assistance and encouragement will be needed to influence educational decisions in the future.

As we have seen, gender, region, community size, social class, and ethnicity all play a role in streaming young Americans into (or away from) postsecondary education. But these patterns are not entirely rigid and unchanging. Government policies have made postsecondary education somewhat more accessible to women and certain ethnic minority groups. Some change has occurred. But the changes must be accompanied by specific *value changes* and the willingness on the part of educational institutions to make accommodations.

Even the ideology underlying education has changed. In the 1960s, postsecondary education for the largest possible number was viewed as a societal responsibility that would bring societal benefits. Now, postsecondary education is viewed as yielding the greatest benefits to the individual graduate, not society as a whole. This view justifies passing an increasing proportion of educational cost back to the "user."

An awareness of the factors that influence other people's postsecondary plans may lead you to examine your own educational choices—past, present, and future—with greater clarity. People may realize that their upbringing has limited their educational horizons, or "incapacitated" them. Alternative educational choices actually available to them might yield greater fulfillment.

The Returns on a Postsecondary Education

When asked what concerns them most about their education, today's postsecondary students usually mention job opportunities first. This section will look mainly at how your postsecondary education will affect employability, income, and job satisfaction. However, you should balance the emphasis here on job-related returns by also examining how higher education will influence the overall quality of your life.

Nonmonetary Returns   Anyone who has received a good education, in whatever field, will say that education can bring many benefits that cannot be measured in dollars. Just like strenuous physical exercise, strenuous mental exercise—the regular exertion of learning, debate, and new ideas—can be exhilarating and fulfilling. Often people find themselves filled with excitement and admiration by what earlier thinkers have accomplished.

With more education, people also feel a sense of greater mastery as they become more able to understand complicated arguments and create their own. Further, by increasing our knowledge through education, we increase our sense of control over our own lives. This is satisfying and reassuring, though it is often daunting as well (for education also teaches us how much we do not know and cannot control).

Education in the sciences gives people more insight into the logic of the universe and the technological revolution that is sweeping everyone's lives. Education in the humanities puts people in touch with the vast variety of human cultures and ideas. It gives us a sense of the continuity of the human race, and allows us to admire how much people have achieved that is good and beautiful. Education in the social sciences helps us understand why we live the way we do and how we can change ourselves—individually and collectively—before we suffer disastrous consequences.

Higher education is more than a ticket to a job. In the space of three or four years, students gain in critical ability, aesthetic sense, and tolerance for divergent values (Bowen, 1977). College graduates are better informed and more politically active citizens. They even make better parents. Along these lines, Bowen (1977: 201) writes:

> The effects of college education on the family are numerous and strong—so much so that these effects may be among the most significant outcomes of higher education. . . . Among the familial impacts are the following:
>
> 1. Narrowing the traditional differences in attitudes and behavior between the two sexes.
> 2. Selection of college-educated persons as marriage partners.
> 3. Delay in age of marriage.
> 4. Slight reduction in the divorce rate.
> 5. Reduction in the birth rate.
> 6. More thought, time, energy and money devoted to the rearing of children.
> 7. Influences on parents, spouses and siblings of the college educated.

These kinds of nonmonetary benefits are not confined to American undergraduates, nor even to people receiving a postsecondary education. Generally, education is a good thing. In a comparative study of six developing nations, sociologist Alex Inkeles (1973) showed that the amount of education a person has received is the single best predictor of how "modern" he or she is likely to be. By "modern," Inkeles means all the characteristics Bowen has mentioned; he also means "capable of living in a modern world." So the more education you get, the better off you will be.

To narrow our sights somewhat, what are the career benefits for students who manage to get a postsecondary education? Is today's liberal arts degree a ticket to a good job, or to unemployment office lineups? Do nontransfer community college programs really give more marketable, job-oriented training? Do recent graduates feel that their postsecondary education was a waste of time?

Job Status Returns   Education is an important "intervening variable" between the social characteristics you start out with in life and the rewards you end up with. Although access is largely restricted by factors beyond your control—gender, place of residence, and SES among them—it is possible to break free from your past by using higher education as a lever. By seizing the opportunity for higher education, you can get on a somewhat more equal footing with people who started life with more advantages.

Let us begin by examining the effects of postsecondary education on social mobility. Education has an important impact on your social status and upward social mobility (Jencks et al., 1979; Gilbert & Kahl, 1982).

Sample SES scores displayed in Table 3.4 show that America's most prestigious and best-paying jobs are typically those that require the most education. The prestige, pay, and educational requirement associated with a job are highly correlated. In other words, higher education is the ticket to higher prestige and pay in America, just as it is elsewhere (Treiman, 1977).

The Duncan Socio-economic Index scale runs from 0 to 96. Olneck (1979) found that among men with a similar SES background, an extra year of elementary and secondary education brings an advantage of 2.0 points on the Duncan scale. Four years of college among men with similar SES move up the graduate's occupational status by 25.4 points. It is important to note that the status benefits of education are *discontinuous*. For example, completing the final year of a B.A. degree is worth far more in prestige and earnings than completing the second-last year and dropping out.

It should also be mentioned that the Duncan Socio-economic Index scores, and Olneck's analysis of the effect of education on occupational status, are based on the characteristics of men in the labor force. They do not reflect occupational segregation by gender or the different income and educational levels of men and women. Further, the occupational structure has changed since the 1950s and 1960s, when these measures of occupational status were taken; in particular, the rate of labor force participation by women has increased dramatically. More recent measures of occupational status, reflecting these changes, are based on the total civilian labor force, including both men and women (see, for example, Nam & Powers, 1983).

A 25–point spread on the Duncan scale is equivalent to the difference between an aeronautical engineer and a stenographer, an accountant and a mail-carrier, and a social worker and a retail sales clerk. Which end of the 25–point spread do you prefer? The occupations at the top of the scale—physicians, lawyers, and university professors, for example—typically require education beyond four years of college.

TABLE 3.4 Duncan's Socioeconomic Index scores for selected occupations. (Source: Duncan, 1961).

Occupation	Socioeconomic Index
Dentist	96
Lawyers and judges	93
Physicians and surgeons	92
Architects	90
Aeronautical engineer	87
Banking and other finance manager	85
University/college professor	84
Social scientists	81
Accountants and auditors	78
Authors	76
Teachers	72
Wholesale trade manager	70
Social workers	64
Real estate agents and brokers	62
Secretaries and stenographers	61
Actors and actresses	60
Funeral directors and embalmers	59
Metal industries foremen	54
Mail-carriers	53
Bank tellers	52
Telephone operators	45
General office clerk	44
Cashiers	44
Police Officer	40
Retail sales clerk	39
Radio/television mechanics and repairmen	36
Electrical equipment assembler	26
Automobile manufacturing worker	21
Bartender	19
Guards and watchmen	18
Food industry processer	16
Waiter/waitress	16
Chefs and cooks	15
Truck driver	15
Janitor	9
Garbage laborers	8

Thus, if you want to increase your job status and income, education appears to be a pretty good "investment" of your time and money. However, since the 1960s, the surplus of B.A. degree-holders seems to have depressed the economic value of a degree. More young college graduates are entering lower-status occupations than they did in the past, and here the potential for increases in earning are limited. The upward mobility of four-year college graduates has declined, but it is likely that they still have a better chance of promotion than the high school graduates. If so, the lifetime returns to higher education are no lower than they were previously (Olneck, 1979). Thus a degree would still be important for people coming from a low SES background. And for persons from a higher SES background, education may serve as a hedge against downward mobility (Harvey, 1984).

University graduates of 20 years ago may have gotten slightly better jobs than they would today, but opportunities for people without a post-secondary education have also shrunk appreciably over this period. A bachelor's degree may now have more value than ever because it provides even greater protection against low-status work and unemployment. But what kind of job security does postsecondary education provide? Will more education reduce the likelihood of your being unemployed?

Employability Returns   With very few exceptions over the past 20 years, the more education a person has, the lower his or her likelihood of unemployment. Even though national unemployment rates have fluctuated over this period, people with more education have always been more likely to hold a job than people with less education, all others things (such as gender, race, and place of residence) being equal. This pattern holds true for people of all ages, including youths (aged 15 to 24), who typically have the highest unemployment rates.

While the college graduates of today may not get jobs as good as the graduates of 20 years ago, unemployment rates for people with at least four years of college or university education are lower than for any other group. This has been so throughout the 1970s and 1980s, even in a sluggish economy such as during the severe recession of the early 1980s. For example, in 1982, when the national unemployment rate reached almost 10 percent, one of the highest since the end of World War II, the lowest unemployment rates were recorded by college graduates—whether men or women, or black, white or Hispanic (Young, 1982). As can be seen in Table 3.5, unemployment rates were 3.0 percent for college graduates, 8.5 percent for high school graduates, and more than 12 percent for those without a high school diploma.

TABLE 3.5 Unemployment rates of persons 25 to 64 years old by sex, race, and years of school completed, March 1982. (Source: Young, 1982, Tables 1 and 2).

	Elementary	*High School*		*College*	
	8 yrs or less	*1 to 3 yrs*	*4 years*	*1 to 3 yrs*	*4 years*
U.S. Total	13.2	12.1	8.5	6.2	3.0
Men					
White	12.0	12.6	8.3	6.0	2.6
Black	17.3	12.9	17.3	14.6	8.9
Hispanic	13.4	14.3	8.8	7.8	4.7
Women					
White	14.5	10.4	6.8	4.6	3.1
Black	11.4	15.1	15.6	10.6	5.4
Hispanic	18.0	18.4	7.0	5.6	4.9

Unemployment rates among the highly educated remained low because postsecondary graduates were willing to take work that had not traditionally called for a postsecondary education (Young, 1982). Highly educated people are increasingly doing work below their levels of skill and ability (Berg, 1970). As more postsecondary graduates enter the labour market, employers demand higher qualifications simply because they prefer to hire the highly educated, and more highly educated people are available today.

Fitting a highly educated person into an undemanding job risks employee boredom, loss of motivation, and rebelliousness. But for several reasons most employers are willing to take this chance. University graduates lend the organization an air of professionalism and credibility. Further, employers assume that postsecondary graduates in general, but university graduates in particular, learn new things faster, have better interpersonal skills, and come from a higher class of family. This makes them more desirable employees.

Beyond this, postsecondary education teaches people to be ambitious and career-oriented (Bowles and Gintis, 1976). Doing work that cannot be closely and continuously supervised, the employee with a postsecondary degree must be relied upon to see personal well-being as linked to the well-being of the organization. The employee must believe that merit will be rewarded and continuous hard work is a worthwhile investment in the future. These views are learned and rewarded in postsecondary institutions, then carried into the work world.

In this way, postsecondary institutions both instill job traits employers desire and select for a good background and high motivation. The evidence an educational credential provides saves the employer a lot of trouble in identifying good candidates for independent work. This is why postsecondary graduates are so rarely unemployed, even if often "underemployed."

Postsecondary education not only influences employability but for women it also influences the degree of labor force participation. Nearly all working-age men, whatever their level of education, work full-time. But the situation is quite different for working-age women. The participation rate for black female four-year college graduates has always been around 90 percent, substantially higher than for their white counterparts. However, in recent years, white female four-year college graduates have increased their rate of labor force participation, from 59 percent in 1970 to 75 percent in 1982. By contrast, the participation rates for black and white female high school graduates are 70 and 62 percent respectively. The participation rate for women, black or white, who have less than four years of high school is less than 50 percent (Young, 1982).

Income Returns   Throughout the 1960s, four-year college or university graduates earned well above the industrial average in their first job. Since then, they have earned relatively less, at first. However, workers with more education catch up soon, and in the long run their earnings surpass others'. Table 3.6 shows that among full-time workers 25 to 34 years old in 1987, men with at least four years of college earn 35 percent more than the male high school graduates, and female college graduates earn 52 percent more than women with four years of high school. The effort is worth it, if higher income is your goal.

As we noted earlier, the financial benefits of educational attainment are, with some exceptions, discontinuous. For most people one more year of pregraduation training does not bring the same reward as one more year of training that completes a degree. Degree completion is very important, as can be seen when you compare columns 3 and 6 with columns 4 and 7 in Table 3.6. An individual who completes all but the last year of a medical degree is not "nearly a doctor" in the work world, entitled to *nearly* the same rewards as doctors. That person must seek nonmedical jobs on a roughly equal footing with high school and community college graduates and with other university dropouts. Such jobs will not be found in the highly protected (or price-controlled) market for medical services, but in the more competitive market for technical or personal services.

TABLE 3.6 Median earnings and earnings ratios* of year-round, full-time workers 25–34 years old, by educational attainment and by race and sex: 1978, 1982, and 1987. (Source: Center for Education Statistics, 1988b, Table 2:8–1).

| Year | Median earnings: 4 years of high school | Earning ratios | | Median earnings: 4 years of high school | Earning ratios | |
		1–3 years college to 4 years high school	4 or more years college to 4 years high school		1–3 years college to 4 years high school	4 or more years college to 4 years high school
		White			Black	
1978	$11,825	1.07	1.20	$ 9,330	1.12	1.38
1982	15,308	1.10	1.33	13,106	1.06	1.27
1987	18,238	1.16	1.41	14,357	1.12	1.49
		Men			Women	
1978	13,472	1.06	1.17	8,662	1.12	1.29
1982	17,664	1.09	1.27	11,755	1.13	1.39
1987	20,540	1.14	1.35	14,424	1.17	1.52

*The earnings ratio is the earnings of those completing 1–3 or 4 or more years of college divided by the earnings of those completing only 4 years of high school.

Moreover, *which* degree you complete is also important. Different degrees not only make you eligible for different jobs, they also make you competitive in different job markets.

Still, incomes increase more or less steadily with the amount of education you attain. Jencks et al. (1979) tried to isolate the effect of education on earnings from that of other factors such as work experience, family background, and cognitive ability (that is, I.Q.). In the job market that prevailed up to 1970, completing four years of high school raised average earnings by at most 15 to 25 percent. Completing four years of college or university could add up to 40 percent, because a bachelor's degree provides access to higher-status occupations—that is, better job markets. Economic downturns of the 1970s and early 1980s, along with the continued supply of college graduates, have probably decreased the size of this income advantage; but graduates are still ahead of the rest.

The income value of a postsecondary education also varies by gender. For every type of education, men earn more on average than women. The male–female wage gap is narrowing, but at a slower pace than in the

1970s and early 1980s. Women earned about 70 percent as much as men in 1989 (San Francisco Examiner, April 16, 1989). Many women earn less because they enter poorer-paying "pink collar" occupations which are traditionally considered female jobs. However, even when women and men are matched for age, training and experience, and hold the same jobs, women earn much less (Thio, 1986). This is true also of the well-paying, traditionally male-dominated professions such as engineering, the physical sciences, medicine, and dentistry. In universities and colleges, male professors earn more than the women faculty at every rank (see Table 3.7).

Predicting income returns on education in the future is difficult. The growing number of young B.A.'s seeking jobs increases the competition, thereby driving down the price that an employer must pay to hire a B.A. The spillover of postsecondary graduates into lower-status jobs probably limits the potential of high school graduates for career advancement. In the long run, college and university graduates will still push ahead of the competition, though probably not by as much as in the past (Olneck, 1979).

Satisfaction Returns   Satisfaction is a more complicated matter. Campbell (1981) found that college graduates are more likely than people with lower levels of educational attainment to describe their lives as happy. They are also more satisfied with their lives than other people.

However, education has a curious influence on job satisfaction. More education does not increase satisfaction with one's work. On the contrary, job satisfaction is high among the least educated, and then tends *downward* as you ascend the education ladder. The lowest point is reached among people with some college education but no degree. The pattern is only reversed by college graduates, who again report high satisfaction with their work.

While college graduates are more satisfied with their jobs than college dropouts, their satisfaction is not as high as those people who did not even go to high school. Those who have only an elementary education are most satisfied with their work because they never harbored any ambitions for an upwardly mobile career. They see no alternatives to their work situation except unemployment. So as long as their present work pays them relatively well—that is, well in relation to what they have come to expect—they would describe themselves as satisfied with their jobs.

On the other hand, the better educated may be less satisfied than expected because they have broader horizons, a richer sense of alternatives, and a wider basis for comparison. As their aspiration levels rise, they may

TABLE 3.7 Average salary of full-time university and college professors by academic rank and sex: 1975–76, 1980–81 and 1985–86. (Source: Center for Education Statistics, 1988a, Table 155).

	Current Dollars					
	1975–76		1980–81		1985–86	
	Male	Female	Male	Female	Male	Female
All ranks	17,388	14,292	24,499	19,996	34,294	27,576
Professor	22,866	20,257	31,082	27,959	42,833	38,252
Associate professor	17,167	16,336	23,451	22,295	32,273	30,300
Assistant professor	14,154	13,506	19,227	18,302	27,094	24,966
Instructor	14,440	12,580	15,545	14,854	21,693	20,237
Lecturer	13,577	11,870	18,281	16,168	25,238	22,273
Undesignated or no academic rank	15,764	14,098	23,170	20,843	30,267	27,171

experience declining levels of satisfaction if they have no means of realizing their hopes and desires. Frustration would be most acute in the case of the college dropouts. The college graduates, however, presumably have higher aspirations than people at the lower educational levels, but their circumstances are also more favorable and conducive to fulfilling their aspirations. For these reasons, they are likely to express job satisfaction.

According to Campbell (1981), people with high incomes have high levels of general satisfaction with life, regardless of their educational attainment. College graduates with high incomes are no more satisfied with life than other people who have equally high incomes but less formal education. However, among people with less than an average income, college graduates report a greater sense of well-being than any of the less-educated groups. Low income seems to have a most severely depressing effect on people with a partial college education: they report the lowest level of satisfaction with life. Again, people with more formal education tend to develop high-income expectations, so we would expect them to be quite distressed by their low-income experience. This is only true of the college dropouts, but not of college graduates.

The high satisfaction researchers find among low-income college graduates may be attributed to the distinctive value patterns they hold. When asked to choose those "things about a job you would most prefer," people at all educational levels below college completion gave their first preference to "a steady income" or "a high income" (Campbell, 1981: 119). By contrast, the majority of college graduates gave their first choice to work that is "important, giving a sense of accomplishment."

So if you want to be satisfied with life in general and with your work, you not only have to attend college but must try at all costs to complete a degree. (Since you are reading this book, you have probably had at least some postsecondary education.)

Above all, try to adopt the value that work in itself is important and can provide a feeling of accomplishment. Then enter into a line of work that is interesting to you, even if it does not pay well. Of course, it may be difficult to find a job satisfying just because it is interesting and fulfilling: we all have to pay our bills. Moreover, as we have seen in Chapter 1, "to make more money" is a very important reason for attending college for increasing numbers of college students today. However, contrary to what you might believe, just making a lot of money is not intrinsically satisfying to most American adults.

Education versus Work Experience   Compared with work experience, how important is formal education in ensuring employability and a good income? When postsecondary graduates are asked the reason they were hired for their current full-time job, they may say "personality" or "educational qualifications." For a great many applicants, hiring is based on personal characteristics, supported by educational qualifications.

People with high school or some postsecondary education tend to believe that work experience matters most, and they may be right about the jobs that are open *to them*. In a world with ever more college and university graduates available to employers, high school or some (uncompleted) postsecondary training is worth little: it is like having no educational qualification whatever. No surprise, then, that for these youths, educational qualifications counted for little!

The earnings for people with a postsecondary degree increase more rapidly with age than the earnings of those with less education (Featherman & Hauser, 1978, Table 5.27). Attending college initially lowers a person's income; work experience yields more income than education does for people under age 30. But after age 30 the situation changes: the relative advantage of work experience declines and the growth in earnings of those without a degree slows considerably. Work experience yields immediate and impressive dividends for those without postsecondary education, but the benefit is short-lived. In the long run, higher education is the better investment of youthful energy (Featherman & Hauser, 1978: 306–308).

However, this is not to deny the value of work experience. For every type of postsecondary education, having prior work experience will increase a graduate's income.

Payoffs to Different Kinds of Education   During the 1970s, the income of those people who had attended college declined relative to the income of high school graduates. This led some critics to say that the economic returns on the college degree had diminished. However, since 1980, the income of those with higher education has been rising relative to the income of high school graduates. Moreover, the relative advantage increases with the amount of postsecondary education. For example, in 1980, males with four years of college (bachelor's degrees) earned 1.25 times the median income of males with only 4 years of high school. Males with 5 or more years of college (graduate school and advanced degrees) earned 1.42 times the median income of high school graduates. By 1985, the corresponding figures of the two groups of college graduates relative to the income of high school graduates were 1.38 and 1.65 (Center for Education Statistics, 1987). This means the income advantage due to a college education had risen!

The employment status of bachelor's degree recipients varies according to the field of study. Those with technical or professional degrees (for example, engineering, business and management, health, education, public affairs and social services) are more likely to be working full-time after graduation than those who have degrees in arts or science. For example, 78 percent of the 1983–84 technical/professional majors were working full-time in June 1985 compared to 55 percent of the arts and science majors. On the other hand, one-fourth of all graduates with degrees in arts and science were still enrolled in school and not working full-time one year after graduation. This was approximately triple the percentage of graduates in technical/professional fields. Among the 1983–84 graduates in arts and science, 38 percent of the majors in biological sciences and 36 percent of the majors in physical sciences and mathematics were found to be continuing their studies in June 1985. This pattern of activities of bachelor's degree recipients during one to two years following graduation has been fairly stable since 1979 (Center for Education Statistics, 1987).

Graduates with B.A. or B.Sc. degrees may have a harder time finding work in their fields than those with technical or professional degrees. Some of them are working in clerical, craft, and service jobs that could have been filled by high school graduates. They are indeed over-qualified and underemployed. However, recent technological advances and changes in the occupational structure have led to an increase in the demand for other skills which require more than a high school education. For example, many sales jobs today require extensive scientific and technical knowledge in order to effectively present and demonstrate the product (Young, 1982).

Finally, the credentialling function of a university education should not be underestimated. The possession of a bachelor's degree is evidence of a job seeker's motivation, perseverance, and aptitude for learning. These are all important attributes for employers to consider in selecting candidates who will then receive on-the-job training for specific positions.

CONCLUDING REMARKS

Investments in higher education will have different values for different people. Some people will place a low value on the nonmonetary benefits of education. Others find ways of achieving employment security and social status without a higher education; for example, by entering the family business. Higher education is not for everyone, then.

Higher education is not certain to increase life satisfaction or work satisfaction. On the one hand, it gives people the many benefits—financial and nonfinancial—that Bowen (1977) described. On the other hand, it gives people too much information about the rewards available in life that other people may be getting. Education raises your standards of comparison, and while it increases your chances of achieving job and income rewards, it may not do so as much or as quickly as you would like. There is a real risk that education will raise your expectations more quickly, and higher, than you are able to satisfy them.

Today, postsecondary education is still a worthwhile investment of time and money. In terms of employability, earnings, socioeconomic status, and potential job satisfaction, a university degree brings the greatest rewards. Even terminal community college graduates are better off than people with a high school education or less, but the university degree provides the highest overall benefit. And from the standpoint of nonmonetary benefits, the more education you get, the better off you are.

Where education is concerned, do people get what they want or learn to want what they can get? On the one hand, people get what they want: how much postsecondary education people get is *primarily* shaped by how much they want (their aspirations), not by tuition costs or other economic concerns. Likewise, the kind of postsecondary education people get is also the kind they want, in most cases. Choices between university and terminal community college programs, between one course of study and another, are "free," subject to limits on the total number of students who will be admitted to any given program.

On the other hand, the amount and kinds of education people want are socially patterned by gender, place of residence, and socioeconomic status, and to some degree by other factors like ethnicity and race. As children we have been programmed to want what we (or our parents) expect we can get. If so, educational "choice" is an illusion. Choices and outcomes are predetermined. Social position is inherited from one generation to the next.

Do people learn to want what they get? Not entirely. If they did, people would not change their choices, as increasing numbers of older students do when they return for additional education or new kinds of training. Further, large numbers of graduates are dissatisfied with their educational decisions, particularly when these decisions do not result in the expected employment and remuneration, or when their training does not prove useful on the job.

The educational decision process starts early. People receiving little encouragement for their educational goals at home would do well to find mentors who could advise them about their goals and help to increase their cultural capital. In many ways, your educational choices will become clearer once you have made some career choices. The next chapter takes us a little further through the life cycle. It will discuss likely changes in the world of work and factors that influence the rewards—the pay, security, status, intrinsic interest, and job satisfaction—people get out of their jobs.

REFERENCES

ASTIN, A. (1982). *Minorities in higher education.* San Francisco: Jossey-Bass.

BERG, I. (1970). *Education and jobs: The great training robbery.* New York: Praeger.

BLOOM, A. (1987). *The closing of the American mind.* New York: Simon and Schuster.

BOURDIEU, P. (1977). *Reproduction in education, society, and culture.* Beverly Hills, Calif.: Sage.

BOWEN, H. R. (1977). *Investment in learning: The individual and social value of American higher education.* San Francisco: Jossey-Bass.

BOWLES, S., & GINTIS, H. (1976). *Schooling in capitalist America.* New York: Basic Books.

CENTER FOR EDUCATION STATISTICS (1987). *The condition of education: A statistical report, 1987 Edition.* U.S. Department of Education, Office of Educational Research and Improvement, CS 87–365.

――――― (1988A). *Digest of education statistics 1988.* U.S. Department of Education, Office of Educational Research and Improvement, CS 88–600.

――――― (1988B). *The condition of education, vol. 2, postsecondary education.* U.S. Department of Education, Office of Educational Research and Improvement, CS 88–625.

COHEN, A. M., & BRAWER, F. B. (1982). The community college as college. *Change,* pp. 39–42.

DIMAGGIO, P., & MOHR, J. (1985). Cultural capital, educational attainment, and mate selection. *American Journal of Sociology, 90*(6), 1231–61.

DUNCAN, O. D. (1961). A socioeconomic index for all occupations. In A. J. Reiss (Ed.), *Occupations and Social Status.* New York: Free Press.

GARDNER, R. W., ROBEY, B., & SMITH, P. C. (1985). Asian Americans: Growth, change, and diversity. *Population Bulletin, 40*(4), 1–43.

GARRET PRESS (1987). *Minority student enrollment in higher education: A guide to institutions with highest percentages of Asian, Black, Hispanic and Native American students.* Garret Point: Garret Press.

GILBERT, D., & KAHL, J. A. (1982). *The American class structure: A new synthesis.* Homewood, Ill.: Dorsey Press.

HALLINAN, M. T., & SORENSEN, A. B. (1987). Ability grouping and sex differences in mathematics achievement. *Sociology and Education, 60*(2), 63–73.

HANSON, K. H., & LITTEN, L. H. (1982). Mapping the road to academe: A review of research on women, men, and the college-selection process. In P. J. Perun (Ed.), *The undergraduate woman: Issues in educational equity* (pp. 73–97). Lexington, Mass.: D. C. Heath and Co.

HARVEY, E. B. (1984). The changing relationship between university education and intergenerational social mobility. *Canadian Review of Sociology and Anthropology, 21*(3), 275–86.

HAVIGHURST, R. J., & LEVINE, D. U. (1979). *Society and education.* (5th ed.). Boston: Allyn and Bacon.

HEYNS, B., & BIRD, J. A. (1982). Recent trends in the higher education of women. In P. J. Perun (Ed.), *The undergraduate woman: Issues in educational equity* (pp. 43–69). Lexington, Mass.: D. C. Heath and Co.

HILTON, T., & LEE, V. E. (1988). Student interest and persistence in science: Changes in the educational pipeline in the last decade. *The Journal of Higher Education, 59*(2), 510–26.

HORTON, P. B., & HUNT, C. L. (1984). *Sociology.* (6th ed.). New York: McGraw-Hill.

INKELES, A. (1973). Making men modern. In A. Etzioni (Ed.), *Social change: Sources, patterns and consequences.* New York: Basic Books.

JENCKS, C., SMITH, M., ACLAND, H., BANE, M. J., COHEN, D., GINTIS, H., HEYNS, B., & MICHELSON, S. (1972). *Inequality: A reassessment of the effect of family and schooling in America.* New York: Basic Books.

JENCKS, C., BARTLETT, S., CORCORAN, M., CROUSE, J., EAGLESFIELD, D., JACKSON, G., MCCLELLAND, K., MUESER, P., OLNECK, M., SCHWARTZ, J., WARD, S., & WILLIAMS, J. (1979). *Who get ahead? The determinants of economic success in America.* New York: Basic Books.

JONES, L. Y. (1980). *Great expectations: America and the baby boom generation.* New York: Coward, McCann & Geoghegan.

MICHALOS, A. C. (1981). *North American social report: A comparative study of the quality of life in Canada and the USA from 1964 to 1974. Vol. 3: Science, education, and recreation.* Dordrecht, Holland: D. Reidel.

MICKELSON, R. A. (1989). Why does Jane read and write so well? The anomaly of women's achievement. *Sociology of Education, 62,* 47–63.

NAM, C. B., & POWER, M. G. (1983). *The socioeconomic approach to status measurement, with a guide to occupational and socioeconomic status scores.* Houston: Cap and Gown Press.

NORA, A., & RENDON, L. (1988). Hispanic student retention in community colleges: reconciling access with outcomes. In L. Weis (Ed.), *Class, race and gender in American education* (pp. 126–60). Albany, N.Y.: State University of New York Press.

OLNECK, M. (1979). The effects of education. In C. Jencks et al., *Who get ahead? The determinants of economic success in america* (pp. 159–90). New York: Basic Books.

PORTER, J., PORTER, M., & BLISHEN, B. R. (1982). *Stations and callings: Making it through the school system.* Toronto: Methuen.

ROSENFELD, R. A., & HEARN, J. C. (1982). Sex differences in the significance of economic resources for choosing and attending a college. In P. J. Perun (Ed.), *The undergraduate woman: Issues in educational equity* (pp.127–57). Lexington, Mass.: D. C. Heath and Co.

SEWELL, W. H., & SHAH, V. P. (1967). Socioeconomic status, intelligence, and the attainment of higher education. *Sociology of Education, 40,* 1–23.

STANDING SENATE COMMITTEE ON NATIONAL FINANCE. (1987). *Federal policy on post-secondary education.* Ottawa: Supply and Services.

SOROKIN, P. A. (1957). *Social and cultural mobility.* New York: Free Press. (Original work published 1927).

THIO, A. (1986). *Sociology.* New York: Harper and Row.

TREIMAN, D. J. (1977). *Occupational prestige in comparative perspective.* New York: Academic Press.

WEST, J., MILLER, W., & DIODATO, L. (1985). *High school and beyond: A national longitudinal study for the 1980s.* An analysis of course-taking patterns in secondary schools as related to student characteristics. U.S. Department of Education, National Center for Education Statistics. NCES 85–206.

YOUNG, A. M. (1982). Recent trends in higher education and labor force activity. *Monthly Labor Review, 106,* 39–41.

CHAPTER FOUR

CAREER CHOICES
What You Want and What You Get

INTRODUCTION

This chapter answers questions about jobs and careers; specifically, What are the long-term employment prospects for different occupations? and What makes a job satisfying? To answer the first question, we will evaluate the forecasts social scientists have made about the future job market. Which kinds of jobs are on the rise, and which on the decline? To answer the second question, we will examine data on job and career satisfaction. These data tell us not only which kinds of jobs seem to satisfy people most but also which kinds of people seem hardest to please.

The kind of job a person gets will be largely determined by personal contacts (see "decoupling") and community resources (see "closure"), both discussed in Chapter 2, and by educational attainment. The kind and amount of education a person takes will be largely determined by factors discussed in Chapter 3: these include gender, place of residence, socioeconomic status (SES), race, and ethnicity. Taken together, these factors have a powerful affect on the first job you get—which, in turn, influences your later work life (Blau & Duncan, 1967).

The kind of job you get is also influenced by forces far larger and even more beyond your immediate control than closure, decoupling, and educational choice. These currently include technological changes and changes in the national and local economy, as well as the effects of international trade.

Chapter 3 noted a new and growing element in the educational system—older students. Increasingly, people who have already "completed" their formal education are returning to school to get additional or different education. Many attend classes part-time, while holding down job and family responsibilities the rest of the time. They are often 10 or 20 years older than the average undergraduate. This may be the first opportunity some have had to get a higher education. Others have returned to school in hopes of, ultimately, supporting themselves or entering another, more rewarding line of work. For these mature readers, what this book has to say about careers may be already familiar.

As before, we will close this chapter with a brief consideration of whether people get what they want or learn to want what they get in the domain of work and careers. Occupationally, many have found the 1980s very uncertain, frustrating, and even chaotic. To predict the future with any degree of confidence, we must assume that many career trends are part of a long, slow pattern of change that began before the 1980s, and will reach their completion long afterward.

The Future Job Market

Among the many changes affecting the job market, changes resulting from technological innovation dominate current discussion. The microchip has already eliminated many jobs, though it also holds the potential to create many new ones. Most Americans probably know that, for better or worse, computer technology will continue to evolve and spread. Will today's job skills become outdated in the near future? Will new technology lead to mass layoffs and firings, or will employers retrain their workers? Will entire industries disappear? These are questions career-choosers should be asking themselves.

Other important changes to the job market have centered on specific regions. The United States has always been a very mobile nation: one American family in five will move every year. By and large, the internal migration patterns have followed economic opportunities. Since the early days of the nation, migration has generally been westward. For decades after the Civil War, people also moved out of the rural South to the Industrial North, and from rural areas to the cities, and then to the suburbs (Thio, 1986). More recently, migration is not only westward but also to the South. During the 1970s, with the energy crisis and the decline of manufacturing industries in the industrial heartland (the states of New York, Pennsylvania, Ohio, Michigan, and Illinois), places in the Sunbelt regions of the South and the West drew many eager job-seekers from across the country. According to projections by the Bureau of the Census (1988), net internal migration gains for the South and West and losses for the Northeast and Midwest will continue into the twenty-first century.

Other changes have centered on particular occupations. As Chapter 3 showed, the 1960s and the 1970s saw a sudden growth in the size of the school-age population. New government policies made higher education more accessible. Because of educational expansion, graduates trained as teachers found positions waiting for them. In the late 1970s, the size of the school-age population declined, and cuts in government funding limited hiring. Many newer teachers lost their jobs, and many would-be teachers had to choose an alternative career path. But with the recent "baby boom of the '80s" (the result of baby boomers giving birth to offspring of their own) signs already point to a growth of new opportunities for elementary and secondary school teachers.

Faced with these examples, common sense says you are better off knowing the employment prospects for an occupation before preparing to enter it. Choosing systematically will help you make better choices, but it cannot guarantee the results you desire. Even though a great deal of social change is slow and gradual, revolutionary changes do occur. Back in 1940, who was predicting the hydrogen bomb, personal computers, a baby boom, or declining American power in the world? No one. Changes that break old trends and set new ones in motion take us by surprise. We would be wrong to consider history an infallible guide to the future. But we would be even more wrong to ignore signs of change that can affect our lives.

Social scientists have devised three ways of "reading" these signs; we will discuss each one in turn.

Three Ways of Guessing the Future   The first method, *linear extrapolation*, assumes recent trends will continue without significant change for some time to come. The recent past is held to be our best measure for the future. This approach assumes historical continuity: no sharp breaks will alter the patterns witnessed up to now.

In the United States, the most ambitious job forecasts of this type are made by the United States Department of Labor, Bureau of Labor Statistics, which publishes periodic bulletins such as *Occupational Projections and Training Data* and other reports. This method predicts high growth between 1986 and 2000 in the following occupations: computer programmers, paralegal personnel, radiologic technologists and technicians, dental hygienists and assistants, medical assistants, computer systems analysts, data-processing equipment repairers, and podiatrists.

On the other hand, it predicts fast decline between 1986 and 2000 in such occupations as electrical and electronic assemblers, railroad conductors and yardmasters, gas and petroleum plant and system occupations, stenographers, farmers and farm workers, and compositors and typesetters (Bureau of Labor Statistics, 1988).

Such linear extrapolation tends to overstimulate labor supply. Many readers of the 1989 forecast may decide to train for the currently predicted "high-opportunity" industries and occupations. Readers of the forecast a year later will make plans without knowing what the 1989 readers had decided; and so on. By 1992, not only are all the vacancies filled but enormous numbers of recruits are caught in the middle of training for the very positions that have since been filled. This is one danger of following the advice offered by a linear extrapolation.

Another danger lies in its short time horizon. Journalistic accounts of the labor market are often unscientific and based on short-term trends. For example, a newspaper article headlined "Headhunters big winners as job market picks up speed" (*Globe and Mail*, August 27, 1987) claimed that "it's a good time to be an accountant or finance expert but a lousy time to be in medicine, dentistry or most kinds of engineering." Allegedly, the demand was "hot" right then for marketing specialists, health-care administrators, and finance executives, but cooler for "many middle-management corporate jobs and in-house public relations positions."

Job-placement experts and spokespeople for various professional groups usually cite short-term changes in the business cycle, or recent oversupplies of labor power, as reasons for these trends. Sometimes factors such as improved foreign trade, growing corporate size, or changed consumer spending are cited, but writers admit that many of these explanations are speculative. General theories of social and economic change are rarely put forward to explain these changes, nor are longer-range predictions attempted.

Such journalistic accounts make interesting reading over breakfast and usually contain some insight, but they share all the weaknesses of systematic linear extrapolation and none of the strengths. Avoid basing your future plans on what you read in the newspaper.

Demographic projection—knowing the changing size and composition of the nation's population—can supplement information on future job opportunities gained by looking at recent trends. Job opportunities are influenced by the ratio of jobs to people seeking jobs. Opportunities will grow with *either* increases in the total number of jobs *or* decreases in the total number of workers. Demographers, who study population scientifically, are particularly interested in the factors that increase and decrease rates of labor force participation and the numbers of working-age people. They make population projections based on assumptions about future trends in fertility, mortality, and net immigration.

Demographers estimate that until the baby-boom generation passes away, around the middle of the next century, the average age of America's population will continue to rise. In 1987, the median age of the American population was at an all-time high of 32.1 years. The median age is projected to reach 36 years by the turn of the century and 42 years in 2030. The percentage of the elderly population (65 years and older) is expected to change from 12.4 percent in 1988 to 13.9 in 2010. From 2010 to 2030, the number of people 65 and over is projected to increase substantially, from 39.4 million in 2010 to 65.6 million in 2030. About 22 percent of the population would be 65 or older in 2030 (Bureau of the Census, 1989).

The elementary-school–age population (5 to 13 years) is projected to be about 3 million larger in 1995 than in 1987 and to remain above the 1987 level for 50 years. The increase is largely due to the higher birth rates among some minority groups and recent immigrants. The size of the population 18 to 24 years old—most important to higher education, the military, and employers of new labor force participants—has been declining since 1980 and will continue to decline to about 24 million by 1995. This group would then rebound to 25 million people in 2000 and 27 million in 2010. However, it would never again be as large as it was in 1980 when it stood at about 30 million (Bureau of the Census, 1989).

How will changes in the age composition of America's population affect your employment opportunities? First, consider that many occupations aim their services and products at specific age groups. We have already noted the effect of demographic change on one such service—the effect of baby boomers (and their children) on jobs for teachers. When children born during the 1950s and early 1960s were at school, teaching was a secure and growing occupation. As the baby boomers graduated from school, enrollments dropped and fewer new teachers were hired. A demographic shift had affected the need for teachers at the primary, then secondary, and then postsecondary levels of education. During the late 1970s, teachers seeking employment experienced great frustration and disappointment. Now, the "baby boom of the '80s" is starting to revive teaching opportunities.

Other industries catering to baby boomers' young children will also thrive until the mid-1990s. By the second half of the 1990s, industries with products and services directed at teenagers should grow more rapidly (Casale & Lerman, 1986: 237–38; Woods Gordon, 1986: 3) and the universities may start to hire significant numbers of new faculty once again.

Industries catering to the aging baby boomers themselves will become increasingly large employers of labor. As the numbers of middle-aged people grow, more service workers in health, leisure, recreation, and travel will be needed. As the same people reach old age, the demand for nursing-home workers, gerontologists and funeral directors will swell.

Population composition also affects the supply of appropriately aged workers. Currently, there are too few young workers compared to middle-aged workers. A great many jobs in our economy—low-paid, unskilled or semiskilled, and often part-time—are normally held by teenagers. The current shortage of teenagers and people in their early twenties, relative to people aged 25 to 45, has strengthened the demand for young workers, increasing pay and improving working conditions (Easterlin, 1980).

On the other hand, there are too many middle-aged workers relative to older workers, resulting in a "promotion squeeze." Because of their large numbers, baby boomers have worse chances than earlier generations had of getting into upper-management positions (Kettle, 1980: 192–93). In the 1960s and 1970s, many managers were promoted to top positions while they were still young. Until these managers retire or die, there is little room for career advancement by workers below them; and these managers have many more years to go before retiring. The result is stifled opportunity for advancement among baby boomers.

Attrition—the movement of workers out of particular occupations—increases younger workers' chances of moving up from below; and it occurs for a number of reasons. Some attrition is peculiar to particular career paths. For example, annual attrition is great in occupations where physical strength and agility (for example, professional sports) or youthful good looks (for example, rock music or various "hospitality" occupations) place a premium upon "juniority" rather than "seniority."

In occupations with large numbers of older workers, attrition due to retirement will eventually create new opportunities for younger workers. However, the process may be a long, drawn-out one. Studies have shown that the percentages of people who leave their occupations for whatever reason within a twelve-month period (that is, separation rates) differ significantly among occupations. Occupations with high separation rates typically require little education and training, offer low pay and status, and have a larger proportion of young, and often part-time workers. In contrast, occupations with very low separation rates typically have high pay and status, extensive education requirements, or a larger proportion of older male workers. There are few part-time workers in these occupations. For example, physicians, dentists, and lawyers are in this group, and these occupations require many years of higher education. However, barbers and mail carriers also have low separation rates. These occupations do not require extensive education, but have relatively large proportions of workers over 45 years of age and are dominated by males (Eck, 1984; Bureau of Labor Statistics, 1984). Thus the attrition in some occupations is slow even if they are presently filled by older workers. Table 4.1 lists 10 occupations with high separation rates and 10 occupations with low rates. Those with lowest separation rates also have low replacement rates, and vice versa for the occupations with high separation rates.

Demographers use the "life table"—a technique for analyzing age-specific probabilities of dying—to predict retirement patterns almost as accurately as they can predict mortality patterns. But they are unable to predict the creation of job vacancies by economic growth, or the filling of job vacancies by automation (the substitution of machines for people)

TABLE 4.1 Occupations with the highest and the lowest separation rates, 1980–81. (Source: Eck, 1984, 8).

Occupations with high rates	Separation rates 1980–81
Child-care workers, private	58.8
Dining room attendants	57.7
Dishwashers	51.7
Hucksters and peddlers	49.8
Food counter, fountain workers	47.2
Newspaper carriers and vendors	47.1
Garage workers, gas station attendants	44.5
Attendants, recreation and amusement	43.0
Child-care workers, except private household	41.7
Waiters and waitresses	40.2
Occupations with low rates	
Dentists	1.2
Physicians	1.4
Firefighters	4.1
Electrical engineers	4.1
Chemists	4.2
Lawyers	4.9
Computer systems analysts	5.3
Mechanical engineers	6.2
Mail carriers, post office	6.4
Barbers	6.8

and immigration (the substitution of people who are somewhere else today for people who are already here). In periods of economic stability and low immigration, this method predicts the future reasonably well.

However, the present is not very stable. Trade deficits experienced by the United States, liberalized immigration laws, and increased workplace automation make demographic projection useful but incomplete. A fuller theory of change is needed, one that meaningfully addresses all of society's parts—social, economic, political, technological, and demographic. That is precisely what futures researchers try to provide.

Futures research predicts changes to work as part of societal change in technologically advanced societies. Sociologist Daniel Bell's (1973) thesis of postindustrial society argues that in today's most advanced societies the economic base is shifting from industrial manufacturing to the production and processing of information. Types of jobs associated with industrial production are disappearing with the rise of information technology and new forms of social organization based on this technology.

According to the postindustrial thesis, the economic emphasis in society will change from producing goods to providing services. Therefore, manual work will decline as a greater portion of the work force engages in cleaner, more interesting white-collar work. Automation will improve the factory jobs that remain; new jobs will require more training and allow workers greater scope for autonomy and creativity.

Many advanced societies have already entered the postindustrial stage. Just as Bell would predict, the proportion of workers employed in the service has steadily increased in the last few decades. Between 1950 and 1980, the proportion of Americans employed in the service sector grew from 52 percent to 63 percent of the total labor force. Most of the increases are in business services, health care, professional services, transportation and communication, and other services. Manufacturing industries meanwhile have declined in importance as employment sources. Goods-producing jobs accounted for 26 percent of all jobs in 1950, but less than 20 percent in 1980 (Bureau of the Census, 1956, Table 256; 1987, Table 632).

America has also seen a significant increase in the proportion of the labor force performing white-collar work, from 43 percent of population in 1960 to 54 percent in 1984. The percentage of blue-collar jobs dropped from 37 percent to 29.7 percent over the same time period (Maris, 1988: 431).

However, larger increases in the service sector and white-collar work have *not* required large decreases in manufacturing jobs in absolute numbers. Between 1959 and 1984, the manufacturing sector actually gained 3 million jobs. But this growth was dwarfed by the 14 million added in the service sector. Furthermore, the manufacturing sector still contributes a sizable share to the Gross National Product. Its share of output dropped less than 1 percentage point from 26.6 percent in 1959 to 25.7 percent in 1984 (Bureau of Labor Statistics, 1986).

Agricultural, not industrial, work has declined as the postindustrial society grew. In 1940, 8.5 million workers were employed in agriculture, forestry, and fisheries, accounting for 19 pecent of all employed persons. By 1984, only 3.3 million workers, 3.1 percent, were employed in agriculture (Bureau of the Census, 1956; Bureau of Labor Statistics, 1986, Table 1).

The postindustrial thesis holds that future jobs will offer more creativity and stimulation by drawing more on people's skills. Yet many of the rapidly growing occupations—for example, truck-driving—are blue-collar jobs, and few among the rest require a higher education. Finally, none is outstandingly creative or stimulating. Many of the growth occupations would have little impact on training volumes. The people who are unemployed could take most of those jobs with no major training or only training in low-level skills. Postindustrial jobs may not really improve Americans' working lives in the foreseeable future. Furthermore, they are relatively low-status, low-paying jobs (see Table 4.2 for currently projected job opportunities).

An interesting finding in relation to the postindustrial thesis is that most workplaces have integrated the new technology painlessly. By 1986, 31 million adults—from business executives to clerks, and from scientists to plant operators—were using a computer at work, and for the vast majority, the experience has been positive. In fact, nine out of 10 people who use a computer at work are happy with the way computers have changed their work lives; 54 percent of them are very happy with their computers. About 8 million people who use computers at work also have them at home (Casale & Lerman, 1986: 126–27).

The postindustrial thesis holds that the refinement and spread of new technology—especially information technology—will radically change work and career prospects. But, in fact, the majority of reported technological innovation has occurred in offices and involve low-cost technologies such as word-processing, personal computers, and office networks. Most establishments introducing new technology (that is, "innovators") say these changes have created new jobs or substantially modified existing ones. But, in fact, noninnovators appear to create more jobs than innovators.

Nor it is clear that technological change has had a major, positive effect on the nature of work, as the postindustrial thesis predicts. In general, most changes prove slight: many new jobs seem to require no more skill than the ones they replace. Nearly all establishments respond to new skill requirements by retraining the affected employees—often through brief, on-the-job programs. But skills that workers learn quickly on the job are

TABLE 4.2 Occupations with the largest job growth, 1986–2000. Numbers in thousands. (Source: Bureau of Labor Statistics, 1988: 57, Table 5).

Occupation	Employment		Change in employment, 1986–2000		Percent of total job growth, 1986–2000
	1986	Projected, 2000	Number	Percent	
Salespersons, retail	3,579	4,780	1,201	33.5	5.6
Waiters and waitresses	1,702	2,454	752	44.2	3.5
Registered nurses	1,406	2,018	612	43.6	2.9
Janitors and cleaners, including maids and housekeeping cleaners	2,676	3,280	604	22.6	2.8
General managers and top executives	2,383	2,965	582	24.4	2.7
Cashiers	2,165	2,740	575	26.5	2.7
Truck drivers, light and heavy	2,211	2,736	525	23.8	2.5
General office clerks	2,361	2,824	462	19.6	2.2
Food counter, fountain, and related workers	1,500	1,949	449	29.9	2.1
Nursing aides, orderlies, and attendants	1,224	1,658	433	35.4	2.0
Secretaries	3,234	3,658	424	13.1	2.0
Guards	794	1,177	383	48.3	1.8
Accountants and auditors	945	1,322	376	39.8	1.8
Computer programmers	479	813	335	69.9	1.6
Food preparation workers	949	1,273	324	34.2	1.5
Teachers, kindergarten and elementary	1,527	1,826	299	19.6	1.4
Receptionists and information clerks	682	964	282	41.4	1.3
Computer systems analysts, electronic data processing	331	582	251	75.6	1.2
Cooks, restaurant	520	759	240	46.2	1.1
Licensed practical nurses	631	869	238	37.7	1.1
Gardeners and groundskeepers, except farm	767	1,005	238	31.1	1.1
Maintenance repairers, general utility	1,039	1,270	232	22.3	1.1
Stock clerks, sales floor	1,087	1,312	225	20.7	1.0
First-line supervisors and managers	956	1,161	205	21.4	1.0
Dining room and cafeteria attendants and barroom helpers	433	631	197	45.6	.9
Electrical and electronics engineers	401	592	192	47.8	.9
Lawyers	527	718	191	36.3	.9

unlikely to increase the work's complexity and challenge very substantially. Most of the retraining is to prepare women for clerical work—mainly data processing and word processing.

Do many jobs disappear when new technology is introduced? Some argue that job losses resulting from the greater efficiency of new technology should be balanced against the jobs created by an increase in the demand for automated activities or functions (Osterman, 1986). Others admit that technological change will drive some workers out of their jobs, especially in industries suffering slow economic growth; but they maintain that economic and market forces, not technology, ultimately determine employment levels (Ontario, 1985: 15; see also Cyert & Mowery, 1987: 86–99).

Many disagree with these views. Critics of new technology point out the grim experience of the 5.1 million displaced workers, mostly from heavy industries, after three years: only 30 percent had landed equivalent jobs; 30 percent had to take a pay cut of 20 percent or more; and 40 percent had found no job, and some of them were still looking for work. Women and blacks numbered high in the last group (Flaim & Siligal, 1985). Leontief and Duchin (1984) estimate that the same combination of goods and services produced in 1980 will require 11.4 percent fewer workers to produce by 2000.

The situation is essentially similar in other countries. In Britain, new technology does not seem likely to create new job opportunities in the service industries to accommodate displaced workers from other industries or new entrants into the labor market (Gill, 1985: 89–116). Between 1980 and 1986, a period when microtechnology was widely introduced, Canadian banks cut 9000 employees (Rinehart, 1987: 85). While each older-generation robot eliminates 2.5 manufacturing jobs in West Germany, newer ones eliminate 5 to 10 jobs (Words Associated, 1986: 20). The Japanese Ministry of Labor found that 40 percent of companies introducing microelectronics later reduced their numbers of employees, and French job losses in banking and insurance due to information technology have been estimated at 30 percent (Schneider, 1984: 164).

Futures research, including the postindustrial thesis, certainly helps us to understand changes in work and careers. Yet the evidence supporting these models is contradictory. What should we conclude from the forecasts we have examined?

What Does the Future (Appear to) Hold?   Different forecasting techniques yield somewhat different forecasts. But if the two most different approaches—linear extrapolation and futures research—point in a similar direction, we should consider taking that direction.

As already noted, linear extrapolation confines its attention to likely changes occurring in the next 5 or 10 years. It assumes that the near future will be a lot like the recent past. Much of our everyday experience shows that this is a reasonable assumption. Unfortunately, it is less helpful when we are planning a career that we hope will last 40 years, not 5 or 10.

In 1984, the Bureau of Labor Statistics (1984) predicted that the following ten occupations would need the most new recruits between 1982 and 1995 (numbers in parentheses are the numbers to be hired): building custodians (779,000); cashiers (744,000); secretaries (719,000); general office clerks (696,000); salesclerks (685,000); registered nurses (642,000); waiters and waitresses (562,000); kindergarten and elementary school teachers (511,000); truck drivers (425,000); nursing aides and orderlies (423,000); and technical sales representatives (386,000).

All of these top-growth jobs, as well as those predicted for large growth in 1988 (see Table 4.2), are in the service sector, not manufacturing. This certainly agrees with Bell's postindustrial thesis. However, most of the top-growth jobs are not highly creative and do not require a lot of postsecondary education.

More worrisome is the fact that the set of predictions made in 1988 (some of which are shown in Table 4.2) does not agree very closely with the earlier version of itself. The predicted need for waiters has grown from 562,000 to 752,000. General managers and top executives are now in the top 10, whereas four years ago they did not appear in the top 40 occupations.

On the other hand, the predicted need for cashiers has dropped from 744,000 in 1984 to 575,000 in 1988; and for secretaries from 719,000 to 424,000. Physicians ranked 26th among the top 40 occupations in 1984 with a predicted need for 163,000, but disappeared altogether from the top 30 in 1988.

These changes may reflect real changes in labor supply and demand, not problems with the prediction method. Moreover, people planning to enter occupations that require little educational preparation—waiter, teller, office clerk—may be able to adjust to a changing labor demand fairly painlessly. But people basing their higher education on the predictions of Bureau of Labor Statistics may find adjustment difficult.

Do we get a better result by consulting futures researchers? An example is given by Cetron (1984), who predicts the 500 best jobs of the future, "where they'll be and how to get them." Cetron's forecast and the Bureau of

Labor Statistics forecast agree that large numbers of additional waiters and waitresses, retail sales clerks, secretaries and stenographers, bookkeepers, chefs and cooks, truck drivers, accountants, and elementary school teachers will be needed in the near future.

In terms of their present numbers, Cetron expects rapid future growth in opportunities for secretaries and stenographers, chefs and cooks, and accountants; but only average or slow growth for the other top-growth occupations identified by the Bureau of Labor Statistics. Cetron also distinguishes between what he calls "new" jobs and old jobs that he believes are becoming obsolete. Among the slow-growing or obsolete jobs, he includes factory assembler (that is, assembly-line worker), bank cashier, farm worker, and farm manager. Although some of these jobs are likely to hire many people in the foreseeable future, they offer a declining prospect for future employment, and hence a poor bet for a career.

On the other hand, some occupations will allegedly hire millions of new workers in the near future and grow very rapidly. Some of these jobs already exist, others scarcely do. They include computer software writer, administrative assistant, energy conservation technician, hazardous-waste disposal technician, and housing rehabilitation technician. Each will need over a million new American workers by the turn of the century. Other relatively unheard-of jobs that Cetron estimates will need more than half a million new workers in the next 20 years include CAD (computer-aided design) product engineer, computer terminal operator, computer operator, industrial laser process technician, engineering and science technician, geriatric-service worker, laser technician, and energy technician.

The picture futurists present, then, is of an industrial economy that is rapidly becoming postindustrial. Agriculture and manufacturing will offer people jobs of very different kinds from the past. Food will be increasingly produced on the ocean floor, in space, or in factories and laboratories. People in manufacturing will build, program, repair, and "supervise" robots. The use and recycling of Earth's limited resources, whether for food or manufactured goods, will require more scientific know-how than ever. Clerical workers in banks and offices will be replaced by computerized equipment.

New technical specialties and new services—in sales and information supply (education, guidance, consulting, and lobbying)—will rapidly establish themselves as major sources of work. Some futures researchers predict that "five of the ten fastest-growing jobs over the next few years will be computer-related, with programmers and systems analysts growing by 70 percent in the next ten years"; "services will account for 92 percent of the jobs and 85 percent of the gross national product by the year 2000, compared with 70 percent of U.S. jobs and 60 percent of GNP today"; and "25 to 35 percent of all paid work in the United States will be be done from people's homes by the turn of the century" (*Outlook '87*, 1986: 5).

This rapidly and profoundly changing world of work demands more and better education, whether you are training for a particular vocation or not. To avoid being replaced by a machine, you have to be more complex and more flexible than a machine. The "basics" of education for a postindustrial work world include learning to read and write effectively, communicate simply, manage information, and operate a computer. Moreover, Cetron advises you to "learn your history and relate it to your future . . . learn to learn . . . learn to think . . . and learn how to do it for the rest of your life" (Cetron, 1984: 129).

What career should you enter? Whatever forecast we use, the estimates of employment opportunity for a variety of traditional *jobs* seem pretty stable. There is much less agreement about the opportunities in nontraditional *careers*. Indeed, the Bureau of Labor Statistics offers us job forecasts, not career forecasts: its time perspective is short. In the face of such uncertainty, get a good general education and examine your own heart. That is what Cetron means by "learn your history and relate it to your future." Pay a lot of attention to what you like doing and what you are good at. If you love, and are good at, a lot of things, use forecasts to choose a career from among your "loves."

Job Satisfaction

Job satisfaction is important. Some Americans consider job satisfaction somewhat less important than marital, familial, and romantic satisfaction. And people learn to compensate for a dissatisfaction in one life domain with satisfaction in another, as we saw in Chapter 1. But satisfaction with your job remains an important part of life satisfaction. For a satisfying life, you will need to know more about job satisfaction—what it is, how you get it, and who has it.

Although many jobs at present are mindless and boring, the majority of Americans are satisfied with their jobs. In fact, four out of five workers are satisfied in some degree with their jobs, and one out of three would describe themselves as "completely satisfied" (Campbell, 1981). In another survey, three out of four people reported that they enjoyed their work (Casale & Lerman, 1986: 117).

At least 3350 articles or doctoral dissertations have been written on the topic of job satisfaction (Locke, 1976). Researchers have looked in three main directions to explain what causes people to be satisfied and dissatisfied with their jobs: *objective job characteristics*, such as working conditions, salary schemes, work schedule, union membership, and supervision patterns; *biographic characteristics*, such as age, gender, marital status, education, and religion; and *personality characteristics*, such as self-esteem, feelings of trust toward others, sense of mastery, and control over one's life (King et al. 1982; Parasuraman & Futrell, 1983; Weaver, 1980).

The bulk of research into causes of job satisfaction has focused on objective job characteristics.

> Previous research indicates that work satisfaction is engendered by work which is varied, allows autonomy, is not physically fatiguing . . . is mentally challenging and yet allows the individual to experience success, and . . . is personally interesting. Satisfaction with rewards such as pay, promotions, and recognition depends on the fairness or equity with which they are administered and the degree to which they are congruent with the individual's personal aspirations. . . . The employee will be satisfied with agents in the work situation (supervisors, subordinates, co-workers, management) to the degree that they are seen as facilitating the attainment of his work goals and work rewards, and to the degree that these agents are perceived as having important values in common with him (Locke, 1976: 1342).

Less is known about the contributions of personality and biographic characteristics to job satisfaction. For example, only one personality variable regularly appears to influence job satisfaction. Locke reports that "high self-esteem individuals will experience more pleasure in their work, other things being equal, than individuals with low self-esteem" (1976: 1344).

Moreover, studies have rarely compared the relative influence of objective job characteristics, biographic characteristics, and personality characteristics on job satisfaction. Two recent studies of job satisfaction—one by King, Murray, and Atkinson (1982), and another by Rice, Near, and Hunt (1979)—try to do this, sorting through the three groups of characteristics to find out which matters most and by how much.

The two studies reach quite different conclusions about the importance of biographic characteristics in predicting job satisfaction. However, the study by King et al.—more believable because it collects more detailed data—finds that biographic characteristics add little to our understanding of job satisfaction, once job and personality characteristics are taken into account.

One biographic characteristic that does predict job satisfaction quite reliably is age—that is, stage in the life cycle (see also Campbell, 1981: 120). As we have noted, people generally become more satisfied with life as they age. As well, older people are often less highly educated than younger people; and the less-educated are usually more satisfied with life (and work) than average Americans.

King et al. find the following objective job characteristics particularly important influences on job satisfaction: occupational category, occupational prestige rating, yearly salary, years on the job, self-employment, union membership, shift-work requirements, regularity of hours, control over the pace of work and overtime, degree of supervision, seriousness of danger, problems with working hours, and job-related mental or physical exhaustion at the end of the work day (1982: 125).

The Role of Personality   Whatever their job, people are able to change their behaviors, attitudes, expectations, desires, and even their values. Many sociological studies have shown the process by which people commit to, and identify with, particular jobs and careers. So, for example, the factory worker promoted to supervisor gradually learns (and tries to adopt) the viewpoint of management; the young academic learns the viewpoint of grader, not graded; the physician or social worker learns to deal with suffering in a more practical, less emotional way.

However, people are rarely able to change their basic personality. For this reason, you have to understand your own personality and try to fit it into the right kind of job or career.

Both King et al. (1982) and Rice et al. (1979) find that personality variables are highly correlated with work satisfaction. Typically, people who feel alienated or feel they have little control over life, and people who harbor negative sentiments about neighborhood, health, and general life course, are less satisfied with their jobs. In the King et al. study, these personality variables are only slightly *less* powerful predictors of job satisfaction than objective characteristics of the job itself; in the Rice et al. study, they are slightly *more* powerful predictors.

People's feelings about their jobs are best understood as an interaction between "individual expectations and traits" and "objective characteristics of their experience" (King et al., 1982: 129). Feelings of alienation, distrust, and external control reduce job satisfaction. They may also combine with objective job characteristics such as danger, unpredictability, long hours, excessive supervision, and low occupational prestige to magnify job dissatisfaction.

Job/personality mismatching may be a cause of "burnout," the ultimate sign of job dissatisfaction and an apparently common malaise of professional and managerial workers (Freudenberger & Richelson, 1981). The internally motivated person who works in a setting that imposes strong external controls and/or random rewards for performance is a prime candidate for "burnout."

People need to know enough about their own personalities and the jobs they are thinking of entering to anticipate whether they will find a given job satisfying. You should not become a police officer if you hate rules and routines, or a novelist if you crave imposed order, or a door-to-door sales representative if you need continuous approval. Of course, less-satisfying jobs should be reorganized to eliminate their dissatisfying characteristics. All in all, universal job improvement and a better allocation of personalities to positions will increase everyone's satisfaction. But for the time being, career-choosers need to be particularly alert to the worst features of the jobs they are thinking of entering.

Unfortunately, social class significantly influences what people get out of their work life, just as it affects the rest of their life. People in the working class and lower middle class are particularly likely to hold jobs with objectively dissatisfying features—low pay, high risk of unemployment, shift work, dangerous or unpleasant working conditions, and so on. Moreover, their jobs typically combine low prestige and a high degree of external control. All these conditions and experiences create feelings of alienation, external control, and even distrust.

By contrast, managers and technocrats are not closely supervised. Nor are most of them required to produce a quota. Usually only a small percentage of them experience unemployment or layoff. The objective conditions of managers and technocrats are very much better—more satisfying—than manual workers, and also much less likely to excite feelings of alienation, external control, and distrust.

The combination of personality and job characteristics may be particularly problematic for working-class people. If working-class life "incapacitates" by giving people low esteem, people in highly alienating and unprestigious work will suffer particularly great job dissatisfaction. They will also substitute "extrinsic" for "intrinsic" job goals, that is, shift away from looking for pleasure in work to looking for decent pay and working conditions.

In jobs where intrinsic satisfaction is generally high, workers are less influenced by the level of extrinsic satisfactions (for example, pay, working hours, working conditions) than in jobs where intrinsic satisfaction is low. "Among unskilled/semiskilled and clerical workers, pay, job conditions, and the social environment of the job are more important than among skilled workers or professional/technical workers. Extrinsic rewards become an important determinant of overall job satisfaction only among workers for whom intrinsic rewards are relatively unavailable" (Gruenberg, 1980: 268).

Managers and workers value extrinsic and intrinsic job facets differently. "Future research must be careful to distinguish between the categories of employees when discussing the contribution of various job factors to employee job satisfaction" (Ronen & Sadan, 1984: 92, 94). People's job satisfaction will reflect the degree to which expectations are being met—lower-status workers will expect satisfactory extrinsic rewards, higher-status workers intrinsic ones. The disappointment of such expectations will diminish job satisfaction.

The key to job satisfaction, like the key to life satisfaction generally, is matching expectations to real possibilities. Given enough time, people can change their expectations; and they can take satisfaction from "substitute" rewards, once they expect them. As we saw in Chapter 1, in order to achieve satisfaction, people commonly learn to want what they can get. Trends in job satisfaction will reflect changes in the match-up between what people are getting and what they have learned to expect. What, then, are these trends?

Trends in Job Satisfaction National surveys have consistently revealed an essentially high and stable level of job satisfaction among American workers since measurements were first taken in the 1930s (Campbell, 1981; Weaver, 1980; Chelte, Wright, & Tausky, 1982). Casale and Lerman (1986: 117) report that almost 8 out of 10 Americans say they are basically satisfied with their jobs.

However, a new trend of job dissatisfaction might have set in during the 1970s. In a large review of the research on changing job satisfaction, Mortimer (1979) reports that

> workers in all occupations are expressing greater discontent with their jobs. This represents a reversal of the previous stability in job satisfaction from the late fifties to the early seventies. Not surprisingly, the younger and college-educated workers are spearheading this new trend. Although there is little evidence that change has occurred in work values, the rising educational attainment of the labor force would suggest that aspirations have risen. What is certain is that workers of today, in all occupational categories, seek both intrinsic and extrinsic satisfaction from their jobs. (p. 16)

Mortimer finds evidence of "declines in satisfaction in virtually all segments of the working population . . . [despite] a continuing high involvement with work as a central focus of life." The biggest decline in job satisfaction was found most recently. Specifically, from the 1950s through the late 1970s, the percentages of managers reporting job satisfaction dropped from 95 to 84, of clerical employees from around 77 to 62, and of the hourly employees from a high of 71 to 59 (O'Neill, 1981).

Quinn and Staines (1979) reached a similar conclusion in their survey of employment. They found that overall job satisfaction declined over the period 1969 to 1978. Moreover, they identified five facet-specific indicators of job satisfaction—comfort, challenge, financial rewards, resource adequacy, and promotion—which also showed a definite and significant downward trend. They argue that there are limitations to the single-question measure of job satisfaction, such as that based on this type of question: "All in all, how satisfied would you say you are with your job?" By contrast the facet-specific indicators probe the underlying factors of job satisfaction.

According to Quinn and Staines, while the decline in job satisfaction has been pervasive and occurred in all the demographic and occupational subcategories, the emerging discontent is more pronounced among men than women. Workers under the age of 21 show no change, but those in all the older age groups are becoming less satisfied with their work. The amount of decline in job satisfaction is almost the same for white and black workers; but the whites continue to be the most satisfied among all the races. While job satisfaction declined at all levels of educational achievement, the drop was greatest among college graduates (but no graduate education). Workers in the high-status occupations (such as managerial, professional, and technical positions) report a smaller decline than those in lower-status occupations such as operators and laborers.

As Staines (1979) suggested, job satisfaction must be understood in the context of larger, society-wide transformation. Near, Rice and Hunt (1980) found in a review of empirical research that a wide variety of non-work factors—outside the sphere of the job and the work organization—affected job satisfaction. Evidence indicates that job satisfaction is influenced not only by demographic background variables such as age (young workers are less satisfied), education, race, and marital status (married people are more satisfied), but also by other nonwork social factors such as religious preference, characteristics of one's community, personal health, participation in nonwork activity, and childhood environment (Bullock, 1984).

Thus the decline in job satisfaction should also be seen as influenced by a combination of social forces. On the one hand, expectations for greater returns on higher education, in terms of both extrinsic and intrinsic satisfaction, were rising in the 1970s. College-educated workers in their twenties and thirties expected their jobs to be interesting, stimulating, and rewarding. On the other hand, there was a significant decrease in opportunities in alternative employment in the 1970s (Quinn & Staines, 1979). As the baby-boom generation began to enter their thirties in the 1970s, they were competing for a fixed and sometimes diminishing number of middle- and upper-level jobs. As a result, this age group perceived fewer opportunities for advancement in the late 1970s. The baby-boomers continued to be most likely to be laid off and least satisfied with their jobs in the 1980s (Casale & Lerman, 1986: 29).

The debate on whether job satisfaction has indeed declined goes on. Regardless of which side of the debate you may be on, you may benefit from knowing a few more facts about work and job satisfaction as you make your career choice. Four out of five people who say they are satisfied with their work and finances also report that they are happy with their lives. And a higher percentage of them than the national average say that they have a great deal of control over their lives (Casale & Lerman, 1986). Nevertheless, work is not the cornerstone of our real values. Glenn and Weaver (1982) found that only 34 percent of the men and 32 percent of women replied "Yes" to the question: "Do you enjoy your work so much that you have a hard time putting it aside?" Moreover, only 8 percent of Americans choose work as the most satisfying aspect of their lives, whereas 31 percent of the people report relationships with their spouses and 30 percent say relationships with children as the most satisfying aspects of their lives (Casale & Lerman, 1986: 117). Work certainly does not tug at our heartstrings in the way the family does.

Can You Find Satisfaction?   Some people believe that no forecasts are of any use. They argue that occupational forecasts often produce unreliable projections because current methods are not sufficiently developed, data are often incomplete or obsolete, and the labor market changes unpredictably. However, others view occupational forecasts as essential to any effective career strategy; this book shares the latter view.

The recent past is not a perfect guide to the near future, much less the distant future. But linear extrapolation has some value. Similarly, demographic patterns are very important in identifying good opportunities. Take them into account if your intended career is geared to a particular group, or is now heavily loaded with young or old workers.

Our economy is increasingly a service economy, and service work depends on flexibility and on cognitive and interpersonal skills (Hunter, 1988), not just a single job skill and credential. Get as much education and as many appropriate credentials as you can; but most of all, learn how to learn, think, and communicate. The bachelor's degree—whether in arts, commerce, or engineering—continues to be a good credential for many career purposes. Increasing numbers are finding that degrees in administration, management, or law offer additional skills and flexibility in a great many service industries.

Occupations that serve capitalism most directly—such as bookkeeping, accounting, financial counselling, and corporate law—are doing well today. Occupations that do not turn a profit—such as jobs in education, social services, and the fine arts—go through better and worse periods. The self-employing, self-regulating professions—medicine and dentistry in particular—continue to be safe, well-paid services, while other professions such as architecture, certain kinds of engineering, and law are much more tied to the business cycle.

Because of the unpredictability of many careers you might choose, you should pay a great deal of attention to your own feelings, interests, and aptitudes. If you can, avoid a career that does not interest you, because it is not likely to satisfy you. Can everyone get job satisfaction? Some jobs are downright dissatisfying. At the same time, some people are harder to please than others; they would not be happy even with a job they had invented for themselves. One way to minimize your own frustration is by being clear on where the problem lies. Know yourself well enough to know whether the problem is you or your job. Know yourself—your interests, aptitudes, and weaknesses—well enough to choose a job that shows off your best features, not your worst.

Futures researchers expect major changes in the objective job conditions that influence satisfaction. For example, technology will likely blur the boundaries between work and play, freeing creativity; "horizontal" (that is, less hierarchical and more egalitarian) organizations will become the new global standard; workers will have legal rights to jobs and affirmative action will expand; job-seekers and managers alike will create (and use) new career categories; part-time work will increase, bringing change to social mores and standards of comparison; training and retraining workers will be an important challenge for unions; and retirement may become obsolete (ASPA, 1984).

The rapidly changing world of work needs people and organizations that can change. Organizational change is a lot easier when employees exercise self-control and have internalized the goals of the employer. Economist Richard Edwards (1979) has called this kind of structure "bureaucratic control."

Bureaucratic control promises career rewards for conformity and effective performance; it is most common in large, complex offices that manage production, provide services, or manipulate information. Employees see that by getting good evaluations and pleasing their supervisors, they can advance up the hierarchy to ever-better more-responsible, and higher-paying jobs. This leads employees to think about the future consequences of their actions. This form of control generates a strong sense of loyalty to the organization, because the fates of the organization and the worker are so closely tied. Such motivations are crucially important in work that cannot be closely or continuously supervised, a characteristic of professional and semiprofessional work.

This kind of control seems most likely to provide highly educated workers with job satisfaction in large organizations. Moreover, it is compatible with technological and organizational change, as long as the organization continues to make good on promises of job security and career advancement. It seems to satisfy a great many of the criteria Locke (1976) has identified as objective job characteristics that lead to job satisfaction. This kind of control certainly seems to have worked well in Japan.

CONCLUDING REMARKS

Choosing the job that is right for you—the job that will satisfy you—is not simply a matter of knowing which fields will be hiring a great many people in the foreseeable future.

An important job characteristic, as we have seen, is the locus of control. You will probably want to find out whether the job (and career) you are intending offers sufficient opportunity for autonomy and responsibility, combined with a secure career ladder. Some jobs and organizations will offer more of these than others. Before starting out on a particular career, be sure to speak to people who are in it and find out their experiences.

Do people get what they want out of their work and careers, or learn to want what they can get? On the one hand, what people get may result from earlier choices, especially educational ones. For women, marital and childbearing choices also influence work and career, as we shall see in the chapters that follow. Yet most people are just as unaware of the long-term consequences of their educational, marital, and childbearing choices as they are of long-term trends in the job market. They need better information about the likely consequences of their decisions.

Moreover, people often choose careers without considering their own aptitudes, passions, or interests. So they often fail to get what they wanted because they did not know all the things they were choosing when they exercised their choice. As well, people are likely to change their minds about what they want as they get older. What they want at one age or stage in the life cycle is not necessarily what they will want at a later stage.

Do people learn to want what they get? To a large degree they do. As people age, they become more satisfied with their work and career. And people who grow up in difficult economic conditions, as have the post–baby boomers, tend to have more moderate, practical goals, so they will always be more satisfied than people with too-high goals.

Although this book aims at helping you make better choices, many problems you face will require collective, not individual, action. Job reform is certainly one area where collective action will be needed. Reforms are unlikely to take place unless the affected workers bring enough collective pressure to bear on management. Unions play this role in many workplaces. Technology will not solve these problems. To solve them completely requires collective action; in the long run, many such problems may get solved.

But we live in the short run. Take collective action but take individual action as well—know yourself, prepare yourself, change. These principles will prove just as important in Chapter 5, which is about another—quite different—domain, the family.

REFERENCES

ASPA (AMERICAN SOCIETY FOR PERSONNEL ADMINISTRATION). (1984). *Work in the 21st century: An anthology of writings on the changing world of work.* Alexandria, Va.: ASPA.

BELL, D. (1973). *The coming of post-industrial society.* New York. Basic Books.

BLAU, P. M., & DUNCAN, O. D. (1967). *The American occupational structure.* New York: Wiley.

BULLOCK, R. J. (1984). *Improving job satisfaction.* Work in America Institute Studies in Productivity Series. New York: Pergamon Press.

BUREAU OF LABOR STATISTICS (1984). *Occupational projections and training data, 1984 edition.* Bulletin 2006. Washington, D.C.: U.S Government Printing Office.

_____ (1986). *Employment projections for 1995: Data and methods.* Bulletin 2253. Washington, D.C.: U.S. Government Printing Office.

_____ (1988). *Projections 2000.* Bulletin 2302. Washington, D.C.: U.S. Government Printing Office.

BUREAU OF THE CENSUS (1956). *Statistical abstract of the United States: 1956.* (77th ed.). Washington, D.C.: U.S. Government Printing Office.

_____ (1987). *Statistical abstract of the United States: 1988.* (108th ed.). Washington, D.C.: U.S. Government Printing Office.

_____ (1988). *Projections of the population of states by age, sex and race 1988 to 2010.* Series P-25, No. 1017. Washington, D.C.: U.S. Government Printing Office.

_____ (1989). Current Population Reports. Series P-25, No. 1018. Population Estimates and Projections. *Projections of the population of the United States, by age, sex and race: 1988 to 2080.* Washington, D.C.: U.S. Government Printing Office.

CAMPBELL, A. (1981). *The sense of well-being in America: Recent patterns and trends.* New York: McGraw-Hill Co.

CASALE, A., & LERMAN, P. (1986). *USA today: Tracking tomorrow's trends.* Kansas City: Andrews, McMeel & Parker.

CHELTE, A. F., WRIGHT, J., & PAUSKY, C. (1982). Did job satisfaction really drop during the 1970s? *Monthly Labor Review, 105*(11), 33–36.

CYERT, R. M., & MOWERY, D. C., Eds. (1987). *Technology and employment: Innovation and growth in the U.S. economy.* Washington, D.C.: National Academy Press.

EASTERLIN, R. A. (1980). *Birth and fortune: The impact of numbers on personal welfare.* New York: Basic Books.

ECK, A. (1984). New occupational separation data improve estimates of job replacement needs. *Monthly Labor Review, 107*(3), 3–10.

EDWARDS, R. (1979). *Contested terrain: The transformation of the workplace in the twentieth century.* New York: Basic Books.

FLAIM, P. O., & SILIGAL, E. (1985). Displaced workers of 1979–83: How well have they fared? *Monthly Labor Review, 108*(4).

FREUDENBERGER, H. J., & RICHELSON, G. (1981). *Burn-out: The high cost of achievement.* Toronto: Bantam Books.

GILL, C. (1985). *Work, unemployment and the new technology.* Cambridge, England: Polity Press.

GLENN, N. D., & WEAVER, C. N. (1982). Enjoyment of work by full-time workers in the U.S., 1955 and 1980. *Public Opinion Quarterly, 46,* 459–70.

GRUENBERG, B. (1980). The happy worker: An analysis of educational occupational differences in determinants of job satisfaction. *American Journal of Sociology, 86*(2), 247–71.

HUNTER, A. A. (1988). Formal education and initial employment: Unravelling the relationships between schooling and skills over time. *American Sociological Review, 53,* 753–65.

KETTLE, J. (1980). *The big generation.* Toronto: McClelland and Stewart.

KING, M., MURRAY, M. A., & ATKINSON, T. (1982). Background personality, job characteristics, and satisfaction with work in a national sample. *Human Relations*, 35(2), 119–33.

LEONTIEF, W. W., & DUCHIN, F. (1984). *The impact of automation on employment, 1963–2000*. Final Report to the National Science Foundation. New York: Institute for Economic Analysis, New York University.

MARIS, R. W. (1988). *Social problems*. Chicago: Dorsey Press.

MORTIMER, J. T. (1979). *Changing attitudes towards work*. Studies in Productivity Series. Scarsdale, N.Y.: Work in America Institute.

NEAR, J. P., RICE, R. W., & HUNT, R. G. (1980). The relationship between work and non-work domains: A review of empirical research. *Academy of Management Review*, 5(3), 415–29.

O'NEILL, H. W. (1981). Changing employee values in America. *Employee Relations Law Journal*, 7, 21–35.

ONTARIO. (1985). Task Force on Employment and New Technology. *Final report: Employment and new technology*. Toronto.

OSTERMAN, P. (1986). The impact of computers on the employment of clerks and managers. *Industrial and Labor Relations Review*, 39, 175–86.

PARASURAMAN, A., & FUTRELL, C. M. (1983). Demographics, job satisfaction, and propensity to leave of industrial salesmen. *Journal of Business Research*, 11(1), 33–48.

QUINN, R. P., & STAINES, G. S. (1979). *The 1977 quality of employment survey*. Ann Arbor, Mich.: Survey Research Center.

RICE, R. W., NEAR, J. P., & HUNT, R. G. (1979). Unique variance in job and life satisfaction associated with work-related and extra-workplace variables. *Human Relations*, 32(7), 605–23.

RINEHART, J. W. (1987). *The tyranny of work: Alienation and the labour process* (2nd ed.). Toronto: Harcourt Brace Jovanovich.

RONEN, S., & SADAN, S. (1984). Job attitudes among different occupational status groups: An economic analysis. *Work and Occupations*, 11(1), 77–97.

SCHNEIDER, R. (1984). Technological development and its aftermath. In P. Ayrton, T. Englehardt, & V. Ware (Eds.), *World view 1985*. London: Pluto Press.

STAINES, G. L. (1979). Is worker dissatisfaction rising? *Challenge*, May–June, 38–45.

THIO, A. (1986). *Sociology*. New York: Harper and Row.

WEAVER, C. N. (1980). Job Satisfaction in the United States in the 1970s. *Journal of Applied Psychology*, 65(3), 364–67.

WORDS ASSOCIATED. (1986). *Workable futures: Notes on emerging technologies* (Catalogue No. EC 22–132/1986E). Ottawa: Economic Council of Canada.

CHAPTER FIVE

SINGLE OR MARRIED:
What You Want and What You Get

INTRODUCTION

Chapter 1 showed that Americans put a high value on family life. It follows that average Americans should attach great importance to getting married, being married, and staying married. Veenhoven (1984: 241–43) points out that the presence of a spouse *can* have some important benefits in modern western society: namely,

- since people are expected to have a spouse, having one avoids being labelled deviant or strange;
- marriage provides a pooling of incomes and a variety of practical services, some of which cannot be purchased;
- marriage provides a variety of new social contacts, especially through the extended family;
- spouses may provide social support in the form of love, caring, and esteem, and the reassurance that these will continue;
- spouses may provide advice and guidance in an unobtrusive way, to prevent and correct "maladaptive behaviors";
- a spouse can give life a sense of meaning, or something to live for.

Pollster Louis Harris (1987: 88) asked respondents why people get married and got the following responses: "love" was cited by 83 percent of those questioned; "to be with a particular person," by 55 percent; and "to have children," by 44 percent. Other responses, which were less common than these, included: it's an easier, more comfortable life when sharing responsibilities and income; it's a better way of living than being on your own; it's better than being lonely; it brings economic security; it provides a satisfactory sexual relationship; and it improves your social life.

On the other hand, marriage can also have effects that are harmful to happiness. For example, it may isolate people from their friends and the wider society, require sexual monogamy and impose rigid role patterns. Given the strong positives and negatives of marriage, and increased opportunities for divorce, it is not surprising to see dramatic changes in family life all around us.

That is not to say that family life in the past was static or uniform. Change is the rule in social life, not the exception. Furthermore, diversity always exists within continuity. Yet change today may be more rapid and diversity more marked than in the past. It may be impossible today to talk about the *typical* family or the *typical* marriage. Major trends include smaller families, more dual-earner families, and more people living alone.

The old-style "monolithic" family model (Eichler, 1981) no longer applies, a fact with far-reaching consequences for the ways we prepare ourselves to live, marry, and make social policy. In short, the prospective marrier faces a confusing array of facts about marriage and its consequences.

Three questions bearing on this topic appear to interest students: (1) Should I marry or remain single? (2) Should I have (many) serious relationships outside marriage? and (3) What should I look for in a partner? Let us restate these questions so they can be addressed with data:

1. **How does marital status (married versus single, separated, divorced or otherwise) affect people's life satisfaction?** Answering this question forces us to examine evidence about whether marriage brings the outcomes or benefits people hope that it will.
2. **Do nonmarital romantic relationships provide as much satisfaction as marital relationships do? and Does "experience" make people more aware of what is needed for marital satisfaction, or better able to choose the right partner?** To answer these, we will need to know something about what Americans actually do—about the prevalence of, duration of, and satisfaction with various kinds of romantic relationships—and what they think about these relationships.
3. **What qualities in a mate produce the maximum marital satisfaction and stability? and Do similarities or differences between mates do more to increase the likelihood of satisfaction and marital stability?**

Readers who are already married may find this chapter interesting if it helps them understand the choices they have already made—when and why they got married, and to whom. Moreover, they may find that the discussion of marital satisfaction helps them understand and evaluate the experiences they are currently having in marriage. As before, this chapter will close by considering whether, in the domain of marriage and family, people get what they want or learn to want what they get.

To Marry or not to Marry

Is marriage really satisfying? Surveys show that marriage runs from the heights to the depths of satisfaction. Marriage is an extremely variable state, but most Americans report being very satisfied with marriage. About six out of ten married people say they are "completely satisfied" and nearly seven out of ten say they are "very happy" with their marriage (Campbell, 1981).

Given the satisfaction marriage appears to bring, one is surprised to discover that by 1988 the rate of first marriage was only 9.9 marriages per 1,000 people, the lowest in 20 years (although marriage rates were even lower in the early 1960s and during the Great Depression of the 1930s; see Figure 5.1).

Writes journalist Blayne Cutler (1989: 26),

> Marriage is still the lifestyle of choice for the average American, who considers herself romantic, traces her first "crush" back to age 13, and is bound to fall in love at least six times in her life . . . She waited until age 24 before tying the knot, but the more educated she is, the longer she waited to marry. At age 32, she has more than a 50 percent chance of becoming single again.

In general, people are marrying later and some people are dramatically less likely to marry than others. From demographic factors alone, and without any information about personal history, values, or psychological traits, one can make the following prediction with a high degree of certainty:

> A highly-educated, non-white Catholic man from an urban background has a set of characteristics that all predict marriage at a relatively late age. Using current national data, his odds of ever getting married are seven to one. In contrast, an individual with all of the opposite characteristics—a poorly educated, white, non-Catholic woman from a rural background has odds of 37 to 1 that she will eventually marry (Kain, 1984: 39)

According to Sweet and Bumpass (1987), around 5 to 6 percent of the people born in the 1930s and 1940s are still single in the late 1980s. Rodgers and Thornton (1985) project that as much as 10 percent of both men and women born in the 1950s may never marry.

The trend of people, particularly young people, opting for common-law unions over marriage partly explains this decline in marriages. As well, there is evidence that people are merely delaying, not rejecting, marriage, so that the average age at first marriage is increasing. In 1988, the average age of first marriages was 25.9 years for men and 23.6 years for women. It was 22.8 years for men and 20.3 years for women in 1950. Even in 1930, when young people were delaying marriages because of straitened economic conditions, the average age at first marriage was only 24.3 years for men and 21.3 years for women (Bureau of the Census, 1988, 1979, 1960).

Historically, late marriage has been associated with high proportions never marrying (Hajnal, 1965). Both are a response to unfavorable eco-

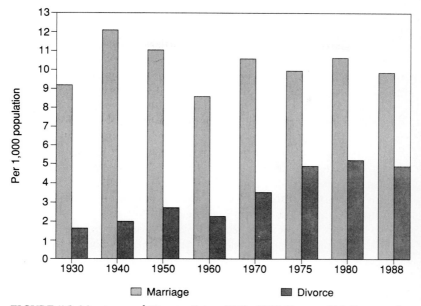

FIGURE 5.1 Marriage and Divorce Rates: 1930–1988 (Source: U.S. Bureau of the Census, 1988.)

nomic conditions that make marrying and childbearing too risky. People who delay marriage beyond a certain age often lose interest in ever marrying; they become accustomed to the single life and, for women, childbearing becomes riskier or impossible. So both increased common-law cohabitation and delayed marriage reflect a flight from marriage and will likely lead to lower percentages of people ever marrying.

On the other hand, one type of marriage has grown much more common—remarriage. The number of marriages in which at least one of the spouses was previously married has doubled since 1960. Given fewer first marriages, remarriages came to represent twice as high a proportion of all marriages in 1984 as they did in 1960. Recently, over 45 percent of all marriages were remarriages for one or both partners (Bureau of the Census, 1987; also, Russell, 1987: 92). London and Wilson (1988: 25) report that men remarry, on average, at age 38—three years after a divorce—and women tend to remarry at age 34—four years after divorce. The older the person at the time he or she divorced, the longer he or she will take to remarry.

About two remarriers in three are marrying remarriers—people who, like themselves, were previously divorced. Again, the likelihood of such a match increases with age: the older the bride or groom, the more likely he/she is marrying a previously divorced person. (Also, the older the groom at remarriage, the wider the age gap will be between him and his bride.)

When spouses have been married and divorced before, there are often children (on one or both sides) coming into the "new" marriage. And, because divorced women tend to remarry when they are still capable of bearing children, their marriage is likely to produce children of its own—hence, complicated new relationships for children with their step-siblings, half-siblings, step-parents, step-grandparents—and so on down the kinship list. Our culture has yet to figure out what to name all of these relationships, much less how to regulate them.

This tendency of the divorced to remarry is one main source of evidence that marriage remains a desired state. Americans who divorce are not rejecting marriage *per se*, but only a particular partner. The search for an ideal mate continues. As well, lower-SES women need remarriage for sheer economic survival (Ambert, 1988). In general, remarriage rates may reflect economic as well as cultural and psychological forces in society. The recent decline in remarriage rates (Leslie and Korman, 1982: 588) may reflect an easing of these economic pressures.

Marriage appears to give most Americans life satisfaction, but it also creates the risk of separation and divorce, two very dissatisfying conditions. In fact, divorced and separated people have on the average the most depressed feelings of well-being of any of the major life-cycle groups. They are much more likely than married people to report that they are "not too happy," and that they have not had their full share of happiness in life. They are much less likely than married people to describe themselves as being "very satisfied" with life in general and with the specific domains of life (Campbell, 1981: 198). So, for many, marriage raises life satisfaction above what they would get by never marrying. But, for many others who remain in bad marriages—for example, the wives who are battered or end up divorcing—marriage lowers life satisfaction. Leaving aside the unhappily married who remain together, how likely is the event of divorce or separation? Marriage is not quite so attractive if the chance of marital breakdown is high.

Rates of divorce have been rising in this century, though not smoothly. The Great Depression depressed divorce rates such that they were lower during the years 1930 and 1933 than in the 1920s. On the other hand, the divorce rates tend to rise in the years immediately following a war. Divorce rates were higher in 1945 and 1946 than either before or for 30 years after that time. (A similar pattern was seen in the years following the Civil War and World War I.) Divorce rates dropped in the late 1940s to the levels at the beginning of World War II and remained steady in the 1950s, not rising again until the mid-1960s. The high rate of 4.3 in 1946 was only surpassed by divorce rates in 1975 and subsequent years (Bureau of the Census, 1975).

More simply, in 1940, before World War II, there was one divorce for every six marriages. In 1970, there was one for every three marriages. Today, about half of all new marriages are expected to end in divorce (Norton and Moorman, 1986).

So far, the peak divorce year was 1979, when the divorce rate was 5.3 divorces per thousand population. Rates levelled off in the 1980s, then began to fall (Bureau of the Census, 1987). However, the slight decline in marriage breakdowns may be more apparent than real. Some couples may be breaking up and forming new (common-law) unions without going through the formalities of divorce.

Simple generalizations about divorce may be misleading, however. People from different regions of the country and different socioeconomic status groups vary widely in rates of divorce. Divorce rates are higher in urban than rural areas. Divorce rates also increase from east to west: rates are lowest in the northeast, followed by the north-central region, then by the south and, finally, by the west (Leslie and Korman, 1982). States with the longest median durations of failed marriages are: Massachusetts (9.2 years), Maryland (8.9), Pennsylvania (8.5), New York (8.4) and Connecticut (8.3). States with the shortest median duration of failed marriages are: Wyoming (5.0 years), Utah (5.1), Idaho (5.2), Kansas (5.3), and Montana (5.3) (Casale & Lerman, 1986: 106–107).

There is an inverse correlation between socioeconomic status and divorce rates: that is, more divorces occur at the bottom of the SES structure. The rate steadily declines as we move upward. Thus, divorce rates are lowest among professionals, managers, and proprietors; among college graduates; and among high-income people. Among blacks, however, the higher the education level, the higher is the divorce rate, except among the black college graduates whose divorce rate is as low as those with little formal education. The inverse relationship between other indices of SES (namely, income and occupational status) and divorce rates holds true among blacks (Leslie & Korman, 1982).

Age is also an important factor: your risk of divorce is higher the younger you are when you marry, and higher too if this is your own (or your spouse's) second or later marriage (Ambert, 1988, Chapter 6).

Divorce rates also vary by race. The incidence of divorce is higher for blacks than for whites. Black married couples also have a greater probability of separating than white couples. Black couples who separate tend to remain separated longer than whites before obtaining a divorce. Once divorced, blacks also tend to take a longer time to remarry. Mexican Americans are less likely than non-Hispanic whites to divorce after separation (Cherlin, 1981; Sweet & Bumpass, 1987).

We used to think about marriage as a relatively permanent state that would occupy most of our adult lives. In fact, our lives are increasingly different, one from another, and increasingly fluid. A Rand Corporation study (cited in Russell, 1987: 86) of living arrangements documented the following facts:

- half of all cohabiting couples change their household status (typically, by marrying) within 1.8 years;
- half of all married-couple households change their status (either by divorcing or having a child) within 4.2 years;
- half of all nuclear families (couples with one or more children) change their status within 6.9 years;
- half of all single-parent families change their status (either by the parent marrying or the children leaving home) within 3.9 years;
- half of all people who live alone change their status (marry, get a roommate, or die) within 4.8 years.

These data suggest that you are likely to pass through a variety of adult household statuses in your own lifetime. Of these, the most likely one of all is marriage.

Determinants of Marital Satisfaction   The recently married will have enjoyed greater freedom to experiment sexually, and to marry whom and when they wanted, than earlier generations were able to do. For this reason, we might think they are more likely to have made the "right" choice for the right reasons. They *should* be more satisfied with marriage. Yet the data do not confirm our expectations. Except for young people in their very earliest years of marriage, older people are slightly more satisfied with marriage, and with life generally, than younger people of the same marital status (Campbell, 1981).

Younger married people (aged 18 to 24), most of them married a short time and without children, are the most likely to feel very satisfied with their marriages. That is, newlyweds without children express the very highest level of marital satisfaction. Let us call that state of mind "enchantment"; it is a state of mind that Dorothy Tennov (1979), who called something similar "limerence," says lasts for about two years on average, among those who experience it at all.

As the years of marriage increase, "enchantment" begins to dissipate. Part of the decline in marital satisfaction is due to childbearing, an effect we shall discuss in length in Chapter 6. As people go through their 30s and 40s, their expression of marital satisfaction is more moderate. Once they are into their 50s, their marital-satisfaction levels turn upward again (Campbell, 1981).

The U-shaped relationship between marital satisfaction and age (or marital duration) is frequently reported by sociologists (see, for example, Lupri & Frideres, 1981). What's more, it is found for both men and women. Among couples who have been married for three decades or more, "enchantment" edges back up again to near the newlywed level. Some of this return to satisfaction with marriage is more apparent than real. People in our society are supposed to be happy with marriage, and are embarrassed to say otherwise. Unhappy people tend to drop out of surveys, are difficult to locate, and are generally less likely to answer questions.

Moreover, findings on marital satisfaction reported here are based on cross-sectional, not longitudinal, data—which is to say that we are comparing different people at different ages, not the same people as they age. Yet the same findings have been obtained in so many different studies that one is reluctant to dismiss the finding out of hand.

Regrettably, most people separate or divorce when their marriage is in the early years, years of declining satisfaction. They often blame falling satisfaction on their mate and, by divorcing and remarrying, try to recapture the enchantment they felt as newlyweds. On average, they will experience another long decline in satisfaction, especially if children are present in the new family. Spouses who last out the bad times may get two periods of enchantment with the same mate, rather than two periods of disenchantment with two different mates. (On the other hand, some couples will remain unhappily married throughout life.)

After the honeymoon is over, the levels of marital happiness of remarried people are about the same as those experienced by people in their first marriages (Benson-von der Ohe, 1987). Likewise, remarried people prove to be no more satisfied with their lives overall than people in their first marriage, and may be even less satisfied when they have children and stepchildren. This fact is reflected in a higher incidence of divorce among the remarried than in first marriages. The failure of remarriage to yield higher average satisfaction does not prove that people should always stay with their first mate. But it does suggest that people's ignorance of the ways marital satisfaction rises and falls over time may lead to faulty decision-making.

Social class has a significant effect on marital satisfaction (see, for example, Ambert, 1988). Generally, lower-SES people (especially women) report the lowest levels of past and current happiness. Further, social class affects the degree to which marital satisfaction influences overall life satisfaction. Marital satisfaction is likeliest to affect the life satisfaction of upper-middle-class people, whether positively or negatively. Prosperous people can afford to be more concerned with self-fulfillment and other intangible (that is, nonmaterial) life goals, including marital satisfaction.

However, the best predictor of marital satisfaction is a marriage's ongoing quality. The day-to-day activities and concerns of spouses affect marital satisfaction far more profoundly than the social and economic characteristics of spouses. Generally, marital satisfaction is lower among husbands and wives who fight a lot and do not show much love for each other (Benson-von der Ohe, 1987). This is not surprising. But does marital satisfaction produce kissing and reduce fighting, or do kissing and shared understanding produce marital satisfaction?

An experiment is needed to answer this question conclusively, so here is some homework. If you have a steady romantic relationship with someone, try kissing your friend more often and fighting less; then measure the changes in your "marital" satisfaction. If you can only kiss more and fight less by suppressing your real feelings, or if your changed behavior fails to improve your relationship, you will have learned something valuable, both personally and theoretically.

"Kissing and fighting" may sound like trivial concerns or a trivialization of important ones until you remember that marriage is a supercharged way of living. Domestic violence—wife abuse, elder abuse, child abuse, and even husband abuse—is a problem we read about in the newspaper every single day. People who never thought they were capable of such acts may find themselves committing them. We know relatively little about rates of domestic violence in the past, so measuring the trend is difficult if not impossible. What we do know, according to reliable statistics, is that more people (especially women) are murdered by their spouse than by a stranger.

Marriage and Life Satisfaction   A comparison of cross-national findings on life satisfaction by Dutch sociologist Ruut Veenhoven (1984) has revealed fairly consistent patterns. A majority of twenty or so studies conducted in the United States show:

- "People who share a household with a steady partner appeared on the whole to be happier than those who do not" (Veenhoven, 1984: 233);
- "Great differences in happiness between married and never married persons . . . in Denmark, the Netherlands and the US. Less strong differences were observed in West Germany and Luxembourg . . . The differences in happiness between married and never married people were generally strongest among young persons" (Veenhoven, 1984: 234);
- "There is no country where the widowed were relatively happier" (Veenhoven, 1984: 234);
- "In western Europe and in the US divorced people appeared very unhappy relatively . . . There is no country in which the divorced appeared equally happy as the married" (Veenhoven, 1984: 234–35).

In the United States as elsewhere, married people are generally more likely than those who are separated or divorced, or who are still single after age 30, to call themselves "very satisfied" with life in general and with the specific domains of life. In fact marriage and family life contribute a great deal to one's general level of satisfaction. After satisfaction with self and with one's standard of living, satisfaction with family life and with marriage have the third- and fourth-strongest relationships with general life satisfaction (Campbell, 1981).

Veenhoven also notes that, in survey after survey, "the never married are generally happier than the widowed and the widowed happier than the divorced" (Veenhoven, 1984: 235). This finding agrees with results of an American survey (Casale, 1986: 31–32) showing that getting married adds 7 points to a person's Happiness Index, but getting divorced subtracts 16 points. (Staying married and having a "serious problem with your marriage" subtracts 22 points!)

The psychological factors influencing marriage's effect on life satisfaction are fairly easy to guess. Veenhoven finds that, generally, people living intimately with another person—whether married or not, heterosexual or not—are happier than people living alone (Veenhoven, 1984: 235–36). Indeed, cross-national research finds no significant difference in the satisfaction levels of formally married and cohabiting couples. So a stable intimate relationship is, in itself, conducive to life satisfaction.

Yet, as you might imagine, "happiness is generally higher when marital partners spend more time together and behave more affectionately to each other . . . The overall happiness of American women has furthermore been related to the 'value similarity with their husband'" (Veenhoven, 1984: 236). Certain characteristics of one's spouse also play a part in marital happiness. For example, married people are happier if they have a happy spouse. According to at least one study cited by Veenhoven, married women are happier if their spouse has a higher socioeconomic status, and is regularly employed but avoids excessive "work demands" (Veenhoven, 1984: 237).

This reminds us that marriage, as Jesse Bernard pointed out, is very different for husbands and wives. The demographic factor influencing marriage's effect on life satisfaction most significantly is gender. On average, married women are more satisfied with life than never-married women who are, in turn, more satisfied with life than divorced and separated women. Overall, husbands are slightly more likely to describe themselves as "completely" or "almost completely" satisfied with their marriages than wives are (Campbell, 1981: 76). Married and remarried women are less happy maritally than married and remarried men (Ambert, 1988).

The correlation between marital satisfaction and overall life satisfaction is much stronger for wives than it is for husbands. Because of structured inequality, marriage is more necessary for women than for men. The most satisfied couples are in egalitarian marriages where the husband and wife share duties equally; the least satisfied are in traditional marriages where the husband is head of the household and the wife is subservient.

Men, not women, benefit more from marriage. Men need and like marriage more than women and are much more likely to remarry. Research shows that men's best friends are their wives, while wives almost never list their husbands as best friends. Moreover, marriage increases men's life expectancy far more than women's. Keyfitz (1988) shows that Canadian men increase their life expectancy five years by marrying, while women increase it only one-and-a-half years. By this measure, marriage is over three times as beneficial to men as to women. Moreover, other measures of physical and emotional well-being (for example, see those cited in Bernard, 1973) point in the same direction.

Marriage has no significant effect on a man's occupational attainment. But it has a definite *negative* influence on a woman's occupational attainment. Women in the full-time labor force who do *not* bear children are unaffected by marriage. With parenthood—the birth and presence of children—young women in dual-career families often find themselves in the "mommy track" with fewer professional opportunities and lower salary scales (Hutter, 1988: 346–49).

Divorced and separated women are much less likely to be highly satisfied with life than divorced and separated men. Although divorced and separated men have much higher rates of emotional problems than divorced and separated women, divorced and separated women tend to suffer many more severe financial and social hardships than divorced and separated men (Gove, 1970; Ambert, 1988). They have greater difficulty finding satisfactory work, getting a living wage, and meeting eligible people of the opposite sex. Further, women suffer more difficulties in aging than men do.

In addition, divorced and separated women more often have the major responsibility for raising the children of a broken marriage. After divorce, about one father in three pays for child support regularly, while about one in two sees his children regularly. At all ages, divorced men have higher remarriage rates than women, and remarry more quickly (on average, about three years) (Cutler, 1989: 25). Their involvement in new families lessens their commitment (financial and emotional) to previous ones. As a consequence, a majority of female-headed, single-parent families live below the poverty line. After a marriage breaks down, men usually continue in the same line of work, more easily meet single (typically younger) women, and are free of most child-raising duties. Women can depend on none of these opportunities.

Marriage remains a greater risk for women than for men. Though women appear to gain more life satisfaction from a marriage's success, they also lose far more if the marriage fails. The psychic costs of a failed marriage fall more heavily on female than male shoulders. Separated or divorced women are far more likely than other women or men to describe themselves as burdened, tied down, or worried (Campbell, 1981: 199).

Should you get married or remain single? To sum up thus far, marriage has riskier, less predictable outcomes for women than for men. Both spouses have the chance of gaining more life satisfaction (as well as less satisfaction) through marriage than the average never-married person can expect to attain. Marriage will also generally increase your income, standard of living, and longevity. Yet men apparently gain most from a marriage that succeeds, and the costs are higher for women—especially for mothers and poorer women—if it fails. So the key to deciding about marriage, especially if you are female, is a realistic assessment of the marriage's chance for survival and your chances of supporting yourself and your children if the marriage fails.

Though never foolproof, gathering evidence during courtship is very important. If you think there is too much fighting and not enough kissing in your nonmarital relationship, marriage will not solve the problem. Remember that the "enchanted newlywed" period is typically followed by many years of declining satisfaction, especially if children are present. The U-shaped data on marital satisfaction tell us that the situation will worsen long before it improves.

Remember, too, that kissing and fighting remain important throughout marriage: in fact, they help to shape marital satisfaction. Morever, they indicate the ongoing quality of the relationship. The costs of a wrong guess are enormous, especially (though not exclusively) if you are female. Learn as much as you can about your relationship before taking the plunge into marriage, get ready to support yourself, and do *not* have children until you are fairly certain that the marriage will not fail. Most important, perhaps, flee a relationship in which physical violence occurs. It is likely to recur.

Trying a Relationship before Marriage

Nonmarital relations today are more varied and sexually active than ever before. New housing patterns make intimate relations and living with someone to whom you are not married easier than ever. Even data on teenagers (Zelnik & Kantner, 1980; Pratt et al., 1984) show a very high exposure to nonmarital sex, including sexual intercourse.

CHART 5.1 What Americans Believe about Marriage and Family (Source: Brink, 1984: 80–83.)

Here are some general views Americans are said to hold about marriage and family life. How many of these views do *you* hold? How would you test the validity of these beliefs with facts?

- Men raise their social class by education and financial success, while women raise their social class by marrying a man of a higher social class.
- People try to get married in order to prove that they are worth loving.
- When people are ready to get married, they will do so with the first person of the opposite sex who meets certain minimum standards and is interested in the venture.
- Men and women do things in front of their spouse that they did not do in front of their fiancé.
- There are no perfect marriages but some are better than others.
- Most divorces occur because neither person has tried hard enough.
- Women who drive large station wagons put their family first.
- If anyone makes your spouse's life miserable, your life will become miserable.
- Most men go to lodges or on hunting/fishing trips to get away from their wives.
- Most men would prefer to be polygamists, if it were legal, socially acceptable, and if they could afford it.
- People without family feel very depressed over the holidays.

Pollster Louis Harris (1987: 178) notes that sex and marriage have become more and more distinct from each other with passing generations.

> A quarter of a century ago, in the early 1960s, 52% of women who had had sex before marriage went on to marry the men with whom they had had sexual relations . . . In the latest period measured, only 21% of all women who have premarital sex go on to marry the men with whom they have had sexual relations. This means that sex among unmarried women is on the rise.

Today, "of all women in the normal childbearing period, those 15 to 44 years old, 61% of those who have never been married nonetheless have had sexual intercourse" (Harris, 1987: 178). By 1979, the percentage was 88.5 percent among never-married black 19 year-old women and 64.9 percent among never-married white 19 year-olds. Their average age at first intercourse was 15.5 years and 16.4 years, respectively. (Similarly, by age 19, 79.9 percent of never-married black men and 77.1 percent of never-married white men had had intercourse) (Zelnik & Kantner, 231).

Contrary to popular expectations, a fear of AIDs and premarital pregnancy has only slightly reduced the sexual activity of unmarried young people. Schwartz (cited in Guber, 1987: 44) reports, for example, that

> Despite the publicity about AIDS and other sexually transmitted diseases, only 48 percent of teenagers believe that sexual activity carries the risks of these diseases. Teenage girls are more concerned about venereal disease than boys. Overall, 55 percent of girls and 42 percent of teenage boys strongly agree that teenage sex carries the risk of disease.

Easier sexuality has gone hand-in-hand with a growing tendency to cohabit with, rather than marry, a romantic partner. Citing research by demographers Bumpass and Sweet, Riche reports that

> Among Americans aged 19 and older [in 1987], 4 percent were currently cohabiting, about one-fifth had cohabited before marriage, and almost one-third had cohabited at some time. Though cohabitation is more frequent among younger people, as many as 5 percent of people aged 60 and older have cohabited (Riche, 1988: 25).

The rates of cohabitation are much higher than average among people aged 25–29. In that age group, "17 percent of the never-married and 20 percent of the previously marrieds are cohabiting . . . Moreover, two in five people in that age group cohabited before their first marriage, and half of those still single had cohabited at some point" (Riche, 1988: 25–26).

Among people marrying in 1980–84, first marriers were four times more likely to have cohabited before marrying than were people who first married between 1965 and 1974.

There is little doubt that people are using cohabitation to delay marriage—perhaps, to better evaluate the strength of their commitment to a given partner. Using data from the Department of Education's National Longitudinal Survey, University of Chicago researchers Willis and Riche found that young adults with certain economic futures are more likely to marry than cohabit. Yet people who start relationships at later ages, and formerly married people, are more likely to choose cohabitation than marriage (Riche, 1988: 8).

Only half of cohabiting couples continue to live together more than a year without marrying. As Riche says, "If the couple is going to marry, they generally do so quickly." And roughly one half of all cohabiting couples *will* marry. But is this choice between cohabitation and marriage of any importance?

What do people experience in serious romantic involvements outside marriage? Compared to marriage, how satisfying are these relationships? Are they satisfying enough to make marriage obsolete? Or are they very much like marriage—no better or worse, but without the legalities?

These are questions you might ask yourself if you are considering a serious romantic relationship. If personal ethics rule it out, a marriagelike involvement outside marriage would probably prove dissatisfying and even distressing. Do not change your ethics or values to test a potential partner. Rather, try to fit the information provided here into your world view. Doing so may help you understand your own goals and opportunities better.

Before discussing the effects of a serious involvement outside marriage, we should take note of a methodological problem. The kinds of people who enter such relationships are probably the kinds of people who value them, want them, and can handle them. So if we discovered, for example, that people in serious nonmarital relationships were twice as satisfied as people in marital relationships, this finding would *not* prove that marriage is obsolete or that *everyone* would be twice as likely to get satisfaction out of a nonmarital relationship. Remember, different kinds of people have—for a variety of reasons—selected either marital or nonmarital relationships. What satisfies one kind of person will not necessarily satisfy another.

General conclusions on this issue are only possible if we experiment with people—randomly putting some into one kind of relationship and similar people into another—or control statistically for all the relevant variables—people's values, personality types, social backgrounds, parental influences, and so on. But we cannot experiment with people in this way, and the complexity of the problem, combined with a shortage of data, makes the second solution almost impossible too.

So our goals will be simpler: we will compare people's experiences in different kinds of relationships, recognizing that the participants are also, conceivably, different kinds of people. Let us look at the results and speculate on what they might mean.

A Canadian Quality of Life survey (1981) asked married respondents and respondents involved in a serious relationship with a "friend" identical questions about their satisfaction with the marital or marriagelike relationship. The data reveal a surprising similarity in responses.

Both groups prove to be equally satisfied (or dissatisfied) with the amount of love shown (31 percent are extremely satisfied) and the way their spouse/friend deals with the respondent's children (32 percent are extremely satisfied). Both are equally likely to disagree many times about money (6 to 7 percent) and how to spend the evening (5 percent) and are almost identically satisfied with the interest their spouse/friend shows in their work (25 to 26 percent are extremely satisfied), the amount of time they spend together (24 to 27 percent), and their spouse/friend's understanding of the respondent's feelings (26 percent of married respondents and 32 percent of unmarried respondents are extremely satisfied).

Overall, married respondents are only slightly more likely to give their relationship the very highest rating—an 11 on the 11-point scale; 25 percent do so, compared to 21 percent of respondents in a nonmarital relationship. On most points, then, married and unmarried respondents are about equally satisfied (or dissatisfied) with their romantic involvement.

However, the two groups differ in other ways. Of the two, married respondents are much more satisfied with the assistance they get working around the house (33 percent are extremely satisfied, as compared with 21 percent of the unmarried respondents). Although the unmarried respondents are more likely to report having been kissed many times in the preceding month, married respondents are more likely to report that all their sexual needs are being met.

Most important of all, perhaps, people in a nonmarital relationship are nearly twice as likely as married people to feel that their freedom is limited by the relationship: 12 percent of the unmarried respondents frequently feel this, compared with 7 percent of the married group. Finally, the unmarried respondents are over five times as likely to report having thought about ending the relationship during the past year: one in three had thought about it, compared with only one in sixteen married respondents.

What happens to these serious, nonmarital relationships in which so many partners think yearly about breaking up? According to these data, a serious nonmarital involvement is almost indistinguishable from marriage in most important respects. Male cohabitors are as violent toward their partners as are their married counterparts. But there is one important difference between the two groups: one relationship is based on a firm commitment and the other is not. People who are married are more likely to have mentally, as well as legally, committed themselves to the relationship and followed up with actions that rest on such a commitment—most especially, having children and incurring major joint expenses (for example, buying a home). As sociologist Max Weber might have said, they have "routinized the charisma."

The Life Cycle of a Relationship   Love tends to follow a self-maintaining course (Collins, 1982). It begins with enchantment—commitment based on very strong, nonrational feelings—and consolidates itself with hard-to-escape commitments—for example, lifestyle, children, and debts. As the nonrational enchantment starts to decline, mounting rational considerations about these commitments assume greater importance in keeping couples together until later on in marriage—with the decline of debts and child-raising burdens—enchantment starts to grow again. Middle age is a time of marital rediscovery for many.

This pattern makes the life cycle of a love relationship very much like the life cycle of a religious or political movement (Max Weber, 1958). Each begins with "charismatic" attachment (to a lover or leader). This powerful, irrational attachment moves people to make extraordinary efforts and commitments. A "routinization" of charisma follows: institutions are created that capitalize on people's faith in the original inspiration. These institutions—increasingly rational and rationalized—are better able than their charismatic, nonroutinized, nonrationalized counterparts to withstand the tests of faith that people experience in everyday life and even the periodic, quite dramatic trials of faith—the major disappointments—they encounter.

From time to time, people renew their faith by fundamentally reassessing it and the lives they have built on it. A major family crisis may be the catalyst for such a renewal of faith; equally, it may destroy the family. And the elimination of long-term family pressures, such as the end of child-rearing and a paid-off mortgage, may also be the catalyst.

In comparing the family to other self-renewing institutions, Collins (1982) is not arguing that married people, having "routinized the charisma" of a relationship, love each other less than people still at the "charismatic," "enchanted," or "limerent" stage. At marriage, people simply enter a qualitatively different phase of the relationship—a phase that is, in most respects, neither more nor less satisfying than the premarital relationship. Later stages of marriage are also qualitatively different. Though routinized, a marriage may be both satisfying and capable of charismatic self-renewal, like any other social arrangement. (Of course, it may also be stable but unsatisfactory and nonrenewing.)

The one area in which marriage excels is in reducing concerns with freedom and new relationships. Commitment to a marriage is simply more serious than commitment to a nonmarital relationship. Therefore, to judge from these data alone, the answer to the question "Should I have (many) serious relationships before marrying?" is "Yes, if you have doubts about your prospective mate or your willingness to make a commitment; but otherwise, no." Marriage is no better or worse than nonmarriage, but it is different.

Trial Marriage versus Early Marriage   Young people often find themselves in a state of love, enchantment, or limerence; in that state, they may have trouble imagining how they can continue living without the object of their affection. What should a person in that situation do? Three solutions suggest themselves: marry your beloved, cohabit but do not marry, or delay making a decision until you have a great deal more evidence about yourself, your mate, and the relationship between you. What choice makes the most sense?

Sociological evidence argues forcefully against early marriage as a solution. "The divorce rate among [those who marry young] is estimated at from two to four times that among persons who marry after 20 years of age. The divorce rate is related to low educational levels, low economic levels, premarital pregnancies, and possibly to personality difficulties" (Leslie & Korman, 1985: 396; see also Scanzoni, 1972: 6–28).

As always, the cost of failure falls most heavily on the woman. By far, the most numerous single parents are separated and divorced women. Single-parent families have become much more numerous lately, and a large proportion live below the poverty line. Single mothers are more likely than other women to have married (and had children) too soon, before getting enough education and job skills for economic independence. "In the longer run, this lack of job-related resources may have limited their power within a marriage or union and, thus, may have predisposed its termination" (Pool & Moore, 1986: 49).

The message is clear: you should not marry before you are ready. Even more important, you should not enter parenthood too soon, or for the wrong reasons. (We will discuss this further in Chapter 6.) Getting married does not ensure the stability of a relationship, and having children does not keep a couple together, much less improve a shaky relationship.

Does this argue that the smitten couple should live together unmarried? Evidence suggests higher-than-average divorce rates for people who live together before marriage (Riche, 1988: 26). This may be a temporary fact, subject to change as people become more accustomed to cohabitation and the wise use of their freedom. Or it may reflect differences in romantic stability between people who are inclined to cohabit before marriage and those who are disinclined. So it may not be cohabitation *per se* that leads to higher risks of divorce. But of two risky choices, early marriage remains the riskier, for obvious reasons.

When is marriage "too early?" Our culture has long promoted the ideal that men should finish their education, get established in a career, and *then* marry; Hogan (1981) calls this the "normative pattern." But many factors conspire against this normative pattern. Wars tend to interrupt young men's formal education and take them away from their loved ones; this separation exerts a powerful pressure to marry before their education is complete and before career-building has gotten under way. In fact, World War II and its aftermath helped destroy the notion that marriage and university attendance were incompatible.

Economic recessions, on the other hand, throw traditional patterns into doubt because they make it harder for young people to find work and achieve economic security. Education and career-building become harder to plan for and control. Such uncertainty breaks the traditional link between economic security and the establishment of a family. Under these conditions, getting married appears no more foolish than not getting married.

Beneath these and other temporary factors, Hogan detects a growing trend toward non-normative sequencing, even in peaceful and prosperous times—a trend toward marriage before the completion of education and career-building. Some reasons may include the progressive lengthening of formal education, the growing availability of student loans and married-student housing, the rising availability of full- and part-time work for students and/or their spouses, the growth of part-time education, and, of course, the increased protection from unwanted pregnancy modern birth control provides.

What happens to the increasing numbers of young men who marry before their education is complete and their career has been set in motion? "Initially, married men who seek employment tend to find better-paying and somewhat higher-status jobs than single men. . . . But the man who is single has greater freedom to seek a better job. Unrestricted by family responsibilities, single men tend to enjoy quicker career advancement" (Hogan, 1981: 200–201).

Additionally, men who (for reasons of marriage) have left school and entered the labour force relatively early tend to rely more on family connections to secure a first job. This tends to situate them in jobs with relatively poorer prospects for career advancement. (Remember Granovetter's findings, discussed in Chapter 2, which show that the "best" jobs travel through networks of acquaintanceship.) Men who marry early and rely on family connections for work are more likely to start out in organizations that are small and limiting. Because they are married, their geographic mobility is restricted and they are less able than the single man to risk moves, changes, and transfers that would increase their acquaintanceships and overall marketability.

How does non-normative, early marriage affect marital stability—specifically, the chance of divorce? Like other commentators on early marriage, Hogan finds that early marriers

> have rates of marital instability more than 50% higher than men marrying on time or relatively late. . . . It seems likely that men who marry early are relatively immature at the time of marriage. Their choice of a marriage partner might be ill-considered because of this immaturity, or problems associated with the sudden entry of an immature man into a marital union may produce strains that result in marital discord. (1981: 204–206)

These risks appear to have lessened somewhat in recent decades. But despite improved chances, the data still argue against early marriage, which continues to increase the risk of career limitation and divorce as compared to the "normative pattern." By implication, the data argue in favour of nonmarital relationships that do not result in pregnancy or limit career mobility, as marital relationships might.

The answer to our second question, then, is in many ways less ambiguous than our answer to the first. Yes, people who feel comfortable with the idea of a serious nonmarital involvement, and feel they cannot delay some kind of living together, should go through with it. Cohabitation gives the participants greater knowledge about each other and the quality of their relationship; half the time, it ends in marriage. By leaving open the door for a decision *not* to marry, it allows for further maturation and thus reduces the risks of becoming parents too early and of hindering careers. But, as we have seen, it does not at present reduce the risks of a divorce later.

There is no reason to fear that nonmarital relationships will prove so satisfying that they will replace the conventional attractions of legal marriage. On average, cohabitation is no more or less enchanting than marriage, other factors (such as childbearing) being equal.

To repeat an earlier point, people who are morally opposed to serious nonmarital relationships such as cohabitation should feel no obligation to change their minds. They will simply have to work harder to get the information they need *before* marriage, and adapt to unforeseen disappointments *after* marriage.

Choosing a Mate

No mate selection process, however sound, will guarantee the survival of your marriage. This is because, throughout life, you are constantly changing, your mate is changing, and the socially structured pressures (constraints and opportunities) surrounding you are changing. But some selections may produce more marital satisfaction than others, and some are riskier than others. For example, people who divorce many times tend to

CHART 5.2 What Americans Believe about Mating (Source: Brink, 1984: 85–90.)

Here are some views Americans are said to hold about mating and, generally, the battle of the sexes. How many of these views do *you* hold? How would you test the validity of these beliefs with facts?

- Women are more concerned about social class than men are.
- Lower-class women are only attracted to macho men, while middle-class women are attracted to men who offer economic security.
- Men of all races prefer lighter-skinned women.
- In a romantic relationship, the person who is less emotionally involved will manipulate the person who is more emotionally involved.
- Few men will offer a seat to a woman on a crowded bus anymore, unless she is attractive or wearing a low-cut dress.
- Most men feel better about looking at themselves in the mirror than most women do.
- When a man is desperate, any woman looks good enough; when a man is sexually stimulated, he may promise just about anything.
- Women with less than a 38D wish they had a bigger bust; men under six-feet-two inches wish they were taller.
- Middle-class people are more embarrassed if their daughters look like sexpots than if they look like slobs.
- Before women became assertive, they fainted.
- If a girl is loose enough with her affections, she can get the attention of men, no matter how homely she is; if a girl is beautiful enough, she can get the attention of men no matter how cold she is.

---

be less careful in their mate selection than people who divorce only once (Ambert, 1988). Bad mate-choosers are probably to be avoided as mates. It is worth our while examining what social science knows about mate selection and the results of better and worse choices.

We shall soon argue that the very idea of "mate selection" is misguided, in the same way that "job selection" wrongly describes how people find work. But for the time being, let us proceed with the metaphor of mate selection, since most people think of mating and marriage as a selection process—which, in a limited sense, it is.

The strongest theory in this area, exchange theory (see, for example, Homans, 1974; Blau, 1964), holds that all social behaviour, even apparently nonrational emotional behaviour like mating and marriage, can be usefully viewed as an interpersonal exchange that must balance. People are self-interested and wish to maximize their well-being in everything they do. When they give up something, they want to get something as good or better in return. Failure to make an equitable or balanced exchange produces disappointment and resentment. Whoever has the greater "resources" in the marriage has the greater power (Blood & Wolfe, 1960; Scanzoni, 1972).

If so, we should expect to find that people mate with and marry others of similar social value, since each stands to gain as much from the relationship. Most mating takes place between people of approximately equal physical attractiveness (Hatfield & Sprecher, 1986). When mates are not equally attractive, the less attractive person usually brings another valued attribute—wealth, power, social position—to the relationship. If balance is not achieved, satisfaction soon declines and the relationship will deteriorate (Hatfield & Sprecher, 1986).

This may explain the so-called "mating gradient"; the mating of attractive young women with more-prosperous, usually divorced, older men. When people of different occupational levels, educational levels, or other status characteristics do marry, men generally marry downward. This fact holds several implications. First, marriage is a more common means of upward social mobility for women than it is for men. Second, cross-class marriage—which, like interracial and other mixed marriages, appears to be increasing—may serve to reduce class conflict in a highly unequal society.

Across societies, the average groom is slightly older than his bride, although this difference is narrowing for first marriages. Sometimes the age differences are very great. In our own society, the age gap between brides and grooms is particularly wide—nearly ten years, on average—

when grooms are marrying for the second time. To such a union, the younger woman brings youthful good looks and childbearing capability; the older man brings social position. The opposite match (bride much older than groom) is less often observed, presumably because older women are less often able than older men to bring high social position to the relationship (see Ambert, 1988, for a discussion on age differences in remarriage). Morever, men may not find high social position alluring in a woman, given our culture's preference for male domination of females.

So in one sense, however unconsciously, mating is a bargain struck between approximate equals. Homogamy, the tendency for like people to marry, "has been verified for age, marital status, social status, race, religion, and ethnic background. . . . [However,] there is some evidence that people seek marital partners who complement themselves in personality" (Leslie & Korman, 1985: 396–97). Thus, psychological complementarity and social likeness may be the norm.

Even so, the question of whether to marry someone like or unlike you is not all that simple. For the mating "bargain" to satisfy, your mate must be as valuable as you in the "marriage market." In practice, balancing a mate's "market value" against your own is a subtle process involving many factors: for example, age, appearance, race, class, and personality. As in many other market transactions, we learn most about a thing's market value by seeing who is bidding for the "good" in question.

Rephrasing the question somewhat gives a slightly different answer. If a market imbalance does exist, it will show itself through instability in the relationship: kissing will decline, fighting will increase, compromises will be few and far between, or one spouse will do all the compromising. In that sense, you will know the viability of an exchange from its ongoing quality, not from some abstract evaluation of your mate's marketability relative to your own.

Evidence about the stability of "mixed marriages" is scanty and somewhat contradictory. As mixed marriages become more common, their acceptance will increase; with acceptance, their viability will increase. If we judge by comparative divorce rates, the difficulties supposed to beset mixed-race or mixed-class marriages are rarely found to be as great as expected. It also appears that age and status differences are more problematic than religious differences between mates (Leslie & Korman, 1985: 397). For example, younger women in marriages with older (usually divorced) men are relatively unhappy maritally, and such marriages display a higher-than-average divorce rate (Ambert, 1988). It is not easy to determine whether the problems are due to age-mixing, bad choosing, or other factors (for example, child support obligations from a first marriage).

Why People Do Not Optimize   The metaphor of a mating or marriage "market" is largely fictional. We learned in Chapter 2 that people find the best jobs through personal contacts, not through impersonal shopping. Similarly, people rarely find mates by shopping for them, as one might shop for a television set. In part, we do not shop for a mate because we do not really know what we want, and will not know until we find it. More important, we could never live long enough to marry if we approached mating as a shopping problem.

Like most rational people, we do *not* seek the ideal or "optimal" solution to our mating problem: that is, we do *not* try to optimize. Rather, we "satisfice": we seek a "good enough" solution, within the constraints life has handed us (March & Simon, 1958). The reasonable person draws no useful distinction between the satisfactory and the ideal: for most purposes, whatever satisfies *is* ideal, under the circumstances.

According to March and Simon, most human decision-making aims at discovering and selecting *satisfactory* alternatives. "Only in exceptional cases is it concerned with the discovery of optimal alternatives. To optimize requires processes several orders of magnitude more complex than those required to satisfice" (1958: 141). This is the difference between searching a haystack for the *sharpest* needle and merely searching for a needle that is sharp enough to sew with.

Choice is certainly a burden and people are not happier for having it. But once they have tried it, they would be very unhappy to go back to a condition in which they had no choice. So the practice, and illusion, of choice remains. But the human race could not reproduce itself and survive if people were "optimizers."

Consider the arithmetic of the problem. Suppose that, as an idealistic adolescent, you listed ten qualities you felt you absolutely must have in a mate. Your mate must be attractive—at least in the top fifth of all possible mates. Your mate must be fun—again, at least in the top fifth of all possible mates. He or she must be interesting to talk to—again, at least in the top fifth of all possible mates. Imagine making up a "shopping list" in this way. Now, what is the probability that your ideal mate actually exists?

If the various qualities you are looking for are uncorrelated, only one person in five to the tenth power—one in 9.8 million—will meet all your requirements. Equally, there is only one chance in 9.8 million that your "perfect" mate will consider *you* the perfect mate. So by this scenario, the chances in favour of meeting and mating with the "perfect mate" are nearly zero: one in 9.8 million squared.

Even more-modest goals will not find you a mate if you seek to optimize. Suppose that, instead of requiring your ideal mate to be among the top fifth in attractiveness, you only require him or her to be in the top half. You similarly lower your standards for each of the other requirements you had listed. This helps to solve your mating problem: now, you only need to look for that one person in a thousand (that is, two to the tenth power). The probability of meeting and mating with an ideal mate who is making similar calculations has improved: it is now one in a thousand squared, or one in a million.

But at most, you only know a few thousand people by their first name. The chance of meeting and mating this way is extremely unlikely. Some people may think they have teamed up with the "perfect partner," and one time in a million they may have. But more likely than not, they have not sought or found their mate by shopping for "the right characteristics," and they have merely decided after the fact that their mate is perfect.

The arithmetic shows that even lowering your original standards will fail to solve your mating problem, if you attempt to optimize. Other solutions are just as fruitless. Some people try meeting more potential partners: if you knew six thousand people instead of two thousand, this would triple your chances. But getting on a first-name basis with six thousand people is very difficult and time-consuming, and the odds are still enormously stacked against you.

Expanding your acquaintanceship network selectively seems to be a way around this. By joining certain kinds of groups, placing or answering personal advertisements, or using matchmaking services, you will more quickly meet new people with the qualities you require. These mating techniques have become much more popular lately, especially among the middle-aged, whose opportunity to meet a large number of new people is seriously restricted. *Take note: postsecondary school will expose you to more potential mates than you will ever pass among again.*

Many people hesitate to shop for mates this way, finding it demeaning or fearing the unpleasantness of blind dates that do not work out. Most people try to solve *this* problem by reducing the number of qualities they require in a mate. Now the potential mate must excel in one or two respects and merely satisfy in half a dozen more. Imagine that you and your "perfect mate" are now looking for someone who excels (is in the top 20 percent) in one quality and is better than average (that is, in the top 50 percent) on just four other particular qualities. The probability of finding a person with the qualities you seek is one in 1250; the probability that you will satisfy his or her requirements is now one in 1250. Even so, the chance of meeting and mating is still less than one in a million (that is, one in 1250 squared).

However you revise the shopping list and extend your range or number of contacts, the chance of mating this way is nearly zero. That tells us that people cannot and do not find a mate in this way. Rather, people fall in love with others who are close-at-hand. As in so many other areas of life, we come to value what we know best and have available—people like ourselves. That is why social homogamy is so common. We become satisfied with the possible, not the ideal.

Even if arthmetic did not rule out shopping for a perfect mate, our other social relationships probably would. For even in an economically rational, "market-based" society like our own, people tend to avoid behaviours that violate customs associated with their household, kin group, religious or ethnic group, and community. This tends to eliminate from consideration—often automatically and unconsciously—potential mates who are quite unlike our friends and family in important ways. We are freer to choose than people who lived in small homogeneous communities in earlier times, because we can more readily bear the costs of social exclusion if our mate is deemed inappropriate. But this factor has by no means disappeared as a limitation on those we consider potential marriage partners.

As well, few of us are psychologically prepared to shop for mates. Among Americans asked "What attracts you to someone of the opposite sex?", "good looks" is the second most common answer (the first is "personality") and, for men, "figure" holds third place (Casale & Lerman, 1986: 75–76). Less visible qualities like intelligence, honesty, or sense of humour are much lower down most people's list. Equivalently, when asked "What turns you off" about a person of the opposite sex, most people mention appearance in their top two or three picks: men are turned off by overweight women or an unkempt appearance; women, by sloppy or overweight men.

What this means is that most people are judging others according to how they look, and they expect that others are judging them the same way. Yet only "54 percent of the nation's adult men are satisfied with the way they look. Only a third of all women like their own looks" (Casale & Lerman, 1986: 76). Nearly two women in three say they need to lose weight, for example; women are also more likely than men to say they need exercise.

In fact, Louis Harris reports that 94 percent of all American men and 99 percent of American women say they would like to change something about their personal appearance. Three women in four (compared to only two men in four) think about their physical appearance quite often, and 40 percent say they spend a lot of time on how they look (Harris, 1987: 3).

Men are somewhat less anxious to change their appearance; after all, women are less likely to judge them by their appearance than they are to judge women in this way. Even so, one-third or more of all men would like to change their weight, waistline, muscles (that is, they want bigger ones), teeth, hair (that is, they want more) or height (that is, they want to be taller).

For their part, three women in four would like to change their weight; nearly half would like to cover up telltale signs of aging; and a third or more of all women would like to change *at least one* of: their thighs, buttocks, teeth, hair, legs, and wrinkles. (Nine percent would even change their ears, if they could.) (Harris, 1987: 5, 6).

Given this national neurosis about appearance, it is natural for people to feel shy about meeting strangers, especially in a mating context. Not surprisingly, then, Louis Harris found that a majority of Americans—five in every six—do not like to be the "center of attention." About two-thirds of the people he interviewed also said they do not like to take the lead in talking socially, or do not like others to notice and comment on their appearance. Concludes Harris, "the evidence here reveals an innate shyness that leads most to pick and choose carefully just where they want to be socially, and especially precisely with whom" (Harris, 1987: 46).

Because they are sensitive about their appearance, expect others to judge them on their appearance, and feel shy at having their appearance noticed, most Americans are going to *avoid* shopping for mates (and being shopped). Instead, they will carefully and quietly take stock of potential mates that are nearby, then satisfice.

This process of satisficing, of marrying the close-at-hand, may sound very cold-blooded and disheartening; but in the actual event, feelings of love are quite genuine. People in love *feel* like they have discovered the one perfect mate, and in a sense they have. But they do not do it, could not have done it, by following a shopping list. Moreover, a person rich and leisured enough to actually shop the world for the "perfect" mate might never be any more satisfied than the "satisficer." The romantic wanderer's exposure to great variety and unlimited expectation might prove profoundly *dis*satisfying.

CONCLUDING REMARKS

The family is changing rapidly. Family life in general is not "dead," as critics of modern life have claimed. But the "traditional" family—two opposite-sex married people living together with their dependent children, neither having cohabited (or been a parent) before, and only one of them (that is, the husband) earning an income—is now experienced by a minority of American adults. It has passed into history; we have no reason to think it will return.

Within the new context, many people still find marriage satisfying: they say so when asked, and remarry after divorce. Although large numbers are entering common-law unions, such unions are largely trial runs for legal marriage, witness the high proportion that end in marriage.

The problems of marriage appear, increasingly, to be problems of doubled career strain—witness the growth of dual-career families—and parenting. In large part, the potential problem a couple faces can be resolved through less, and more carefully timed, childbearing. Evidence suggests that voluntary childlessness may increase further, a matter Chapter 6 will discuss at greater length. Spousal sharing of duties is even more important, and norms on this score seem to be changing, though behaviours change more slowly.

The most interesting changes so far have involved women. Women have already changed their conception of and relationship to marriage in significant ways. More women than ever have equipped themselves for independence. Even working women who have married are placing less importance on that relationship in the overall scheme of their lives (Baruch, Barnett, & Rivers, 1983: 294). In future, the most interesting and far-reaching changes will involve men. They have yet to catch up to the gender revolution at work and at home.

Across modern societies, divorce remains one of the most significant life events, affecting large numbers of adults in traumatic ways. Worse, it is an event for which we scarcely prepare ourselves. The North American mythology of romantic love and mating—one true love 'til death do us part—ill prepares young people for the everyday realities of married life, within which divorce looms as an ominous, ever-present risk. Few are prepared for the strains and difficulties of married life, much less the hardships of divorce.

Like marriage rates, divorce rates reflect a preoccupation with personal fulfilment. If our culture continues to value personal freedom and continuous gratification as much as it has in the last few decades, people will continue to change their marital status as often as they can afford to. The motivations to end a marriage will remain just as high, only the costs of doing so will vary. A healthy economy makes all status-changing—marriage, divorce, career-shifting, geographic relocation—easier and safer. Therefore, the key to predicting the future may lie in the economy's health and vigour. High divorce rates may be a more-or-less permanent feature of our marriage system.

Do people get what they want from marriage, or learn to want what they can get? On the one hand, people are increasingly free to marry or not to marry; to have the kinds of marital and nonmarital relationships they want to; to choose the kind of mate they wish. On the other hand, what we want is certainly patterned. Americans learn to want marriage as the preferred form of adult life. We mate with people who are nearby and socially like ourselves (because they are nearby), not with "ideal" mates. Some divorces may occur because mating is constrained by proximity. More occur because most of us have also learned to expect things out of life that marriage can scarcely provide—especially, the freedom to develop as individuals.

Do we learn to want what we get? Largely, we do. We fall in love with the close-at-hand, believing that we have discovered the "perfect" mate. On the other hand, people rarely get what they expect from divorce. Women, who rarely choose divorce, are particularly hurt by it; but even males who divorce and remarry find the same marital satisfactions and dissatisfactions as males who had never divorced and remarried. People are slow to learn new wants.

The only solution science can offer at present is more information about reality. And this solution is best where free choice is involved. Chapter 6 examines problems of parenthood: what you want and what you get.

REFERENCES

AMBERT, A. M. (1980). *Divorce in canada.* Toronto: Academic Press.

————. (1988). *Ex-spouses and new spouses.* Greenwich, Conn.: JAI Press.

BARUCH, G., BARNETT, R., & RIVERS, C. (1983). *Lifeprints: New patterns of love and work for today's women.* New York: Signet Books.

BENSON-VON DER OHE, E. (1987). *First and second marriages.* New York: Praeger.

BERNARD, J. (1973). *The future of marriage.* New York: Bantam Books.

BLAU, P. M. (1964). *Exchange and power in social life.* New York: John Wiley.

BLOOD, R. O., & WOLFE, D. M. (1960). *Husbands and wives: The dynamics of married living.* New York: Free Press.

BRINK, T. L. (1984). *The middle-class credo: 1000 "All-American" beliefs.* New York: Fawcett Gold Medal.

BUREAU OF THE CENSUS. (1960). *Statistical abstract of the United States: 1960.* 81st ed. Washington, D.C.: U.S. Government Printing Office.

————. (1975). *Historical statistics of the United States, colonial times to 1970.* Part I. Washington, D.C.: U.S. Government Printing Office.

————. (1979). *Statistical abstract of the United States: 1979.* 100th ed. Washington, D.C.: U.S. Government Printing Office.

————. (1987). *Statistical abstract of the United States: 1988.* 108th ed. Washington, D.C.: U.S. Government Printing Office.

————. (1988). *Statistical abstract of the United States: 1989.* 109th ed. Washington, D.C.: U.S. Government Printing Office.

CAMPBELL, A. (1981). *The sense of well-being in America: Recent patterns and trends.* New York: McGraw-Hill Co.

CASALE, A. M. & LERMAN, P. (1986). *Tracking tomorrow's trends.* Kansas City: Andrews, McMeel and Parker.

CHERLIN, A. J. (1981). *Marriage, divorce, remarriage.* Cambridge, Mass.: Harvard University Press.

COLLINS, R. (1982). *Sociological insight: An introduction to non-obvious sociology.* New York: Oxford University Press.

CUTLER, B. (1989). Bachelor party. *American Demographics*, February, pp. 22–26, 55.

————. (1989). Meet Jane Doe. *American Demographics*, June, pp. 25–27, 62–63.

EHRENREICH, B. (1983). *The hearts of men: American dreams and the flight from commitment.* Garden City, N.J.: Anchor Books.

EICHLER, M. (1981). The inadequacy of the monolithic model of the family. *Canadian Journal of Sociology*, 6(3), 367–88.

————. (1988). *Families in canada today.* (2nd ed.). Toronto: Gage.

GOVE, W. R. (1970). Sex, marital status, and psychiatric treatment: A research note. *Social Forces*, 58, 89–93.

GUBER, S. S. (1987). The teenage mind. *American Demographics*, August, pp. 42–44.

HAJNAL, J. (1965). European marriage patterns in perspective. In D. V. Glass and D. E. C. Eversley (Eds.), *Population in history* (pp. 101–43) London: Edward Arnold.

HARRIS, L. (1987). *Inside America.* New York: Vintage Books.

HATFIELD, E. & SPRECHER, S. (1986). *Mirror mirror: The importance of looks in everyday life.* Albany: State University of New York Press.

HOGAN, D. P. (1981). *Transitions and social change: The early lives of American men.* Studies in Population Series. New York: Academic Press.

HOMANS, G. C. (1974). *Social behavior: Its elementary forms.* (rev. ed.) New York: Harcourt Brace Jovanovich.

HUTTER, M. (1988). *The changing family: Comparative perspectives.* (2nd ed.) New York: MacMillan Publishing Co.

KAIN, E. L. (1984). Surprising singles. *American Demographics,* August, pp. 16–19, 39.

KEYFITZ, N. (1988). On the wholesomeness of marriage. In L. Tepperman and J. Curtis (Eds.), *Reader in sociology: An introduction.* Toronto: McGraw-Hill Ryerson.

LESLIE, G. R., & KORMAN, S. K. (1985). *The family in social context.* (6th ed.) New York: Oxford University Press.

LONDON, K., & WILSON, B. F. (1988). D-I-V-O-R-C-E. *American Demographics,* October, pp. 23–26.

LUPRI, E., & FRIDERES, J. (1981). The quality of marriage and the passage of time: Marital satisfaction over the family life cycle. *Canadian Journal of Sociology,* 6(3), 283–305.

LUXTON, M. (1980). *More than a labor of love: Three generations of women's work in the home.* Toronto: Women's Educational Press.

MARCH, J. G., & SIMON, H. A. (1958). *Organizations.* New York: John Wiley.

MITCHELL, A. (1984). *The nine American lifestyles.* New York: Warner Books.

NORTON, A. J., & MOORMAN, J. E. (1986). Marriage and divorce patterns of U.S. women in the 1980's. Paper presented at the annual meeting of the Population Association of America, April 4.

PRATT, W. F., MOSHER, W. D., BACHRACH, C. A., & HORN, M. C. (1984). Understanding U.S. fertility: Findings from the National Survey of Family Growth, Cycle III. *Population Bulletin, 39,* 1–42. Washington, D.C.: Population Reference Bureau.

POOL, I., & MOORE, M. (1986). *Lone parenthood: Characteristics and determinants (Results from the 1984 Family History Survey).* (Statistics Canada, Catalogue No. 99–961). Ottawa: Supply & Services.

QUALITY OF LIFE SURVEY. (1981). Unpublished raw data from large survey of life satisfaction conducted at the Institute for Behavioural Research, York University, Toronto.

RICHE, M. F. (1988). The postmarital society. *American Demographics,* November, pp. 22–26, 60.

RODGERS, W. L., & THORNTON, A. (1985). Changing patterns of first marriage in the United States. *Demography, 22,* 265–79.

RUSSELL, C. (1987). *100 predictions for the baby boom.* New York: Plenum Press.

SCANZONI, J. H. (1972). *Sexual bargaining: Power politics in the American marriage.* Englewood Cliffs, N.J.: Prentice-Hall.

SEWARD, R. R. (1978). *The American family: A demographic history.* Beverly Hills: Sage Publications.

SWEET, J. A., & BUMPASS, L. L. (1987). *American families and households.* New York: Russell Sage Foundation.

TENNOV, D. (1979). *Love and limerence.* New York: Stein and Day.

VEENHOVEN, RUUT. (1984). *Conditions of happiness.* Dordrecht, Holland: Reidel Publishing.

WEBER, M. (1958). *From Max Weber: Essays in sociology*, Gerth, H. & Mills, C. W. (Eds. and Trans.). New York: Oxford University Press.

ZELNIK, M., & KANTNER, J. F. (1980). Sexual activity, contraceptive use, and pregnancy among metropolitan area teenagers: 1971–1979. *Family Planning Perspectives, 12,* 230–37.

CHAPTER SIX

CHILDLESS OR PARENT:
What You Want and What You Get

INTRODUCTION

Raising a child is a unique experience. It is time-consuming and often expensive. It can be frustrating, grueling, and disappointing; also, thrilling, surprising, and delightful. In all of these respects, raising a child is like falling in love, running a business, learning a trade, writing a book, tending a farm, and mastering a musical instrument or sport. So even though the decision to raise a child is unique, other decisions you have already made are similar; you can bring your own experiences to bear on the parenting decision.

Moreover, many of the decisions you have already made *should* influence your decision to raise children. After all, you have only so much time, money, and energy to spend in living; you must decide how to spend these scarce resources in the most satisfying way. For you, raising children may *not* be among the most satisfying ways.

This chapter will limit itself to two very important questions about parenthood, out of many that might be discussed: (1) Should I have children, and if so, how many? (or, Should I have any children at all, and if so, why?) and (2) Are people with children able to find a satisfactory balance between home and career responsibilities, and if so, how? (or, How does the presence of children affect people's—and particularly women's—abilities to enjoy other important domains of their lives, especially work and marriage?)

Answering the first question will force us to consider what people say about parenthood and what they do; national and international trends in childbearing; and the results of decisions people are currently making. People throughout the modern world have been addressing similar questions about parenthood for over a century. Thus these questions, and the solutions people have considered, are far from new or uniquely American. You will not be the first (or last) person to ask them.

Answering the second question will return us to concerns we addressed in earlier chapters on education, work, and marriage—concerns about gender inequality and the particular problems modern women face in meeting their obligations. Again, people—especially women—throughout the world have been grappling with these issues for much of this century. Gender-based parenting problems are far from solved, but knowing that they are widely shared may put your own thoughts about the matter into clearer perspective.

As in previous chapters, we conclude by considering whether, in the domain of parenthood, people get what they want or learn to want what they get. But we must note from the outset that many people who become parents do not freely choose parenthood at all. For some, parenthood results from an unwanted pregnancy and a sensed responsibility to bear the child, rather than abort it. For others, parenthood results from marriage to a person who already has children.

Likewise, many people do not choose the conditions under which they end up raising their children, particularly mothers whose spouses desert them, abuse them, abuse their children, fail to take part in child-rearing, or maintain heavy commitments to children of an earlier marriage—in short, a great many mothers.

So people do not always choose what they get, or get what they choose. They are not necessarily to blame when parenthood goes wrong. The following analyses are intended to help when people *do* have a choice in the matter, in the hopes they will choose wisely.

Should I Have Children?

The survival of humanity has historically depended on a continuing "Yes!" in answer to this question. But parenthood is not as widely desired or needed today as it was in the past.

Four centuries ago, when mortality rates were very high, many births were needed for a family, community, or society to stay at its original or desired size. A large proportion of all children died in infancy; many others failed to reach adulthood, marry, or reproduce. As a result, about as many people entered parenthood in one generation as had entered it in the previous generation, and the total population stayed at a fixed size. With this, the ratio of people to land, and to the food supply, remained the same for long periods of time, allowing traditional social relations to continue.

But around the seventeenth century, mortality rates in Western Europe began to drop. Despite fluctuations due to famines, epidemics, and wars, they have continued to drop ever since. Today, a larger-than-ever proportion of children survive to childbearing age, and a larger proportion of their children survive infancy; as a result, the people-to-land ratio has changed dramatically.

What some theorists (for instance, Malthus, 1798/1959) considered poverty due to overpopulation first became a social and political problem around the beginning of the nineteenth century. Since then, debates between Malthusians and Marxists have raged over whether the "population problem"—a problem of scarcity—could best be solved by limiting childbearing or by sharing wealth more equitably, thereby increasing the world's productive capabilities. To some degree, the "Green Revolution" (Boulding, 1981: 328) has already solved some of these problems by improving food production methods.

Yet these debates continue today, particularly in respect to the rapid population growth of less-developed countries. Though some believe that the world's current population can be adequately fed and housed by redistributing the world's wealth and technology, few would hold that current population growth rates can continue indefinitely. Even within countries like the United States, where overpopulation and rapid growth are not a problem, most people have an awareness of population (and related environmental) issues their parents lacked thirty years ago.

Childbearing is not always the result of a conscious decision. But when carried out by design, childbearing is one of several decisions people will make that has an enormous impact on their extended family, community, nation, and world. As these impacts become more obvious and pressing, do not be surprised if governments come to play a part in this decision by offering very strong incentives or disincentives to childbearing. Quebec has recently offered tax incentives for bearing three or more children. Such policies have also been put into effect in other countries—for example, in Nazi Germany, to encourage (Aryan) childbearing, and in the Republic of China, to discourage it. Public policies affecting access to abortion already influence childbearing decisions in the United States.

So while the survival of the human race once depended on an almost universal "Yes" answer to the question "Should I have children?", today it increasingly depends on the answers "No," "Maybe," or "Not many." People have to choose parenthood more carefully today, with a greater awareness of the reasons for their choice, and its consequences for their lives.

What People Think about Childbearing   To the extent that childbearing *is* a decision, and a purely personal one, what people think about parenthood will remain very important. What do children—the next generation of parents—think about parenthood? Of more than 600,000 American schoolchildren who participated in a "future survey" (Johnson, 1987), "The great majority, over 80%, expect to marry, although boys were slightly less likely than girls to indicate that. Most children expect to have two, one, or three children, in that order of preference; again, boys were considerably more likely to choose 'none'" (Johnson, 1987: 37).

Children from Grade 4 and up were asked who will care for their children and who will hold another (that is, nonchildraising) job when they grow up and marry. Like the rest, most Grade 4 children are likely to answer that "both" parents will care for the child; but over 40 percent expect the mother to be solely responsible for child care, and only one in three Grade 4 pupils thinks that mothers will hold another job in addition to parenthood. After Grade 6, two pupils in three think that both parents will be responsible for child care, and half say that mothers will hold another job as well.

Schoolchildren soon become aware that modern marriage requires shared parental responsibility and two incomes. But even the young children who seem to know that spouses will need to cooperate in raising children and earning a family income fail to recognize how these facts will affect married life. Surveyed schoolchildren and adolescents routinely reveal that girls expect to get married and have children, and few expect a career even if they do work (Johnson, 1987).

Results from a longitudinal study of the marriage role expectations of college women reveal some interesting trends in the United States over the past two-and-a-half decades. While the 1960s were years of dramatic social change, the beginning of the 1980s witnessed the emergence of a new traditionalism and conservatism (Weeks & Botkin, 1987). "The 1984 group was slightly more traditional on homemaking, personal characteristics, social participation, employment and support, and overall expectations [than the 1978 group]," say researchers Weeks and Botkin (1987: 49).

Whatever their expectations of the marriage role, women have on average indicated a desire to bear fewer and fewer children, at least since 1960—from about 4 children to less than 2 each today (Leslie & Korman, 1985: 462). However, research shows that fathers, older people, and people raised in traditional (often large) families to which they remain strongly attached are least changed in their thinking about parenthood.

Parkhurst and Houseknecht (1983) discuss what they call the "New Right familism" movement that has emerged in the last few years. The New Right is against premarital sexual freedom, abortion, and "career women who utilize some form of day care for their children—or perhaps even worse, draw their husbands into the tasks of housecare and childcare" because these changes "threaten the old norms of patriarchy" (27). Whether the New Right wins out—that is, succeeds in reversing the universal changes in family life and parenthood—will depend on developments in the organization of society and the norms and values that guide social behavior.

Sociologist Jean Veevers (1980) finds an "emerging counterculture" she calls *antinatalism* at the other end of the attitude spectrum. A concrete manifestation of this "antinatalism" is the founding, in 1971, of the National Organization for Non-Parents (NON). This organization was established to give psychological support to couples who prefer to remain childless (Leslie & Korman, 1985: 464). That these couples need a support group indicates that there are strong social pressures against childlessness.

Couples choosing to remain childless are put under intense social pressure to make the opposite decision. Far from starting out as women's liberationists, many voluntarily childless women become more sympathetic to the goals of women's liberation after experiencing this pressure. Sentiments about parenthood have been polarizing in the last few decades, then. But sentiments aside, what do people do, and with what consequences?

What People Do: World Trends in Fertility   The story of modern parenthood really begins when the worldwide decline in childbearing got its start. Around 1871, marital childbearing in Europe and North America began a significant and never-to-be-reversed fall. Starting dates varied somewhat, with France in the lead. No one knows precisely why the massive change centers on 1871, or how the onset of change in one region connected with change in another region. (For a review of the historical findings, see Coale & Watkins (Eds.), 1986.)

Yet the fact remains that since 1871, marital childbearing has almost steadily decreased to a current level that, in the United States and many other developed countries, is well below the number needed to replace the parental generation. In the United States, this trend has been interrupted only twice—by the Great Depression of the 1930s, which produced far fewer births than one might have expected; and by the baby boom of the 1950s and 1960s, which produced far more births than expected.

"Demographic transition theory" (Coale, 1969; Coale & Watkins, 1986) argues that nineteenth- and twentieth-century fertility declines really began with eighteenth- and nineteenth-century mortality declines due to improved sanitation, public health, nutrition, and medical care. As mortality fell and childbearing continued at its earlier level, total populations grew very rapidly, putting enormous pressures on each nation's economy. With more infants surviving, each family's economy also came under greater pressure. One result of this growing population pressure was migration to the New World. Another was international warfare to capture neighboring countries and colonies for resources, markets, and room to live.

Reduced infant mortality and industrialization made large families unnecessary, even a liability. To merely maintain a family over generations, parents needed only two children, not the four or more that were needed when many children died before reaching adulthood. Increasingly, urban middle-class parents decided that their children would do better in life if fewer, so that each received more of the family's care, encouragement, and financial support (Banks, 1954).

The particulars of change have been quite different in the Third World. There, mortality has fallen far more quickly than it did in the West, thanks to modern medicine. In these countries too, parenthood today is a mainly motivational issue. Modern technology allows people to prevent all but the pregnancies they want, though this technology is still imperfectly distributed or utilized (especially among the young), even in our own society. In developing societies, the distribution of birth control devices (pills, IUDs, condoms) is progressing rapidly, due to pressures to promote family planning. For example, the World Bank requires a national commitment to birth control before giving out funds to enable industrialization in Third World countries. (On the other hand, recent pressure from American fundamentalists has simultaneously led to the withdrawal of funds from family planning organizations distributing contraceptive devices.)

Presumably, Third World parents will see the advantages in limiting their childbearing—just as parents in the West have done since 1871— and they will freely limit their childbearing. Yet change is slow in coming, with the result that world population is rising rapidly. The 5 billionth person was added to the world's population around July 11, 1987; United Nations demographers predict the 6 billionth in 1998, the 7 billionth in 2010, and the 8 billionth in 2023. This is amazing growth, given the history of the human population up to this century.

Futurist Ralph Hamil (1987: 36) tells us that the newborn 5 billionth human may be called Mohammed Wang, "using the world's most popular given and family names." He will be male, since slightly more males are born than females; and Asian, for most of the human species—over half—lives in Asia today. The balance of world population is shifting dramatically and, according to some, so may the balance of world power (Wattenberg, 1987).

What People Do: American Trends in Fertility   The United States' fertility also started declining significantly over a century ago (Day, 1964: 15–18; Coale and Zelnik, 1963). Since then, the total fertility rate has fallen from an average of 6 births per woman to about 1.7 today, below the level required to replace the American population. This fall to smaller family sizes has been punctuated by phases of faster and slower decline. Even the enormous baby boom was a mere deviation from the downward trend.

Understanding this historical trend is critical if we are to predict and/ or influence the future of childbearing in the United States. But scholars disagree on whether a declining or stationary population is desirable, given its tendency to "age" the population.

Many, such as the members of the National ZPG (Zero Population Growth) movement believe that a stationary population is indeed desirable. They note the benefits of zero population growth: a rising average income, greater opportunities for women to pursue careers (rather than being tied down to the home), fewer unwanted children, and less (or stabilized) pressure on the environment (Rosenthal, 1973), all of which points to an improvement in the quality of life of the average American (Lincoln, 1972). Others, who view population growth as a desirable or necessary condition for national prosperity, but also think low fertility an inevitable condition of industrial societies, advise more immigration. Others still look for ways of stimulating population growth within the society. For this last group, selecting and implementing the "right" pronatalist policy again depends on the outlook of the observer.

As noted, the United States' total fertility rate today is well below the level of 2.1 births needed to replace generations (Bouvier, 1981: 18). A pattern of delayed childbearing is also emerging. More women are having their first child after the age of 30. The youngest birth cohorts—American women born after 1952—may not bear enough children to replace themselves, but some are merely delaying parenthood (Wilkie, 1981; Bloom & Bennett, 1986: 24). Increased educational and occupational opportunities for women are the main causes of delayed parenthood. Whatever the causes, in the long term, delayed parenthood will most likely result in a drop in the fertility rate.

Predicting the future depends on some understanding of the past and present. Because their understanding of the past is incomplete, demographers disagree about the likely future level of childbearing and immigration in the United States. Assuming the current low level of fertility—below 1.8 children per woman—continues and the net annual migration to the United States remains constant, we can expect to reach 310 million people by the year 2030 and 335 million in 2080. A 10 percent increase in the fertility rates would mean population sizes of 336 and 409 million Americans in the years 2030 and 2080 respectively (Bouvier, 1981: 17–21).

Although the total American population will continue to grow, average family size will continue to decline. "So far in the 1980s, couples with children [as a proportion of the population] are declining even faster than they did in the 1970s, as the baby boom continues to postpone marriage and childbearing, [and] divorce breaks up families" (Russell & Exeter, 1986).

Whatever model you believe is most accurate, there is little doubt that America's future includes continued population growth, and the prospect of an enormous baby-boom generation moving into old age and economic dependency as you work your way through adulthood.

How will individual Americans experience these societal trends? In general, we will all be surrounded by more old people and problems of aging. Deaths will occur more frequently than births. Concerns with aging parents and friends will outweigh our concerns with growing children. Especially for females, loneliness and isolation in old age may become widespread problems. Fulfilling our duties as good children will become more onerous than fulfilling our duties as good parents.

You will spend a larger portion of your life being a spouse but not a parent. Instead of bearing children for 10 to 15 years, as in earlier generations, women today already bear children over a mere 5 years or less. The period when one or more children are present in the home has dropped from 30 to 20 years. And perhaps most important, instead of spending almost no time alone with a spouse in the "empty nest," married people can expect to average 20 to 30 years in that state (Gee, 1986: 277).

This means spending more years alone with your spouse than in the company of children, the opposite of what most married people have experienced in the past century and a half and, perhaps, for most of human history. To fully appreciate the significance of this reversal, we need to consider how the presence of children affects people's lives.

Consequences of Parenthood   At first glance, satisfaction appears to increase with the number of children a parent has produced—the more, the merrier. For example, fathers of three or more children appear more satisfied with life and marriage than fathers with only one or two children—who are in turn more satisfied than married men without any children (Quality of Life survey, 1981). Mothers with varying numbers of children express no statistically significant differences in satisfaction.

But further analyses show that the relationship between satisfaction and number of children has to be interpreted in the opposite direction. It is not that having children makes people (especially fathers) satisfied, but rather that satisfied people are more likely to have children. Couples who are very satisfied with their marriage are more likely than other couples to bear children and also more likely to feel satisfied with life. Couples dissatisfied with their marriage who bear many children are no more satisfied with life than equally dissatisfied people who bear fewer children. And maritally satisfied people with *many* children are only slightly more satisfied with life than maritally satisfied people with fewer children.

So the parenting decision is largely an effect, not a cause, of marital and life satisfaction. Moreover, parenting will not make you more satisifed with life if you are dissatisfied with marriage, and it will contribute little to your marriage if you are already satisfied.

We saw in the last chapter that marital satisfaction is a very important component of life satisfaction. Looking only at couples with at least one child living at home with them, we find that marital satisfaction does not increase with the number of children (Campbell, 1980: 90). Similarly, enjoyment of parenthood does not increase as the number of children increases. Even taking the "quality of the experience" into account, quantity of childbearing has no clear effect on life satisfaction. Parents who report "always" enjoying parenthood do *not* report increasing life satisfaction as their number of children increases. Among respondents reporting that parenthood has only "usually" been enjoyable, life satisfaction actually decreases with the addition of more children.

The mothers of many children are least likely of all mothers to report enjoying parenthood. The number of children at home has less effect on fathers' enjoyment of parenthood, suggesting that the unenjoyable burdens fall mainly on mothers (Campbell, 1980: 91).

Enjoyment of parenthood declines sharply during the children's preschool years, recovers a bit when the children are between 6 and 17, and is at its peak when the children have left home. Whereas "men seem to be about equally positive about their role as parents whatever the age of their children, . . . mothers of preschool children are much less positive than fathers of children at that age" (98). In general, mothers' parenting satisfaction is lower when the children are young, while fathers' satisfaction is unaffected. This difference reflects the uneven distribution of childbearing responsibilities between women and men.

Accordingly, older mothers are less likely "to admit that they ever wished to be 'free from the responsibilities of being a parent'" (Campbell, 1980: 98). This reflects a change in thinking about childbearing and more immediate experience with raising children. Older women can readily advise bearing many children because they are farther removed from child-raising burdens (Campbell, 1980: 191).

Many factors—gender, age, and marital satisfaction among them—are mixed up together, so that drawing a simple conclusion is impossible. The best single bet, however, is that a happily married couple will find no children or one child nearly equally enjoyable. Their enjoyment of life, marriage, and parenthood may lead them to think that more children would be even better, but our data do not support such a conclusion. With more children, their satisfaction with life and marriage will remain unchanged or decline; it will not increase, in most cases.

Both husbands and wives are more likely to be "very satisfied" with their marriage if some or all of their children are living away from home (Campbell, 1980: 191). Moreover, the marital satisfaction of husbands and wives is highest before parenthood begins and after the children have left home. This too argues that children diminish marital satisfaction in the average family. Bearing this out, four parents in ten would *not* like to see their "living-away" children more often than they already do. One in five parents say their children have upset them in the past month; of these, about half report that their children have upset them more than once or twice (Quality of Life survey, 1981).

How many children should you have? That's like asking how many businesses should you run, how many mates should you have, how many books should you write, how many musical instruments should you master. Just because one (of each) is wonderful does not mean that two will be twice as wonderful or three, three times as wonderful. In fact, each addition may bring less new satisfaction than the one before it; the novelty wears away and you have ever fewer resources to give each one.

From the children's own standpoint, fewer may be better. We are all familiar with arguments in favour of large families: most often cited are the "economies of scale"—that is, children come cheaper by the dozen. For example, older children can help take care of the younger ones and give each other companionship.

On the other hand, the rivalry between children for their parents' attention and love will be less in smaller families. Families with only one or two children—currently the most common sizes—do not contain "middle children," who often feel less loved than their first-born and last-born siblings. Proportionately more children are first-borns, who (psychologists have shown) tend to be competitive, sociable, and eager to win approval—traits you may find appealing.

Research consistently shows a small but significant negative effect of family size on adult status attainment. The smaller the family your child comes from, the more likely he or she is to attain high educational and occupational status. An analysis of the results of seven United States national surveys indicates that only children, aside from getting more attention (and money), are more likely to develop self-esteem in childhood; and they are more likely to achieve high educational and occupational status in adulthood. Even after controlling for economic status, adults with one or more siblings consistently score lower on measures of well-being than only children (Glenn & Hoppe, 1984). The more care and encouragement a child receives, the more likely that child is to succeed, as we saw in Chapter 4. This is another reason for having few rather than many children, if any at all.

Stages of Parental Satisfaction   The onset of parenthood is a particularly trying time. "Young parents . . . express more feeling of strain at this stage than at any other period of their married lives" (Campbell, 1980: 187). Campbell reports a particularly strong difference between the mothers of young children and young, married women still without a child. The young mothers are more likely to find life hard, feel tied down, express concern about financial matters, and worry about having a nervous breakdown (Campbell, 1980: 187–88).

Raising small children also strains the marriage: disagreements become more common, both husband and wife feel they get less companionship from their mate than they once did, and both marital satisfaction and enjoyment of parenthood are declining or low. "Two out of five of these mothers of small children go so far as to admit they sometimes wish they could be free of the responsibilities of being a parent, a much larger proportion than is found among mothers of older children" (Campbell, 1980: 188).

In some ways, this period is the hardest parenthood will ever get. Once mother resumes paid employment, financial pressures begin to lighten. Balancing a job and child care is complex, but the parents of a school-age child feel less tied down, less strained or burdened by parenthood, and more likely to enjoy it. Once their children reach ages 6 through 17, spouses start to feel they understand each other better. "But they do not regain the strong sense of companionship . . . they had as young couples until they reach the next stage of life, when the children have grown up" (Campbell, 1980: 189).

Marital satisfaction generally declines with the passage of time, whether children are present or not. However, at all ages and marital durations, married women without children are more satisfied with their marriages than women with children (Polonko, Scanzoni, & Teachman, 1982). Married men without children are also more satisfied than same-aged fathers except between the ages of 45 and 65, but the effects of parenthood on marital satisfaction are generally weaker for men than for women.

Nye (1963) argues that the lower marital satisfaction among working mothers is due to role conflict—namely, the conflict between their role of wife/mother, on the one hand, and employee on the other. But it's probably simpler than that: mothers who work outside the home typically do most of the housework and childrearing too (Townsend, 1985). The less help they get from their husbands, the more dissatisfied they are likely to be with their marriage.

Thus it is primarily the couple with children whose marital satisfaction declines over time, then recovers sharply in middle age, around the time the children leave home. Marital satisfaction falls lower for women who work outside the home than for those who do not. In all cases, marital satisfaction bottoms out when the children are adolescents. Feeding, clothing, and educating the children becomes increasingly burdensome. The greater need for money in middle age, at the very time when family income has started to level off, is often called the "life-cycle squeeze."

Two kinds of marital conflict arise out of parenthood as children reach adolescence. A woman who does *not* work outside the home may start to feel greater marital satisfaction at the very time her husband, smarting under a greater financial burden, is feeling the lowest satisfaction ever. A woman who *does* work outside the home may feel declining marital satisfaction, due to combined pressures at home and on the job, at the very time *her* husband is starting to feel greater marital and life satisfaction.

How long these conflicts last will be determined by the time it takes all the children to pass through adolescence and leave home. The fewer the children and the more closely they are spaced, the shorter the period of minimal satisfaction for one or both spouses and the briefer the marital conflict parenthood produces.

The "generally high level of satisfaction with life and with the various domains of life which we find associated with . . . [later] married life is probably more strongly influenced by the simple fact of growing older than it is by the departure of the children" (Campbell, 1980: 191). Yet freedom from responsibility to their children certainly contributes to this increased sense of well-being. Parenthood, then, is a story with a happy ending; the early and middle parts are a bit more difficult.

For this reason, parenthood should be chosen carefully and for good reasons. Avoid having any children, or too many children, for the wrong reasons—to make you satisfied with marriage or life, for example. Childlessness can be chosen and parenthood avoided if you put your mind to it. People are increasingly able to distinguish between marriage, sex, and childbearing as aspects of intimate life. Each activity can be carried on separately from the others, and each demands a separate choice based on good reasoning. No one will thank you for making the wrong choice, even if you make it with the best intentions.

Table 6.1 contains some questions you might ask yourself to determine whether you are "parent material." Whether you are currently contemplating parenthood or not, you may get something out of answering these questions.

TABLE 6.1 The NAOP (National Alliance for Optional Parenthood) "Am I Parent Material?" test. (Source: Veevers, 1980: 162, 164.)

Raising a child? What's there to know?

1. Do I like children? When I'm around children for a while, what do I think or feel about having one around all of the time?
2. Do I enjoy teaching others?
3. Is it easy for me to tell other people what I want, or need, or what I expect of them?
4. Do I want to give a child the love (s)he needs? Is loving easy for me?
5. Am I patient enough to deal with the noise and the confusion of the 24-hour-a-day responsibility? What kind of time and space do I need for myself?
6. What do I do when I get angry or upset? Would I take things out on a child if I lost my temper?
7. What does discipline mean to me? What does freedom, or setting limits, or giving space mean? What is being too strict, or not strict enough? Would I want a perfect child?
8. How do I get along with my parents? What will I do to avoid the mistakes my parents made?
9. How would I take care of my child's health and safety? How do I take care of my own?
10. What if I have a child and find out I made a wrong decision?

Have my partner and I really talked about becoming parents?

1. Does my partner want to have a child? Have we talked about our reasons?
2. Could we give a child a good home? Is our relationship a happy and strong one?
3. Are we both ready to give our time and energy to raising a child?
4. Could we share our love with a child without jealousy?
5. What would happen if we separated after having a child, or if one of us should die?
6. Do my partner and I understand each other's feelings about religion, work, family, child-raising, future goals? Do we feel pretty much the same way? Will children fit into these feelings, hopes, and plans?
7. Suppose one of us wants a child and the other doesn't. Who decides?
8. Which of the questions in this test do we need to *really* discuss before making a decision?

What's in it for me?

1. Do I like doing things with children? Do I enjoy activities that children can do?
2. Would I want a child to be "like me"?
3. Would I try to pass on to my child my ideas and values? What if my child's ideas and values turn out to be different from mine?
4. Would I want my child to achieve things that I wish I had, but didn't?
5. Would I expect my child to keep me from being lonely in my old age? Do I do that for my parents? Do my parents do that for my grandparents?
6. Do I want a boy or a girl child? What if I don't get what I want?
7. Would having a child show others how mature I am?
8. Will I prove I am a man or a woman by having a child?
9. Do I expect my child to make my life happy?

(continued)

TABLE 6.1 *(continued)*

Does having and raising a child fit the lifestyle I want?

1. What do I want out of life for myself? What do I think is important?
2. Could I handle a child and a job at the same time? Would I have time and energy for both?
3. Would I be ready to give up the freedom to do what I want to do, when I want to do it?
4. Would I be willing to cut back my social life and spend more time at home? Would I miss my free time and privacy?
5. Can I afford to support a child? Do I know how much it takes to raise a child?
6. Do I want to raise a child in the neighborhood where I live now? Would I be willing and able to move?
7. How would a child interfere with my growth and development?
8. Would a child change my educational plans? Do I have the energy to go to school and raise a child at the same time?
9. Am I willing to give a great part of my life—AT LEAST 18 YEARS—to being responsible for a child? And spend a large portion of my life being concerned about my child's well-being?

Balancing Parenthood and Work

We have seen that parenthood intrudes on other domains of life—marriage and career in particular. Another question students commonly ask about parenthood is how they will be able to balance the demands of raising children and succeeding in a career.

This problem of balance is getting harder as more and more women enter the full-time paid labour force. Statistics reveal that male and female work patterns are converging: men are spending less time in the labor force and women more. The percentage of working-age women in the paid labor force rose from 43 percent to 55 percent between 1970 and 1985 (Francese, 1987); while men between the ages of 24 and 44 today are less likely to be in the workforce today than they were in 1970. Young men are freer now to pursue an education while the wife works outside the home (Bryant & Russell, 1984).

Demographers predict that by 1995, 80 percent of women between the ages of 20 and 44 will be in the labor force, as opposed to just two-thirds today. And, women of all ages are expected to make up 47 percent of the labor force (Bryant & Russell, 1984). The result is that the labor force participation of women will become increasingly similar to that of men.

Most interesting of all, the participation rate of women with children under six years old rose from 42 percent in 1980 to 54 percent in 1985—twelve percentage points in a mere five years (Russell & Exeter, 1986: 28).

It is these women, with young children to care for, who are most likely to work for pay and will have the greatest difficulty balancing domestic and job demands.

The problem of balance first appeared with changes in family life three or four centuries ago. In the Middle Ages, the extended household was more common than any other kind and much more common than it is today. Even in Western Europe, households often included grown children, aunts and uncles, and servants, as well as fathers, mothers, and children. Child care and making a living were familial, even communal, activities. People took responsibility for other people's children, freeing adult men and women to work in the fields or, if in a town, at a trade.

Child care was not seen as requiring a lot of attention. It is only in recent centuries that people have regarded childhood as a special period requiring special care (Ariès, 1962). For these reasons, children could be cared for while women went about their normal daily work (producing subsistence). Children who could not be taken care of and could not be afforded were sent into "service." These arrangements made early marriage and unlimited childbearing feasible.

Around the sixteenth or seventeenth century, the "European marriage pattern" established itself (Hajnal, 1965). Characterized by a high age at marriage and a high proportion of people never marrying, the rise of this arrangement seems to coincide with the rise of nuclear families in Western Europe. The traditional "non-European pattern" continued for several centuries more in Eastern Europe, Africa, and Asia, but it has been disappearing even there during this century.

In the European pattern, marriage depends on economic independence—for farmers, on having a piece of land, and for craftsmen, on having a trade and shop. Marriage and childbearing are delayed until economic independence is assured. For many in the past, that meant a long delay in marrying and, for many women, delay beyond the age when childbearing was possible. In these cases, postponement might turn into a permanent state.

The precise sequence of changes from one family pattern to the other is unknown, but several key changes are interrelated. First, unlike the extended family, the nuclear family is relatively small and needs size limitation. Late marriage reduces the average size of a family that is not practising contraception (Henry, 1976: 90–121); so it was useful for groups that could not (or would not) practice other forms of birth control.

Second, even more than the extended family, the nuclear family demands a coordinated division of labor between domestic and other duties.

Without grandparents, uncles and aunts, or sisters and brothers to help raise the children, one or both parents have to assume the domestic chores for their own family. Historically, the sexual division of labor may have become more marked in this kind of family than it had been in the extended family.

Finally, the nuclear family requires more understanding and cooperation between spouses. Spouses rely on each other for more assistance, support, and care. Despite the sexual division of labor, marriage tends to evolve in a direction demanding more and better communication between spouses.

Elizabeth Bott (1957) illustrates the nature of this problem in a classic study of marriage, *Family and Social Network*. She compares two sets of families. One lives in a stable working-class London community full of childhood friends, parents, and other relatives—essentially, an extended family setting. The other set, from a similar background, lives in a new community full of socially and geographically uprooted people.

Spouses in the first—the "traditional"—community maintain their childhood ties and rely heavily on parents, relatives, and old friends for support, child care, and sociability. Husbands and wives have somewhat limited, stereotypical communication with each other, and rigidly define their roles and duties along gender lines. For example, husbands do not change diapers or cook; wives do not repair the car or go out much with friends. Spouses in the second community, cut off from old friends and family ties, form new networks of friends-in-common. They share activities and interests and even share domestic duties more. In general, their isolation from old relationships, sharing of new friends, and greater reliance on each other for support produces new kinds of communication and cooperation within the household.

In going from the old-style, quasi-extended family in the traditional community to the nuclear family in a new community of strangers, people gain privacy, independence, and more chance of upward social mobility. As a consequence, spousal communication and sharing have increased. Survey data indicate that more young married people today endorse the *idea* of communication and sharing—indeed, equality between spouses—than would have done so a generation ago. And, as the Bott study and others have since shown, spouses have started to *act* differently too. But American families are a long way from spousal equality, as we shall see. This inequality becomes particularly noticeable and troublesome when wives take paid work.

As more women enter the paid labor force, this "new family" comes under even greater pressure to balance its various activities. The desire for privacy, independence, and upward mobility spreads to nearly everyone—male and female, child and parent all want more of each. So far, "democracy, individualism and meritocracy, the values most closely identified with two centuries of Western history, are conspicuous by their absence from the family" (Degler, 1980: 471). But all of this is changing.

To achieve a balance, families now purchase many domestic services from "outsiders"; but they still need to find better ways of integrating members' diverse interests and schedules. The problem of scheduling arises out of one simple fact: the day contains only 24 hours. Male and female time use differs markedly in two main respects—time spent in paid work and time spent housekeeping and parenting (Robinson, 1988; Michelson, 1985).

Survey data reveal that, in the average American family, women are solely responsible for deciding what is for dinner and preparing it, managing the household budget, and raising the children. Women and their partners are jointly responsible for major expenditures—where to go on vacation, how much to spend on major purchases, how much to save, how much insurance to carry and where to buy it, and how to invest savings. Men are solely responsible for deciding what to watch on television (Casale & Lerman, 1986: 94).

In a young dual-earner family, the presence of young children makes an enormous difference to the average number of hours wives work each weekday (counting both paid work and unpaid housework/child care). Husbands' home duties increase very little when their wives work full-time for pay, even when small children are present. Instead, wives work an average of two hours per day more, the standard of familial housekeeping and child care may drop, and more services may be purchased from outside sources—nannies, cleaning services, fast-food restaurants, and so on.

So mothers with full-time paying jobs work longer hours than husbands or any other kinds of wives. They have little free time during their waking hours. As a result, time pressures cause these women extreme tension. With more activities to complete within 24 hours, they are less able to tolerate unforeseen snags or hitches. But life with children is *full* of snags and hitches. Not surprisingly then, employed mothers report a lot of tension in activities that would be easy if time were plentiful—activities like waking the children, getting them ready for school or daycare,

TABLE 6.2 His and Hers
Women spent 7.5 fewer hours a week doing housework in 1985 than in 1965, while men spent 5.2 hours more. (Source: 1985: Americans' Use of Time Project, Survey Research Center, University of Maryland; 1965, 1975: Americans' Use of Time Project, Survey Research Center, University of Michigan)

(time men and women aged 18 to 65 spent doing household tasks, in hours per week, 1965–1985)

FEMALE-DOMINATED	Men			Women			Ratio Done by Women*		
	1985	1975	1965	1985	1975	1965	1985	1975	1965
Cooking meals	2.0	1.3	1.3	6.9	7.8	8.4	77	86	87
Meal clean-up	0.4	0.2	0.3	1.9	2.5	4.1	83	91	92
Housecleaning	1.4	0.7	0.4	5.1	6.2	6.7	78	90	95
Laundry, ironing	0.3	0.1	0.1	2.2	3.0	5.1	88	96	98
Subtotal	4.1	2.3	2.1	16.1	19.5	24.3	80	89	92
MALE-DOMINATED AND SHARED									
Outdoor chores	1.4	1.4	0.5	0.5	0.4	0.2	26	22	33
Repairs, etc.	1.8	2.2	1.0	0.4	0.7	0.2	18	24	18
Garden, animal care	1.0	0.3	0.2	0.9	0.6	0.5	47	63	67
Bills, other	1.7	0.8	0.8	1.6	0.5	1.8	48	36	68
Subtotal	5.9	4.7	2.5	3.4	2.2	2.7	37	32	51
Total	9.8	7.0	4.6	19.5	21.7	27.0	67	76	85

* Assuming equal numbers and backgrounds of men and women, percentages, subtotals, and totals may vary due to rounding.

caring for the baby and for the older children, preparing food, cleaning the house and getting to work on time (Michelson, 1985).

People feel more tension than usual in activities they cannot control, or have not chosen. Not only are women involved in more activities than men; they generally have less choice about when and where to spend their time, and suffer more tension as a result. For their part, husbands suffer less tension than their wives and their tensions are more often work-related. Among a mere four activities that cause men greater-than-usual tension, two—commuting to and from work, and doing their job—are directly related to paid employment. Husbands involve themselves more fully in their jobs because they suffer fewer competing pressures. More-over, husbands typically contribute to housework at their convenience; their activities include house maintenance, repairs, and gardening, which

TABLE 6.2 *(continued)* Married to Their Work
Married men now do more housework than unmarried men. (Source: 1985: Americans' Use of Time Project, Survey Research Center, University of Maryland; 1965, 1975: Americans' Use of Time Project, Survey Research Center, University of Michigan)

(time men and women aged 18 to 65 spent doing household tasks, by marital status, in hours per week; 1965–1985)

	Men			Women			Ratio Done by Women*		
MARRIED	1985	1975	1965	1985	1975	1965	1985	1975	1965
Female tasks	4.2	2.1	1.8	18.8	21.3	27.2	81	91	94
Cooking	2.0	1.1	0.9	8.1	8.9	9.6	80	89	91
Cleaning**	2.2	1.0	0.9	10.7	12.4	17.6	83	93	95
Male/shared tasks	6.9	4.7	2.7	3.6	2.9	4.4	3	38	62
Total	11.1	6.8	4.5	22.4	24.2	31.6	66	78	87
UNMARRIED									
Female tasks	3.9	3.7	3.3	12.2	14.9	14.2	76	80	81
Cooking	2.1	2.2	1.5	5.2	6.1	4.6	71	73	75
Cleaning**	1.8	1.5	1.8	7.0	8.8	9.6	80	85	84
Male/shared tasks	4.0	4.2	1.4	2.7	2.2	1.3	40	35	48
Total	7.9	7.9	4.7	14.9	17.1	15.5	65	68	77

* Assuming equal numbers and backgrounds of men and women, percentages, subtotals, and totals may vary due to rounding.
** Cleaning includes meal clean-up, housecleaning, laundry, and ironing.

they are inclined to view as leisure or semileisure (Horna & Lupri, 1987; Robinson, 1988).

A prime tension-producer for both spouses is daily travel. Many family responsibilities disproportionately carried out by women—such as shopping for food or taking children to and from daycare—require travel, and "women often travel with less efficient resources and fewer choices" (Michelson, 1985). They less often have access to the family car or enough choice over where daycare, shopping, and work will be located.

Somehow, working women get all their chores done. Contrary to expectations that working parents would feel guilty about giving their children too little time and attention, a majority of parents in dual-career families feel otherwise. About half feel their children are just as well off as children from homes in which only one parent works for pay, and about

TABLE 6.2 *(continued)* Children's Hour
Mothers are doing less housework than they once did while fathers are doing more. (Source: 1985: Americans' Use of Time Project, Survey Research Center, University of Maryland; 1965, 1975: Americans' Use of Time Project, Survey Research Center, University of Michigan)

(time men and women aged 18 to 65 spent doing household tasks, by presence and age of children, in hours per week; 1965–1985)

	Men			Women			Ratio Done by Women*		
NO CHILDREN	1985	1975	1965	1985	1975	1965	1985	1975	1965
Female tasks	4.4	2.4	2.6	14.5	17.3	18.7	77	88	88
Cooking	2.3	1.5	1.4	6.4	7.4	6.4	74	83	82
*Cleaning***	2.1	0.9	1.2	8.1	9.9	12.3	79	92	91
Male/shared tasks	6.0	4.7	2.1	3.4	3.0	2.6	36	39	55
Total	10.4	7.1	4.7	17.9	20.3	21.3	63	74	82

ALL CHILDREN AGED 5 AND OLDER									
Female tasks	3.9	2.2	2.0	16.6	22.0	27.0	81	91	93
Cooking	1.9	1.1	0.9	7.1	8.9	9.6	79	89	91
*Cleaning***	2.0	1.1	1.1	9.5	13.1	17.4	83	92	94
Male/shared tasks	6.5	5.4	3.3	3.3	1.9	3.3	34	26	50
Total	10.4	7.6	5.3	19.9	23.9	30.3	66	76	85

CHILDREN UNDER AGE 5									
Female tasks	3.5	2.4	1.6	20.0	22.3	29.2	85	90	95
Cooking	1.4	1.2	0.8	8.4	8.9	9.9	86	88	92
*Cleaning***	2.1	1.2	0.8	11.6	13.4	19.3	85	92	96
Male/shared tasks	5.5	3.5	2.3	2.5	2.8	2.8	31	44	55
Total	9.0	5.9	3.9	22.5	25.1	32.0	71	82	90

* Assuming equal numbers and backgrounds of men and women; percentages, subtotals, and totals may vary due to rounding.
** Cleaning includes meal clean-up, housecleaning, laundry, and ironing.

one-quarter feel their children are even better off (Casale & Lerman, 1986: 125).

The major problem modern parents face is not guilt, then. For single parents, it is typically the shortage of money. For married parents, it is the strain of too many duties, conflicts arising out of unequal parental arrangements, and financial concerns arising out of increased reliance on paid child-care and housekeeping services. Married parents most often fight about financial matters (53 percent), job demands (50 percent), disciplining children (50 percent), and the demands of their spouse's job (47 percent). Problems in the marital relationship are primarily caused by poor communication (22 percent), not seeing each other enough (12 percent), not doing enough together (12 percent), and money (12 percent) (Casale & Lerman, 1986: 97).

Too little time for marital interaction may sometimes be a blessing. Many couples report that their brief time together is pleasant precisely *because* they lack the time or energy to argue. Most want to make their time together as pleasant, or at least quiet, as possible (Casale & Lerman, 1986).

During an average adulthood starting in 1980, a married woman can expect to work 14 percent more hours than her husband, if present levels of childbearing and related work patterns continue (Meissner, 1985). So if you are an employed woman, you are likely to work harder and get less pay and recognition for each hour worked than your spouse. Many of your most stress-filled activities, especially parental ones, will yield no career advancement, pay, or public recognition. In fact, they will steal time and energy from your career.

When asked, most people report that they are satisfied with their lives, and since women are unable to alter the domestic inequity, they cope and regard it as inevitable. What will the effects on their children be? Most adolescents continue to hold traditional sex-role ideals (Johnson, 1987). But there has never yet been a generation of American adolescents raised in dual-earner families. What sense do they make of their parents' (or mother's) frustration, and how will they live as adults? We will learn the consequences of this in due course.

Individual and Collective Solutions Women do a number of things about this problem of balance. Some career-oriented women choose to marry but not to bear children. Others bear one or two children in a very short time, to limit the interruption of their careers.

Many of these latter women return to full-time work almost immediately after bearing children. This pattern is most common among highly educated women with careers (not merely jobs) whose salaries are large enough to pay for high-quality child care. Less educated and less career-oriented women are more likely to leave the paid work force until their children begin attending school full-time (Schwartz, 1986). Accordingly, labour force participation is much higher for women with children over five years old than it is for mothers of younger children (O'Connell, Orr, & Lueck, 1982). However, at no age do average mothers ever attain as high a level of labour force participation as similarly educated women without children (Townsend & Riche, 1987). This difference may be due to the parental obligations and tensions that continue even after children are in school full-time. But increasingly, women are returning to work immediately after childbearing: this appears to be the trend of the future.

Another, and apparently growing, solution to the problem of balancing parenthood and work is part-time work. While the total number of workers aged 20 and older increased 35 percent between 1970 and 1982, the number of part-timers increased 42 percent during the same period. It is noteworthy that while women are four times more likely to work part-time than men, the *proportion* of women in the labor force who work part-time declined slightly between 1970 to 1982 (from 21.5 percent to 20.1 percent) while that of men rose during the same period (from 4.8 percent to 5.2 percent). The two trends may be related: as more women work full-time, their husbands have more opportunity to pursue other interests, or fulfill other obligations such as raising a family (Bryant & Russell, 1984: 20).

Labor unions generally oppose the expansion of part-time work because it may reduce the availability of full-time work, may not be fully voluntary, and currently allows employers to avoid paying the fringe benefits full-time workers normally receive. As part-time work becomes even more common, we will probably see the prorated payment of fringe benefits to part-time workers, and some of these objections will disappear. At present, part-time work guarantees women's continued subordination in poorly paid, low-status jobs by continuing to make them primarily responsible for child care.

Most female part-time workers aged 25 to 54 appear to want part-time, not full-time, work for a variety of reasons, among them the need to fulfil personal and family responsibilities. Few female part-time workers want more hours of paid work per month than they already have. Part-time work allows enormous flexibility and many varied patterns and, under the best circumstances, can almost be tailored to a worker's timetable needs. Part-time work helps women to fulfil domestic obligations and meet income needs when virtually single-handed child-rearing makes full-time paid work extremely difficult (McLaughlin et al., 1988: 101).

Indeed, if part-time work continues to increase, gets unionized, and pays benefits prorated to time spent on the job, it will become an increasingly attractive option for both fathers and mothers. One can imagine future generations organizing their life cycles differently from today's, moving in and out of jobs and, within jobs, between full-time and part-time status, to accommodate changing domestic demands and personal well-being. Gender-based differences in work life may disappear, replaced by differences based on education or social class instead. Flexible job-sharing is one way this change may come about.

However, such flexibility does not suit current thinking about careers, much less existing institutional arrangements. Today highly educated professional and managerial women who seek part-time work are not likely to be considered serious about their work. Even if given the part-time work they want, women may significantly hinder their prospects for major responsibility by allowing that impression to stand. This means that employed mothers, the main voluntary part-time workers, must weigh carefully whether they want to have a career and, equally important, be *perceived* as having a career.

British women employed full-time are much more likely than their husbands to prefer more time off over more pay in their current job (Young & Willmott, 1975: 115). Moreover, employed women are more likely than their husbands to put thoughts of a career out of their minds. Compared with their husbands, female full-time employees are much less likely to say there is a "career ladder" in their work, report they have "a lot of say at work," feel "pressed" or "sometimes pressed" at work, report doing overtime work during the previous week, or travel more than 10 miles to their job. Such differences are even greater between female *part-time* employees and their husbands (Young & Willmott, 1975: 116).

By and large, wives are less likely than husbands to hold jobs that interfere with their domestic duties. Avoiding such interference is easier in some jobs—for example, clerical and manual jobs—than it is in professional and managerial work (Young & Willmott, 1975: 117), suggesting that highly educated mothers will be the most pressured women of all.

Most women continue to work in traditional, female-dominated occupations—for example, in eating establishments and service industries; but this occupational sex-segregation has already started to break down. Write McLaughlin et al. (1988: 102):

> Growing numbers of women in the baby-boom cohort are investing in their own human capital—through extended periods of education, delayed family formation, and continued labor force participation during the childbearing years—in order to gain access to and achieve success in traditionally male occupations.

However slow to emerge, this reflects a shift in women's work-versus-family priorities which, in the past, have been tilted very much towards family.

For these reasons, the employers of educated women face increasing demands for company-sponsored or public child care, and more-flexible work schedules. As well, rising numbers of dual-income couples make joint decisions about domestic task-sharing, work time, job transfers, and relocation. Child-rearing needs demand employer accommodation through "flextime," part-time work, sabbaticals (for both women and men), and more working at home.

Partners in two-career families are increasingly resistant to job transfers requiring relocation, long regarded as central to career development. Companies will find it increasingly necessary to ease the burdens of relocation by providing job-search assistance for the accompanying spouse, child-care and real-estate arrangements, relocation counselling, and orientation to the new community.

Goods and services to make housekeeping easier are increasingly demanded. To take a well-known example, the fast-food industry is growing more rapidly than most. In the 1980s, North American restaurants have seen a dramatic increase in their breakfast business over previous years. The use of daycare for preschool children is also increasing and good daycare seems unlikely to result in serious emotional disturbance for the child (Rutter, 1981). But even so, good daycare is hard to find and, for many parents, impossible to afford.

Proposed Solutions   Without other institutional and societal changes to ease the burdens of motherhood, the flight from parenthood may continue and even accelerate. Some solutions are economic. One is to provide more goods and services directly to the families of women who work outside the home—for example, more, better, and cheaper daycare. Another is to pay women higher wages, enabling them to purchase the services they need. This, in turn, requires legislation to prevent and remedy income discrimination against women, and to ensure that payment for part-time work is prorated against full-time pay and benefits.

A more contentious proposal involves paying for housework. At present, women's housework and child care provide a substantial unpaid benefit to their husbands' employers. Married male workers show up for work regularly, in good health, and well turned-out *because* their wives do the unpaid work needed to ensure it. Employers can expect husbands to take work home and work until finished, travel as part of their job, and think more or less continuously about their work *because* wives keep up unpaid housekeeping and child care services regardless. Some observers believe that employers should pay their employees for wives' services by raising salaries, or governments should pay wives directly through taxes raised on corporate earnings.

Perhaps the ideology of parenting as mother's responsibility must change, as should society's definition of the "clockwork of careers" (Hochschild, 1975), to accommodate child-raising and respect it as a collective, societal responsibility, not an individual's problem. More generally, people who care for dependants—whether children, the phsycially infirm, or the very old—should be paid by the state for their labours, whether performed at home or in an institution. It is not so obvious that wives should be paid for taking care of husbands who are perfectly able to take care of themselves.

Resistance to all these alternatives is strong. Most men still take for granted the services mothers and wives provide, and devalue them because they do not yield a cash income. Further, many oppose increasing services to employed women or paying wages for child care on the grounds that these actions would raise income taxes and/or the prices of goods and services. Yet what is at issue is the distribution of benefits between the genders.

More moderate proposals include improving public transportation to make employed women's travel easier and faster; loosening zone restrictions so that shopping and child care will be closer to people's homes; allowing round-the-clock shopping for goods and services, to give employed women a greater opportunity to get their household chores (for example, food shopping) done when most convenient; and increasing flextime to allow paid work and work-related travel to mesh more easily with domestic duties (Michelson, 1985). Universal high-quality, low-cost daycare is much needed and is unlikely to harm children, even preschoolers (Rutter, 1981).

Many of these changes require public spending and/or impose new burdens on other workers. This means they will be resisted, at least in the short run. Whether they are implemented or not, duties will have to be redistributed within the household. Particularly, fathers will have to become more involved in child care and assume a greater share of the tensions associated with too little free time. This will force men to spend less of their time and mental energy on their work or leisure.

In the short run, men may view such changes as uneconomic or irrational. After all, why should a man sacrifice an hour of his time for household duties and child care to save his spouse an hour, even if she spends it on paid work? When both are employed full-time, the typical man is earning about 42 percent more per hour than the typical woman. To give up $1.42 of family income to get $1.00 back seems hardly sensible, some men might argue.

A larger, longer-run perspective answers this argument. First, to do otherwise exploits married women at home, and they are already exploited and discriminated against at work. Second, it gives employers a false message about the true cost of work and a false conception of what they can reasonably expect their workers, whether male or female, to do. Such misinformation delays the search for humane solutions to the problem of integrating parenthood and work. Third, the present arrangement perpetuates traditional stereotypes of marriage in the eyes of children, ensuring that daughters will suffer the same tensions as their mothers.

Women today are working more hours than their grandmothers did and the gap between male and female hours of labour is increasing each year (Meissner, 1985). That the workload is becoming more burdensome is reflected by a general decline in women's attitudes toward homemaking. Further, more women are worrying about having a nervous breakdown (Campbell, 1980: 130, 133). Women are also much more likely than men to report feeling depressed, worried, or frightened (Campbell, 1980: 131).

Yet on the whole, "most women seem to be in the role they prefer, and those who have chosen homemaking are as satisfied with their lives as those who have made the other choice" (Campbell, 1980: 139). Further, given the injustices women face in our society, what is surprising is how close women's sense of well-being comes to men's.

Freer choice has allowed women who want to work outside the home to get the satisfactions paid employment can bring. Many women who remain in the home are just as satisfied, which leads to several major conclusions. The first is that, *given a choice*, people look for and sometimes find the life situation that will give them the most life satisfaction. Second, people largely accommodate themselves to what their life demands, especially if they have chosen it. Finally, adulthood is becoming more complicated and stressful for women, whichever adult role they choose to play.

CONCLUDING REMARKS

This chapter has presented a somewhat bleak picture of parenthood, in order to counterbalance the unrealistic picture of parenthood presented by the mass media.

In reality, parenthood can be extremely gratifying, exciting, and educational. One learns a lot about life, other people, and oneself in raising children to adulthood. Further, parents typically fall in love with their children, just as they did with their mate, not because of the child's ideal qualities, but because he or she is lovable, loving, needy, and close-at-hand. On the other hand, parenthood is extremely demanding of time, money, and emotional energy. It may require important sacrifices.

Some of the difficulties associated with parenthood can be remedied by a better sharing of household duties between spouses. Other difficulties can be remedied by the government provision of better daycare facilities, the assurance of paid maternity (or parental) leave, and other assistance. But ultimately the problem will rest in parents' own hands. People will have to choose more carefully between parenthood and other demanding, fulfilling activities—romance, leisure, career, education, and so on. No one can do everything well, or enjoy trying. People should make the parenting decision with that simple fact in mind.

Do people get what they want out of parenthood? Though some people are undoubtedly pressured into it, more and more people are freely deciding whether or not to become parents. As a consequence, more people are likely to be satisfied with the result—to feel they have gotten what they wanted. Moreover, a majority of people feel quite satisfied with their decision.

Yet this satisfaction varies. The people most responsible for parenting—mothers between the ages of 30 and 45—are least satisfied. Their satisfaction declines the more children they have: more is usually not better. Further, mothers with paid jobs are least satisfied. Balancing marriage, parenting, and paid work calls for tremendous energy and patience. Few people find such continuous demands satisfying. So working mothers are least likely to get what they wanted.

Chapter 7 will address questions having to do with residence: where people choose to live, and with what results.

REFERENCES

ARIES, P. (1962). *Centuries of childhood: A social history of family life.* New York: Vintage.

BANKS, J. A. (1954). *Prosperity and parenthood: A study of family planning among the Victorian middle classes.* London: Routledge & Kegan Paul.

BLOOM, D. E., & BENNETT, N. G. (1986). Childless couples. *American Demographics,* August, 22–25.

BOTT, E. (1957). *Family and social network.* London: Tavistock Publications.

BOUVIER, L. F. (1981). Immigration at the crossroads. *American Demographics,* October, 17–21.

BRYANT, R., & RUSSELL, C. (1984). A Portrait of the American worker. *American Demographics,* March, 16–21.

CAMPBELL, A. (1980). *The sense of well-being in America: Recent patterns and trends.* New York: McGraw-Hill.

CASALE, A. M., & LERMAN, P. (1986). USA today: Tracking tomorrow's trends. Kansas City: Andrews, McMeel, & Parker.

COALE, A. J. (1969). The decline of fertility in Europe from the French Revolution to World War II. In S. J. Behrman, L. Corsa, and R. Freedman (Eds.). *Fertility and Family Planning* (pp. 3–24). Ann Arbor: University of Michigan Press.

COALE, A. J., & ZELNICK, M. (1963). *New estimates of fertility and population in the United States: A study of annual white births from 1855 to 1960 and of completeness of enumeration in the censuses from 1880 to 1960.* Princeton: Princeton University Press.

————— & WATKINS, S. C. (EDS.) (1986). *The decline of fertility in Europe.* Princeton, N.J.: Princeton University Press.

DAY, L. H., & DAY, A. T. (1964). *Too many Americans.* Boston: Houghton Mifflin.

DEGLER, C. (1980). *At odds.* New York: Oxford University Press.

FRANCESE, P. (1987). How many working women? *American Demographics,* March, 16.

GEE, E. M. (1986). The life course of Canadian women: An historical and demographic analysis. *Social Indicators Research, 18,* 263–83.

GLENN, N. D., & HOPPE, S. K. (1984). Only children as adults: Psychological well-being. *Journal of Family Issues,* September, 363–82.

HAJNAL, J. (1965). European marriage patterns in perspective. In D. V. Glass and D. E. C. Eversley (Eds.), *Population in History,* pp. 101–43. London: Edward Arnold.

HAMIL, R. E. (1987). The arrival of the 5-billionth human. *The Futurist, 24*(4), 36–37.

HENRY, L. (1976). *Population: Analysis and models.* London: Edward Arnold.

HOCHSCHILD, A. R. (1975). Disengagement theory: A critique and proposal. *American Sociological Review, 40,* 553–69.

HORNA, J., & LUPRI, E. (1987). Father's participation in work, family life, and leisure: A Canadian experience. In C. Lewis & M. O'Brien (Eds.), *Reassessing fatherhood: New observations on fathers and the modern family.* (pp. 54–73). London: Sage Publications.

JOHNSON, L. (1987). Children's visions of the future. *The Futurist, 21*(3), 36–40.

LINCOLN, R. (1972). Population and the American future: The commission's final report. In *Family Planning Perspectives,* Col. 4, No. 2, April, pp. 10–15.

LUPRI, E. & FRIDERES, J. (1981). The quality of marriage and the passage of time: Marital satisfaction over the family life cycle. *Canadian Journal of Sociology,* 6(3), 283–305.

_____ & MILLS, D. (1987). The household division of labor in young dual-earner couples: The case of Canada. *International Review of Sociology,* New Series, No. 2, 33–54.

MCLAUGHLIN, S. D., MELBER, B. D., BILLY, J. O. G., ZIMMERLE, D. M., WINGES, L. D., & JOHNSON, T. R. (1988). *The changing lives of American women.* Chapel Hill: University of North Carolina Press.

MALTHUS, T. R. (1959). *Population: The first essay.* Foreword by K. E. Boulding. Ann Arbor: University of Michigan Press. (Original work published in 1798.)

MARSHALL, K. (1987). Women in male-dominated professions. *Canadian Social Trends,* Winter, 7–11.

MEISSNER, M. (1985). The domestic economy. In M. Safir, M. T. Mednick, D. Izrael, & J. Bernard (Eds.), *Women's Worlds: From the New Scholarship.* New York: Praegar.

MICHELSON, W. (1985). *From sun to sun: Daily obligations and community structure in the lives of employed mothers and their families.* Totowa, N.J.: Rowman & Allanheld.

NYE, F. I. (1963). Marital interaction. In F. I. Nye & L. W. Hoffman (Eds.), *The employed mother in America.* Chicago: Rand McNally, 263–81.

O'CONNELL, M., ORR, A. C., & LUECK, M. (1982). The children of working mothers. *American Demographics,* April, 26–31.

PANKHURST, J. G., & HOUSEKNECHT, S. K. (1983). The new family, politics and religion in the 1980's: In fear of the new individualism. *Journal of Family Issues, 4,* 5–34.

POLONKO, K. A., SCANZONI, J., & TEACHMAN, J. D. (1982). Childlessness and marital satisfaction: A further reassessment. *Journal of Family Issues, 3,* 545–73.

PORTER, J., PORTER, M., & BLISHEN, B. R. (1982). *Stations and callings: Making it through the school system.* Toronto: Methuen.

QUALITY OF LIFE SURVEY. (1981). Unpublished raw data from a large survey of life satisfaction conducted at the Institute for Behavioral Research, York University, Toronto, Canada.

ROBINSON, J. P. (1988). Who's doing the housework? *American Demographics,* April, 24–28, 63.

ROSENTHAL, J. (1973). Each change has a vast impact. *New York Times,* March 7, E9.

RUSSELL, C., & EXTER, T. G. (1986). America at mid-decade. *American Demographics,* January, 22–29.

RUTTER, M. (1981). Social-emotional consequences of day care for preschool children. *American Journal of Orthopsychiatry, 51*(1), 4–28.

SCHWARTZ, J. (1986). Back to work. *American Demographics,* November, 56–57.

TOWNSEND, B. (1982). Working Women. *American Demographics,* 1982, 26–31.

_____, & RICHE, M. F. (1987). Two paychecks and seven lifestyles. *American Demographics*, August, 24–29.

VEEVERS, J. E. (1980). *Childless by choice.* Toronto: Butterworth.

WATTENBERG, B. J. (1987). *The birth dearth.* New York: The American Enterprise Institute, Pharos Books.

WEEKS, M. O., & BOTKIN, D. R. (1987). A Longitudinal study of the marriage role expectations of college women: 1961–1984. *Sex Roles, 17*, 49–58.

WILKIE, J. R. (1981). The trend toward delayed parenthood. *Journal of Marriage and the Family, 3*, 583–91.

YOUNG, M., & WILLMOTT, P. (1975). *The symmetrical family.* Harmondsworth: Penguin Books.

CHAPTER SEVEN

LOCATIONS AND LIFESTYLES:
What You Want and What You Get

INTRODUCTION

Many students are interested in questions related to where they might live: in what country or state; whether in a city or suburb; whether alone or with friends or family. This chapter will argue that where you live is how you live. It will discuss patterns of location in American society—where people live and why—and the lifestyles associated with different locations. Finally, it will consider the satisfactions associated with each kind of location.

People are not completely free to choose where they live. For many, location is determined by the availability or cost of housing; for others, by the availability of an appropriate job; and for others still, by the location of family and friends. As in so many aspects of life, choice is also limited by social class: the rich have a wider variety of choices than the poor.

But within this context of unequal opportunity, both rich and poor try to locate themselves where they believe they will be most satisfied. Because they have some choice in this, their locations reflect their life goals and concerns. Typically, people who move from one location to another are seeking more satisfaction as their goals and opportunities change. To answer the question "Where should I live?" we must consider what kind of life you want to live and what opportunities you have for living that life. That is the reason this chapter treats questions of location and lifestyle together.

Like earlier chapters, this one will end by considering whether people usually get what they want or learn to want what they get.

Locations

Location as a State of Mind   Where you live both affects and reflects your state of mind. First, where you live is an *environment*, a stage on which you play your social roles for many hours each day. Location determines what you will see, hear, smell, and touch when you are at home. Where you live is not merely a physical environment, but also a social environment, determining *who* you will see and interact with regularly, what ideas you will be exposed to, and what behaviours will be observed, as well as what and who you will *not* be exposed to, see, and learn from. Such selective contacts will capacitate you in some ways and incapacitate you in others.

Beyond that, where you live is an *opportunity structure*. By bringing you into contact with some people and activities, it makes some futures more likely than others. Your acquaintanceships, friendships, and social networks are largely shaped by where you live. These networks are important in coupling you to or decoupling you from major institutions, as we learned in Chapter 2. Further, where you live will reflect your class (and ethnic) group and keep you part of it. Locked into your own community, you are also locked out of other communities.

Finally, where you live is a *state of mind*. Where you grow up shapes your ideas about how and where you want to live as an adult. Maturing ideas about *how* you want to live take material form in *where* you choose to live. The choices we make about where to live—on the coast or inland, in a small or large place, alone or with family or friends, and so on— express concretely the future we desire and the good life we intend to live. For example, "the upwardly mobile executive who moves from one res- idence into another, more elegant one is moving in psychological as well as physical space" (Campbell, 1980: 159).

In all these respects, your location is like your social class: both shape and reflect choices, capacitate and incapacitate, close in and out, couple and decouple. But other factors besides social class will influence your idea of the good life and, with it, your location. They include age, stage in the life cycle (for example, marital and parental status), and the strength of your ethnic or regional identity.

Despite their similarities, social class and location are different enough to justify separate treatment. Asked "Where would you like to be 10 years from now?" a person might answer in social class terms (for example, the owner of a successful business) or locational terms (for example, living in a big old house just outside Seattle). The two types of answers fit together, but they are not the same. Moreover, social class influences your choice of location; but within a given social class, different kinds of choice are possible.

The notional character of location—how location reflects life plans— first became apparent to us through a battle between two communities we shall call "Littletown" and "Metropolis."

Metropolis had grown very rapidly and needed more room to expand. It also needed a larger tax base. To gain land and tax revenues, Metropolis asked the state to let it annex several surrounding communities, including Littletown. Each of the threatened communities hired consultants to help them argue their case before a state board that would decide the matter. Our job was to challenge the conclusions Metropolis's consultants had drawn from a survey of Metropolis and Littletown residents.

The Metropolis-sponsored survey established that about two-thirds of employed Littletowners commuted to work in Metropolis every day. In Metropolis's eyes, this made Littletown just a "bedroom suburb" of

Metropolis. Littletowners also used Metropolis for shopping (especially large purchases) and certain kinds of recreation. But Littletowners felt their community was socially and culturally distinct from Metropolis. They claimed that Metropolis was poorly planned and governed, in comparison with their own community. They feared that annexation would destroy Littletown's unique cultural heritage. In rebuttal, the Metropolis consultants argued that unjustified antiannexation attitudes were promoted by a few who stood to gain from continued Littletown independence.

Yet Littletown's lifestyle *was* different from Metropolis's. A large proportion of Littletowners had previously lived in Metropolis. They had left Metropolis to live in a style they believed was possible in Littletown and not in Metropolis. Less concerned with achieving the goals Metropolis's government had staked out—chiefly growth, business, and a "big-city air"—Littletown's government provided just what people had come to Littletown to get: a small community with satisfying schools, services, and recreation.

Littletowners had the best of both worlds: a large city and its work opportunities on their doorstep, and a small, close-knit, well-run community where they could sleep and relax. They feared losing control over local institutions and becoming just another neighbourhood among the many that made up Metropolis.

When you think about it, small communities often depend on larger, adjacent communities for jobs; their economy relies on selling goods and services to their neighbour. And people in small communities often prefer their own way of life to the one available next door. People usually want the best of both worlds. So the Littletown *versus* Metropolis confrontation was a classic battle of lifestyles.

Littletown was the environment Littletowners preferred, and it represented an alternative to the Metropolis lifestyle and way of governing. In fact, most people's choices about location are choices against something as much as choices in favour of something else. What locations are average Americans choosing for and against, then?

Where Americans Live Today   Today over one-third of all Americans live in a mere five states—California, New York, Texas, Florida, and Pennsylvania. The Census Bureau reports that, if current trends continue, these states will continue to rank among the top six (Pennsylvania is expected to drop to sixth place and Illinois to replace it in fifth place) at least until 2010. The reason: except for Pennsylvania, each of these states is gaining population very rapidly. For example, California's population is expected to grow by 15 percent in the next decade and Florida's by 20 percent, as compared with a national growth of only 7 percent. Other expected rapid gainers are Arizona and North Carolina.

Demographers expect these gains to continue at the same rate for the next twenty years at least. Evidently these are the states where people want to live. Some of these states offer people a climate they enjoy, others job opportunities that cannot be matched elsewhere.

By contrast, some states are expected to lose population in the next decade. For example, Iowa and West Virginia are projected to lose about 7 percent of their population. Other population-losers include North Dakota, Wyoming, Montana, and also some of the large industrial states, especially Pennsylvania and Ohio. Presumably the same factors that are pulling people into some states are pushing them away from others.

The net result will be a redistribution of the American population and a greater concentration of Americans in fewer states than ever. But how much faith should we have in these predictions? Some predictions have a way of going wrong. Journalist Judith Waldrop (1989: 21) points out that if someone had used the 1900–1910 growth rates to predict the five top-ranking American states in 1990, they would have put Washington state in first place, followed by Oklahoma, California, Idaho, and North Dakota. Obviously, they would have guessed right on only one state: California.

If we do this same exercise using growth rates from 1910 to 1920, 1920 to 1930 and so on—coming closer and closer to 1990—the guess rate gets better. Someone predicting the top five-ranking states from growth rates in 1950–60, for example, would have guessed California, Florida, New York, Texas, and Ohio would top the list in 1990. That is, they would have guessed right about four out of five states. So guessing the probable ranking of states in 2010, a mere twenty years from now, may not be so error-prone after all.

What's more, we have theoretical reasons for predicting these continued shifts in population. Businesses are increasingly attracted to growth regions offering lower wages, available labor, energy savings, lower tax rates, political encouragement, and more comfortable life styles. For these reasons, economists and geographers predict a continued migration from the Northeast and North Central ("frostbelt") states to the South and West. In 1981, a Harvard–MIT group (Jackson et al., 1981: 62) was predicting the Mountain and South Central states would be chief gainers from this process. The most recent census data seem to bear out their predictions.

As a result of migration (and also continued low fertility), young workers have become increasingly scarce in the population-losing regions. Recruitment costs have escalated and labour shortages have led employers to relocate to areas where labour is more plentiful and, generally, the economic climate is more receptive. This has, in turn, increased the unemployment rate and led other young people to leave the "frostbelt" for southern climes.

This movement continues a long trend in American history: the western movement of population. In 1790, the midpoint of the American population was located just east of Baltimore, Maryland. By 1900, it was a few miles southeast of Columbus, Ohio, and in 1960, it was just outside Centralia, Illinois. By 1980, the midpoint had moved south and west to DeSoto, Missouri. By the year 2000, the population center of the country is bound to be south and west of DeSoto.

Both jobs and job applicants have increased most rapidly in cities like Houston, Phoenix, San Diego, San Jose, Salt Lake City, West Palm Beach, Orlando, and Tampa. Job growth has particularly benefited the bedroom suburbs, or Littletowns, of the nation. By far, the fastest-growing opportunities are in white-collar work located in suburban communities. On the other hand, opportunities for blue-collar (manufacturing) work in central city cores are shrinking.

In whatever part of the country they inhabit, most people live in family households as the spouse or child of the household head. Next most common is living alone. The percentage of Americans living alone has risen rapidly since 1940. Roughly one person in four lives alone today. As a result of this and lower rates of childbearing by couples, the average household size is much smaller today—about 2.64 people—than it was a generation ago and it is still shrinking.

The reasons for this change are apparent from our earlier chapters on marriage and parenting: today, people are marrying later and, because of more common divorce, spending less of their lives in a married state. Over one-quarter of all adult men and about one-fifth of all adult women are single today, compared with 19 percent and 14 percent respectively, in 1970. Six percent of adult men and 8 percent of adult women are divorced today, in both cases double the figures for 1970.

These changes are reflected in a housing revolution. For example, between 1980 and 1985, the proportion of households occupied by a male (without spouse) aged 25–34 increased 78 percent. The proportion of households occupied by a male (without spouse) aged 35–44 increased

44 percent; and those occupied by a female (without spouse) aged 35–44 increased by one-third (Russell & Exeter, 1986: 25).

As household size declines, the total number of households in America increases. At over 90 million today, the number of households has grown by about 10 million in the last decade. As well, nontraditional housing arrangements have become more common, especially in large cities. The growth in housebuilding and sales has declined as fewer people have been able to afford to buy their home. *American Demographics* reports (July 1989: 12) that the hardest hit are people under age 40. If current patterns keep up, we may see a return to conditions that existed in 1920, when fewer than half of American households were owner-occupied, though today over 60 percent own their own homes.

The type of household you live in is influenced by your age and stage in the life cycle. Increasingly, the marital household—with two spouses present—is a transitional stage in adult life between singlehood and divorce, remarriage, or widowhood. As the data in Table 7.1 show, being married with a spouse present is growing less common with each passing decade. For example, today only two-thirds of men and women aged 30–34 are married with a spouse present, compared with nearly 90 percent in 1960.

The patterns of marriage, family, and living arrangements established in the 1970s have not reversed in the 1980s. However, no changes as

TABLE 7.1 Percentage of adults who are married, with spouse present, by age. (Source: Bureau of the Census, *Current Population Reports*, P-20, No. 423; Donald Bogue, *The Population of the United States, Historical Trends and Future Projections*, The Free Press, New York, 1985.)

WOMEN	1987	1980	1970	1960
30 to 34	68.2%	72.7%	83.5%	88.7%
35 to 44	71.5	76.2	82.8	87.1
45 to 54	72.4	75.0	77.9	79.9
55 to 64	67.1	67.1	63.7	66.0
65 and older	39.2	38.0	33.7	37.4
MEN				
30 to 34	64.7	72.6	84.4	85.7
35 to 44	74.7	80.9	86.0	88.7
45 to 54	80.5	81.9	84.6	87.8
55 to 64	81.3	82.4	83.0	84.0
65 and older	74.9	75.5	68.4	70.8

profound as those of the 1970s have occurred either. As 1970s trends have continued, families consisting of a husband, wife, and one or more children have shrunk to about 30 percent of American households. More than half of these families include a working wife. In fact the "traditional family"—with a housewife mom, a working dad, and two or more kids— today accounts for only 6 percent of all households (Schwartz, 1987).

As we have seen in earlier chapters, the traditional family is being replaced by family arrangements that better suit today's lifestyles. To some degree, people have continued to cling to traditional notions of family and household nonetheless.

The Population Composition of American Places   In America, people have always relocated as their dreams and choices have changed. For example, the Bureau of the Census reports that between March 1986 and March 1987, 18 percent of the population—or over 42 million people— changed locations.

The majority of these movers moved within the county. But fully 3.7 percent of the American population moved within the state (outside the county) and 2.8 percent changed states. Black and Hispanic Americans were the most likely to move during the year, but white Americans were more likely to make the long-distance (interstate) moves (*American Demographics*, September 1989: 14).

Every separation and divorce brings someone a change of location or at least a change of households, and sometimes even a change of cities, states, or regions. Beyond these, increases in family size (through birth), decreases in family size (through death or children leaving home), changes in family income, and new job opportunities also lead to changes in location. With so many economic and demographic changes taking place, it is no wonder geographic movement is so common.

Another factor affecting the population composition of different states and cities is immigration. The size and characteristics of groups immigrating to different American states and cities varies greatly. During the 1980s, legal immigration has averaged just under 600,000 people a year, a figure which is 30 percent higher than during the 1970s and much more than in any year since 1924.

As well, hundreds of thousands of aliens with nonimmigrant status— students, temporary workers, visitors, and others—live legally in the United States. Finally, millions of illegal aliens live in the United States. In 1980, the number was estimated at between 2.5 and 3.5 million, and it has increased since then, if anything (Allen & Turner, 1988: 24).

The largest numbers of recent immigrants have come from Mexico, Central and South America, Africa, and Asia—especially China, Viet Nam, and Iran. New York City is the most popular destination for new immigrants, averaging nearly 100,000 per year between 1984 and 1986. Of the nine other most popular destinations in the top ten, six are in California. (The other three popular destinations are Chicago, Washington, D.C., and Miami.) (Allen & Turner, 1988: 24.)

These immigrants have tended to settle in particular locations, producing unusually high concentrations. For example, compared to other destinations, New York City has received particularly high concentrations of immigrants from Guyana, the Dominican Republic, Ecuador, Haiti, and Jamaica. Not surprisingly, Texas and Arizona have received particularly high concentrations from Mexico, and Florida has received particularly large numbers from Cuba. Washington, D.C., has received particularly high concentrations of immigrants from Cambodia, Laos, and Thailand, as has Minnesota.

To some degree—as in the case of Mexicans coming to California, Cubans to Florida, and Filipinos to Honolulu—these flows are shaped by simple geographic proximity. But in many cases—as, for example, in the case of concentrated Polish immigration to Illinois and Michigan—the flow illustrates the "chain migration," whereby immigrants follow family, friends, and acquaintances who have immigrated before.

These clustered new immigrants are often particularly visible in their new surroundings. As Allen and Turner (1988: 60) report, "The infusion of immigrants to the U.S. is transforming many metropolitan areas and affecting politics, the labor force, and consumer behavior." It is shifting the future population balance even more dramatically.

The black, Hispanic, and Asian populations of America have higher birthrates than the white population. Combined with current high rates of migration and immigration, this high fertility will have important effects on the racial and cultural make-up of the country by 2010. Schwartz and Exeter (1989) write that "By the year 2010, as many as 38 percent of Americans under the age of 18 will belong to minority groups. In seven states and the District of Columbia, more than half of children will be minorities. In an additional 19 states, at least one-quarter of children will be black, Hispanic, Asian or other minorities."

For example, children (under 18) in four of the five state populations projected to be largest in 2010 will be predominantly minorities: in California, 56.9 percent; Texas, 56.9 percent; New York, 52.8 percent; Florida,

53.4 percent. Only in Pennsylvania, which is losing population, will the proportion of children belonging to minority groups be low: a projected 18.7 percent. Where migration is causing the minority populations to grow and concentrate most, racial and cultural mixing will probably be greatest in future.

Migration reflects a desire for both economic opportunity and a particular lifestyle. But what, exactly, do sociologists mean by "lifestyle," and why are they interested in the topic?

Lifestyles

Origins of Interest in Lifestyle   Sociological interest in lifestyle can be traced to at least two main sources in classical sociology. The first source is Max Weber and his writings on "commensalism" and "status group"; important followers include Karl Mannheim. The second source includes a stream of researchers on "community," beginning with the German sociologists Ferdinand Tonnies and Georg Simmel, then the "Chicago school" of sociology, including Louis Wirth and his disciples.

In contrast to Marx, who held that economic and class relations determined all other social relations, Weber was convinced that social organization is founded on a triad of principles: economic (or class), political (or party), and status group. People have economic and political allegiances, to be sure; but they also have status group affiliations that influence their view of life and their behaviour. These status groups do not simply organize people vertically—the way we now think of "social status"—they organize people horizontally as well.

A person's status group might be organized around language, ethnic, religious, or racial differences from the rest of society, or around other symbolic and noneconomic principles. What defines a status group is its degree of *commensalism*: literally, the degree to which its members eat together, or more generally share activities and a common world view. A "status group" in Weber's terminology might today be called a "subculture." When we study the common behaviours of that group, we study a common "lifestyle."

Thus, what sociologists consider lifestyle today is nothing more or less than subculturally shared patterns of behaviour that flow from a common, underlying world view. Such common behaviours serve to signify the boundaries of the group. People who live the same way are considered part of the group, while people who live differently are outsiders.

Thorstein Veblen's *Theory of the Leisure Class* (1934) shows how lifestyles come to define group boundaries. The very rich devise ways of consuming their wealth that are "conspicuously wasteful" in order to clearly define who is, or is not, within their group. By its nature, such consumption is exclusive to the very rich. Moreover, the people with the most established wealth continue to devise new forms of "conspicuous consumption" to delimit the boundaries of the "leisure class." To be a member, you must have enough time and money to keep up with this endless revision of fashions in conspicuous waste; you must also want to try.

Not all status groups test "candidates" so rigorously to determine who is in the group and who is out; but lifestyle behaviors, including consumption patterns, always distinguish insiders from outsiders. For this reason, sociologists have long claimed that you can tell a person's social position from his or her living room. Living-room furnishings display both a "taste" (hence, status group background) and the pretensions (or desired status group affiliation) of the householder. (For a humorous update of living-room assessment, see Fussell, 1983.)

Most members of a culture can "read" the status signals a person emits. This fact is demonstrated by community studies conducted by Chicago sociologist Lloyd Warner and his students since the 1940s (Davis, Garner, & Gardner, 1941; Warner, Meeker, & Eells, 1960). In one community after another, researchers found community members could easily sort local townspeople into groups based on "reputation." In doing so, they regularly identified the same numbers of distinct status groups and sorted people into groups in similar ways.

Moreover, they told researchers similar things about the characteristics of each grouping: for example, how "upper-upper-class" people differed from "lower-upper-class" people. Thus, status groups, their membership, and behaviours appropriate to members, were well-known to people living in small, stable communities.

In large, new, or transient communities the boundaries of such groups are harder to specify and their membership, constantly turning over, is harder to agree on (Jaher, 1982). That is why people in large, mobile communities must rely more on visible behaviours to convey their actual or intended status. Such behaviours not only signal who they think they are or want to be taken for but also what kinds of people they want to interact with, and in what ways.

For this reason, people—especially younger people—wear clothing with the designer labels prominently displayed or easily inferred: for example, Polo, Roots, Club Monaco. Or they wear clothing and hair styles that convey a point of view: for example, punk versus preppy. Increasingly, people spend their time and money to convey an impression of who they are and who they want to be.

Sociologists studying lifestyle often focus on how people spend their time and their money. Each kind of spending indicates commitment, since few people have unlimited time and money. So spending behavior is clearly the making of important choices under constraints. We shall now consider the two kinds of spending behavior in turn.

Lifestyle and Money-Spending Behavior   Researchers in marketing spend an enormous amount of energy figuring out how to influence people to buy particular goods or services. In this respect, market researchers and advertisers are "captains of consciousness" (Ewen, 1976). For example, in order to promote household products more effectively, one particularly gruesome piece of market research helped a publisher of romance magazines find out the secret fears and desires of working-class wives (Rainwater, Coleman, & Handel, 1962).

Marketing research has become more sophisticated with the development of VALS (Values and Life Style) surveying. Mitchell (1983) conceives of nine American lifestyle groups. Based loosely on Maslow's theory of a need hierarchy, Mitchell's typology relates buying behavior to the social, economic, and demographic characteristics of each group.

Consider the group Mitchell calls "experientials." Comprising roughly 7 million Americans, or 11 percent of the adult population, the "experientials" are an important chunk of the baby-boom generation. A majority occupy the middle or upper class and over two-thirds have some postsecondary education, compared to 43 percent of the adult population. Experientials tend to live alone or cohabit, and they are city people, not suburbanites or rural residents. What lifestyle goes with their class and geographic location?

Compared to average American adults, experientials are liberal and independent (that is, party-free). They are very unlikely to think that unmarried sex is wrong, or too much money is spent protecting the environment. They get a great deal of satisfaction from nonwork activities, especially friends; but TV-watching is not their main entertainment.

Their financial status is also distinctive. Experientials' incomes are well above the national average. They are unlikely to have a credit card balance (owing) under $100, and are more likely than others to owe $1500 or more. The experientials are less likely than others to own their home or have a home mortgage, but more likely than any other group to owe over $50,000 in loans. This highly varied group contains some very wealthy and very upwardly mobile people. Experientials are a good credit risk and they borrow regularly against their credit. Much of their income (and credit) is consumed by higher-than-average rates of leisure activity.

In its activities, "this group is in many ways a more mature, less extreme version of the I-Am-Mes" (Mitchell, 1983: 130). Experientials swim, play racquet sports, and ski. "They engage more in yoga and home meditation than any other group and are distinctly concerned with the health aspects of food. They are more likely than any other group to work at a second job or free-lance" (Mitchell, 1983: 132).

How do "experientials" like to spend their money? Mitchell (1983: 132) remarks that "key characteristics of the Experientials—such as the search for direct and pleasurable experiences, their try-anything-once attitude, preference for process over product, and active outdoor orientation—are evidenced in their pattern of product ownership and use." Experiential households are much more likely than average to own compact, subcompact, and small specialty cars. More than any other group, they buy quality European cars, especially used ones. They are also above-average purchasers of motorcycles and racing bikes.

At home, experientials commonly purchase dishwashers, garbage disposals, recreational equipment, video games, stereos, and blank recording tapes. Wine and beer are their preferred alcoholic drinks, with tequila as an alternative. Experientials avoid coffee (with or without caffeine), sugared foods and drinks; they make above-average use of frozen Chinese and Mexican foods. You can sell experientials a lot of eye makeup and shampoo, but forget about aerosol underarm deodorants, feminine-hygiene sprays, after-shave lotions, or room air-fresheners. Experientials use veterinarians a lot, but rarely buy canned dog foods. And if you invite an experiential home for dinner, hide the margarine, Jello, and Planter's peanuts (Mitchell, 1983: Table 16).

If you have not guessed yet, Mitchell's "experientials" are young urban professionals—"yuppies"—finished with being "I-Am-Mes" and on their way to becoming "Societally Conscious."

The VALS approach to analysing lifestyle captures a wide range of attitudes and spending patterns, and relates them to social and demographic identifiers. Such research tells businesspeople what prospective clients "look like," where they can be found, and what psychic buttons to push to make a sale. But what about the nonmonetary aspects of daily life? We learn more about these by studying the ways people spend their time.

Lifestyle and Time Use   "Time budget research" asks ordinary people to keep a detailed, running record of each day's events: what they did, for how long, and in whose company. The resulting data offer sociologists a rich insight into the variety of everyday lifestyles.

The first thing they discover is that the same kinds of people (for example, employed mothers) lead similar lives throughout the modern world (Robinson, Converse, & Szalai, 1972). Industrialization tends to erase national differences, causing lifestyles around the world to converge. Accordingly, international differences in time usage mainly reflect differences in the degree of industrialization and related processes: urbanization, media availability, education, family planning, and female labor force participation, among others. For example, in industrial societies, mass media are widely available, and the more mass media are available, the more time people will spend consuming them. A case in point is the time spent watching television.

However, we also find interesting, sometimes unexplained variations among industrial nations: for example, despite widely available programming, average West Germans watch a lot less television than average Americans (Robinson & Converse, 1972).

Domestic relations also seem to vary among industrial nations. People differ markedly in the amount of time they spend at home with their spouse, and the amount that is spent in the spouse's company alone, without children, relatives, or friends present (Varga, 1972). In countries where married couples spend more time alone together, divorce rates are lower. This suggests that divorce is caused, at least partly, by spouses spending too little time in intimate, "courtship" behaviour.

Time budget data also show cross-national variations in the amounts of sociability at work and at home. North Americans are more likely than most people to retreat from an intensely interactive work life into solitude or relatively passive family activity. But in many European cultures, leisure is as intensely interactive as work.

Finally, mothers who work outside the home enjoy more leisure and more control over their domestic duties in countries with good public daycare, where friends and relatives are readily available, or spouses cooperate more than in North America (Michelson, 1985; Szalai, 1972).

Lifestyles vary most between industrial and preindustrial societies, but they also vary *within* industrial nations. Time budget data show that even neighborhoods vary in lifestyle.

In choosing a place to live people are influenced by such characteristics as education, occupation, and income, but also by values and stage in the life cycle: whether married or single, childless or parent, older or younger. These characteristics lead them to move into some neighborhoods and types of dwellings rather than others. Though often unanticipated, such moves may produce major lifestyle changes.

Consider the lifestyles of homeowners, whether suburban or downtown. "They have above average interests in gardening, go to church on Sundays, and spend time with their neighbors, who are similar to themselves. . . . Husbands (especially in suburban homes) exchange several kinds of mutual aid with their neighbors, and expect the same in return. The husband knows a number of people in his neighborhood well. He participates actively in organizations" (Michelson, 1977: 307–308).

Lifestyles consist of activity *dimensions*. For example, they may be person-centered (and if so, either family-centered or centered on other people) or centered on ideas or objects; passive or active, public or private, formal (organized) or informal, productive or consumptive; and in motion or at rest, at home or away from home, and indoors or out-of-doors (Reed, 1976).

People living in each type of residential environment—downtown apartment, suburban single-family dwelling, and so on—end up living in different activity dimensions. So, for example, a married woman who moves to a new house in the suburbs takes on a new package of activities. She is much more likely to spend her weekday hours preparing food, cleaning house, repairing the home, doing laundry, and caring for children than a married woman who lives in an apartment downtown. Conversely, the apartment-dwelling woman is more likely to spend her time travelling to work, working for pay, reading books, and attending to personal hygiene. "Relatively typical of wives moving to downtown apartments is a very weak emphasis on domestic tasks. . . . The same holds for child care activity" (Reed, 1976: 202).

The married suburban woman is more likely to spend *Sunday* preparing food, cleaning house, attending church, and visiting friends and relatives than her counterpart who lives in a downtown apartment. Conversley, the apartment-dwelling woman is more likely to spend Sunday catching up on weekday duties (laundry, infant care, home repairs), preparing meals at home, attending to personal hygiene, and relaxing. Stated otherwise, the married apartment-dwelling woman's Sunday is more solitary, recuperative, and family-centered; the suburban housewife's Sunday more broadly sociable (Rubin, 1982).

The activities of married men are much less "patterned" than those of their wives. Mens' activities also differ from their wives' in content. Still, their lifestyles also vary by location. On weekdays, married suburban men are busy working, travelling to work, and repairing the home—"a relatively active life style in common with their wives," but with less emphasis on social, home-centered, or passive activities. By contrast, downtown apartment-dwelling husbands are more likely to shop and visit friends during the week and to spend less time than other married men on "work, personal hygiene, at-home meals, and newspaper reading" (Reed, 1976: 207).

In choosing a place to live, people usually display different kinds of concerns. But interestingly, lifestyle "appears to operate more as a latent than as a strongly explicit consideration in residential choice-making" (Reed, 1976, Abstract). When people choose a place to live, they choose it with particular features in mind: house price and size, convenience to work, schools, and shopping, and so on. According to Reed, when choosing a place to live people do not take the likely lifestyle changes into account, perhaps because they are unaware of them.

Regional Variations in Lifestyle   Lifestyles vary most between industrial and preindustrial societies, and also vary within industrial societies, as we have just seen. Moreover, they vary regionally within continents. Consider Garreau's (1981) evidence that North America contains nine "nations," not two. Many straddle the national border dividing Canada from the United States.

Garreau argues that political boundaries are no longer very useful in defining the regions of North America. Increasingly, distinct regional lifestyles derive from two main factors: economic forces and regional traditions. Both of these are, in turn, rooted in different land surface conditions and environmental concerns. In each region or "nation," wealth is generated differently, leading to different—even opposing—political and environmental concerns.

This suggests that state, and national borders are highly artificial and, today, have little basis in either economic or cultural life. Garreau claims that people are more attached to their regions and regional ways than they are to the nation as a whole. But are the Canada/United States and Mexico/United States borders as culturally blurred as Garreau makes out? And do North America's regions really differ from one another in lifestyle?

Let us travel the continent from east to west, as Garreau did, seeking patterns as we go. First comes the "nation" Garreau calls "New England." For Garreau, the essential thinking of New Englanders (including Canadian Maritimers) is captured in words written by nineteenth-century

Massachusetts philosopher and recluse Henry David Thoreau. Thoreau wrote: "The town's poor seem to me often to live the most independent lives of any. . . . Cultivate poverty like a garden herb, like sage. Do not trouble yourself much to get new things, whether clothes or friends. Turn the old; return to them. Sell your clothes and keep your thoughts. God will see that you do not want society" (cited in Garreau, 1981: 47).

Continuing west, Garreau arrives at the region or "nation" he calls the Foundry, America's industrial heartland. "Enormous quantities of time, sweat and money have been invested in making this region what it is, and the Foundry's future will be determined by the extent to which North Americans decide they should, or will, walk away from that" (Garreau, 1981: 74). Since, according to Garreau (1981: 75), "the whole point of living in the Foundry is work," what determines people's state of mind and willingness to stay here is precisely whether they can find employment.

West of the Foundry, Garreau groups parts of Canada, and the States of Alaska and the Rocky Mountain region into the "Empty Quarter." Here, energy interests form a powerful lobby and fuel a strong, ongoing conflict with the federal government and Eastern financiers. According to Garreau, people in the Empty Quarter are enthusiastic, optimistic, and committed to material progress. Resources were made to be exploited, in their view.

The Breadbasket—North America's grain-farming and ranching region—includes the Canadian prairies and the states of the Great Plains. "As people stumble toward an explanation of what they value in their friends and neighbours around here, the words are *always* 'open,' 'friendly,' 'hardworking,' 'there when you need them,' 'down to earth.' . . . [There are] pressures not to flaunt wealth, or to ascribe success to 'luck'" (Garreau, 1981: 350).

The American south and southwest, that recipient of so much recent migration, also contains three nations. Garreau calls them Dixie, the Islands, and Mexamerica.

He reports (1981: 130) that "the South has changed so much in the past decade or two that change itself has become Dixie's most identifiable characteristic . . . Dixie is now best described as that forever underdeveloped North American nation across which the social and economic machine of the late twentieth century has most dramatically swept."

Because it is sociologically, climatically, historically, politically, topographically, and racially diverse, Dixie cannot be defined in terms of any single activity, resource, or environment. It defies definition in terms of standard politics and geography. Rather, "Dixie's boundaries are defined more by emotion than any other nation" (Garreau, 1981: 131). If a state at all, Dixie is a state of mind, indeed a state of preoccupation.

South and east of Dixie are "the Islands." They include southern Florida, centering on Miami; Puerto Rico; and several other territories not typically considered part of the United States—among them Cuba, the Bahamas, Jamaica, and Haiti. What connects them is, first, a common climate and terrain. Tourism is very important because of this pleasant climate and terrain.

Second, they are tied together by a flow of Hispanic and Caribbean peoples. As Garreau (1981: 172) says, "This is why the geographic reorientation that South Florida has undergone in the last decade has been the most sweeping of any not caused by war in North American history. The economy and culture have turned completely around, and are now facing due south. They now look to Cuba, Puerto Rico, Columbia, Venezuela—even Argentina—for their future."

Third and equally important, the Islands are linked by covert American political, military, business, and criminal organizations operating out of Miami. Each has its own reason for wanting to use the Islands nearby. Per person, more secret, illegal or semilegal activities may be going on in this "nation" of North America than in any of the other eight.

No less Hispanic but rather less covert is the nation Garreau calls "Mexamerica." It includes all of Mexico and a band of southern states running from Houston and Brownsville, Texas, in the east to San Diego and the San Joaquin Valley, California, in the west. The first feature unifying this nation is its roots in Spanish civilization and the prevalence of Spanish language use. Like Quebec in the north—that "nation" of French traditions nestled in a continent of Anglos—Mexamerica is virtually bilingual and bicultural. And, like Quebec, it is fighting to keep its traditions from melting in the great pot of Anglo-American culture.

Some of the fastest-growing metropolitan areas in the United States are located in Mexamerica, Phoenix, Los Angeles, and San Diego. This is a second defining feature of the Mexamerican nation: Anglos view it as the "promised land." Says Garreau, "It's not hard to envision a near future in which the MexAmerican Southwest becomes the continent's dominant region—replacing the Foundry" (Garreau, 1981: 218).

Part of MexAmerica's continental importance is due to the dominant role Los Angeles plays in creating television and film images of America. If New York City is the financial center of North America and the Foundry its industrial center, California is the continent's postindustrial, ideological center.

Finally, Garreau comes to Ecotopia, which includes most of North America's Pacific coastline. This region is an "ecological utopia," full of majestic mountains, rivers, and forests: here, the quality of daily life is a central concern. People focus on how the natural environment should be used to give everyone the greatest pleasure now and in the future. This concern about life quality also produces extremes and smugness, Garreau says. "Even [Ecotopia's] search for new futures is burdened with some moralistic selfrighteousness. It's not hard to find people in the Northwest who get as rigid with distress over the idea of a person eating an additive- and sugar-laden Twinkie as a devout Empty Quarter Mormon does about someone imbibing strong drink" (Garreau, 1981: 272).

The Clustering of America   The claims that many lifestyles coexist in North America and lifestyles are interwoven with locations, would find ready acceptance from the marketing community. Increasingly, people with goods and services to sell are able to find particular locations where the demand for their product is likely to be greatest.

The ability to do this effectively has been revolutionized by a marketing technique called PRIZM, which attaches social, economic, and demographic information to the nation's 36,000 ZIP codes. By computer it is possible to find the ZIP codes containing the highest fractions of people viewing "Miami Vice," eating fat-free yogurt, or buying used cars (among other things). With this information in hand, marketers can focus their advertising, product tryouts, or merchandising efforts on particular parts of the country where the probable payoff is highest.

This computerized procedure has redefined the ways marketers view American society. Claritas Corporation, in particular, has devoted a great deal of effort to finding out how many different "kinds of neighborhoods" exist in the United States, and how they differ from one another in values and lifestyles. The result of this effort is described in a book about the "clustering of America" (Weiss, 1988).

Researchers at Claritas Corporation have found that location is important to lifestyle. They have identified 40 distinct neighbourhood (or lifestyle) clusters among the 36,000 American ZIP code areas, not a mere 9 as Garreau had suggested. Empirical research conducted for nearly two decades has shown Claritas that regional differences, though important, are not the only important ones.

People living in one neighbourhood may have almost nothing in common—in terms of values and lifestyles—with people living in the same "nation" (as Garreau would define things) ten miles away. Yet, they may have a great deal in common with people living in another "nation" on the

TABLE 7.2 America's Forty Neighborhood Types (Source: Weiss, 4–5.)

Cluster	Thumbnail Description	Percent U.S. Households
Blue Blood Estates	America's wealthiest neighborhoods includes suburban homes and one in ten millionaires	1.1
Money & Brains	Posh big-city enclaves of townhouses, condos and apartments	0.9
Furs & Station Wagons	New money in metropolitan bedroom suburbs	3.2
Urban Gold Coast	Upscale urban high-rise districts	0.5
Pools & Patios	Older, upper-middle-class, suburban communities	3.4
Two More Rungs	Comfortable multi-ethnic suburbs	0.7
Young Influentials	Yuppie, fringe-city condo and apartment developments	2.9
Young Suburbia	Child-rearing, outlying suburbs	5.3
God's Country	Upscale frontier boomtowns	2.7
Blue-Chip Blues	The wealthiest blue-collar suburbs	6.0
Bohemian Mix	Inner-city bohemian enclaves à la Greenwich Village	1.1
Levittown, U.S.A.	Aging, post-World War II tract subdivisions	3.1
Gray Power	Upper-middle-class retirement communities	2.9
Black Enterprise	Predominantly black, middle- and upper-middle-class neighborhoods	0.8
New Beginnings	Fringe-city areas of singles complexes, garden apartments and trim bungalows	4.3
Blue-Collar Nursery	Middle-class, child-rearing towns	2.2
New Homesteaders	Exurban boom towns of young, midscale families	4.2
New Melting Pot	New immigrant neighborhoods, primarily in the nation's port cities	0.9
Towns & Gowns	America's college towns	1.2
Rank & File	Older, blue-collar, industrial suburbs	1.4
Middle America	Midscale, midsize towns	3.2

Household percentages are based on 1987 census block groups and estimated to the closest 0.1 percent. Source: PRIZM (Census Demography), Claritas Corp., 1987.

other side of the continent—so much so that if they woke up in their twin community, it would take a while before they realized they had left home at all. As Claritas founder Jonathan Robbin puts it, "You can go to sleep in Fairfield, Connecticut, and wake up in Pasadena, California, but except for the palm trees, you're really in the same place" (quoted in Weiss, 1988: 14).

Consider the neighbourhood type Claritas calls "Two More Rungs."

In the affluent cluster of Two More Rungs—consisting of communities like Skokie, Illinois; Rancho Park, California; and Flushing, New York—resi-

TABLE 7.2 *(continued)*

Cluster	Thumbnail Description	Percent U.S. Households
Old Yankee Rows	Working-class rowhouse districts	1.6
Coalburg & Corntown	Small towns based on light industry and farming	2.0
Shotguns & Pickups	Crossroads villages serving the nation's lumber and breadbasket needs	1.9
Golden Ponds	Rustic cottage communities located near the coasts, in the mountains or alongside lakes	5.2
Agri-Business	Small towns surrounded by large-scale farms and ranches	2.1
Emergent Minorities	Predominantly black, working-class, city neighborhoods	1.7
Single City Blues	Downscale, urban, singles districts	3.3
Mines & Mills	Struggling steeltowns and mining villages	2.8
Back-Country Folks	Remote, downscale, farm towns	3.4
Norma Rae-Ville	Lower-middle-class milltowns and industrial suburbs, primarily in the South	2.3
Smalltown Downtown	Inner-city districts of small industrial cities	2.5
Grain Belt	The nation's most sparsely populated rural communities	1.3
Heavy Industry	Lower-working-class districts in the nation's older industrial cities	2.8
Share Croppers	Primarily southern hamlets devoted to farming and light industry	4.0
Downtown Dixie Style	Aging, predominantly black neighborhoods, typically in southern cities	3.4
Hispanic Mix	America's Hispanic barrios	1.9
Tobacco Roads	Predominantly black farm communities throughout the South	1.2
Hard Scrabble	The nation's poorest rural settlements	1.5
Public Assistance	America's inner-city ghettos	3.1

dents shun the extravagant trappings of success. With its high concentration of Jewish, Irish, Italian and Slavic stock, this cluster is filled with professionals who dedicated their lives to sending their kids to college. Today they're comfortably settled in a paid-for condominium or split-level. Two More Rungs is filled with success stories of first-generation Americans living near the port cities to which their parents emigrated (Weiss, 1988: 51).

As this example shows, neighborhood types are partly defined by location—in this case, closeness to a port city. They are also defined by varying combinations of socioeconomic status, stage in the life cycle, and racial or ethnic origin. For example, people who live in Two More Rungs neighborhoods—and Claritas has found that about 7 in every 1000 American households are located here—hold particular values and live in particular ways.

> They often spend more than $100 weekly on groceries, although their shopping carts reflect Old World tastes—rye bread, corned beef hash and spaghetti sauce. They frequently travel to their ancestral homelands in Europe, but they tend to take discounted chartered plane trips or cruises. At home, Two More Rungs residents read *Scientific American* and *Atlantic Monthly* twice as often as the general populace, and they would rather host a family dinner than a cocktail party. In this tradition-bound neighbourhood type, status is still a son who grows up to be a doctor, lawyer or college professor—junior-high teachers don't cut it (*ibid*).

Why are these patterns so regular and predictable? And why do people with certain characteristics live together in similar ways? The answer is that people seek out neighborhoods and neighbors who are most like themselves. Demographically similar neighborhoods share the same consumer patterns because people with particular educational or ethnic backgrounds, at similar stages in the life cycle and with similar amounts of money to spend, have similar conceptions of "the good life" and similar abilities to attain that good life.

Though people continuously move in and out, neighborhoods stay more or less the same. That is because, over time, the same kinds of people are likely to find the neighborhood appealing, and move into it, as found it appealing five, ten, or twenty years ago but are now moving out.

Are different locations and lifestyles equally satisfying? And do people become more satisfied with their location and lifestyle over the course of their lives?

Location and Satisfaction

People who are free to choose a location and lifestyle as they wish should be generally satisfied with where and how they live. In this section we briefly examine people's satisfaction with various aspects of their location, including macrostructures (state and city) and microstructures (neighborhood, dwelling, and household).

A Basis for Comparison   Before discussing Americans' satisfaction with their location and related lifestyle, we must situate the problem in its proper historical context. That is because the American people have a very distinctive history and culture, and many "myths" about location circulate in American society.

Recent years have seen a fascination with traditional values and rural life in the United States. This is occurring despite—or perhaps because—American society is changing faster, becoming more urbanized, and reaching higher levels of technological sophistication than ever in its history. In this respect, America is not unique, nor is the surge of sentiment favouring old ways—for example, rural versus urban life—a new thing. From at least the start of the twentieth century, writers and artists have been looking back at the rural homey ease they left behind for city riches.

It is not surprising, then, to find that people entertain many erroneous ideas about the lives they are *not* leading. Dutch sociologist Ruut Veenhoven (1984) has surveyed 245 empirical studies of happiness and life satisfaction and reports the following "myths about happiness"—widely held beliefs that are consistently proved false by empirical research.

First, he argues against the myth that "modern Western society is a sink of unhappiness" and against "long-lived romantic ideas that life is better in primitive societies." Unfortunately, we do not have the high-quality data on life satisfaction from 1840, 1890, or even 1940 that would allow us to determine scientifically—with comparable data from 1990—whether people really *were* happier in the "good old days." However, we do have current data that seriously call into question some of the assumptions of those who look wistfully backward.

Specifically, data show Veenhoven (1984: 396) that "In spite of the evident perils of industrialization and economic growth, people in developed nations are generally happier than people in underdeveloped countries." Second, "Contrary to the 'urban malaise theory,' people in the country are no more satisfied with life than people in towns . . . Neither are the inhabitants of small towns happier than people living in big cities." (However, Veenhoven notes the opposite is true in developing societies.) Finally, research shows "No unhappiness because of hurry . . . The ones who feel most harassed [by hurry] do not take less pleasure in life."

Against this backdrop of global research, the United States is slightly off-center. Research in the United States has, more than anywhere else, tended to find people happier in rural than in urban areas, and in small rather than large communities. Veenhoven reports (1984: 174) that some of the differences disappear when other factors—such as health, marital status, ethnicity, income, and church attendance—are taken into account. It is not so much that rural or small-town life is more satisfying, rather, people who remain in these communities may be easier to please.

Yet, even allowing for this, "In the US, inhabitants of large metro-politan areas appeared to be slightly less happy than average." He notes that "The lower happiness level of people in big metropolitan areas in the US was largely accounted for by people who moved from small towns to a big city. These people appeared to be relatively poor, while the ones who left the cities were relatively well off" (Veenhoven, 1984: 175).

Since the Second World War, city populations have become poorer as affluent whites have left for surrounding suburbs. It is not city life but poverty and racial discrimination that accounts for the relationship be-tween location and satisfaction. What's more,

> Though an influx of poor people may depress average happiness in US metropolitan centers, the poor do not appear particularly vulnerable to the hazards of city life. Poor Americans living in the big cities rather took more pleasure in life than their fellows in misfortune in small towns, while well-to-do inhabitants of big cities appeared slightly less happy than compatriots living in smaller towns (Veenhoven, 1984: 175).

So, in general, research reveals little correlation between location and satisfaction. In the American case, what correlation there is can be ex-plained by selective migration. Clearly, popular beliefs about location and satisfaction are "myths." Where location is concerned, people are largely getting what they set out to find. Their pleasure in living where they want to, or looking forward to doing so, is moderated only by a peculiar Ameri-can ambivalence that Tocqueville was first to notice, and far from last to mention.

Alexis de Tocqueville, a young French aristocrat, was fascinated by everything he saw in America during his nine-month visit in 1831–32. His book *Democracy in America* (1945 [1833]) reports on what he learned, and includes some thoughts on how the American experience could be used profitably elsewhere.

Though clearly impressed with many aspects of the American repub-lic, Tocqueville expressed concern about some of the peculiar products of democracy.

For example, he noted (1945, Volume 11: 136) that democracy in America had created a general "passion for physical well-being" which has certainly not abated in the century and a half since then. "When . . . the distinctions of ranks are obliterated and privileges are destroyed, when hereditary property is subdivided and education and freedom are widely diffused, the desire of acquiring the comforts of the world haunts the imagination of the poor, and the dread of losing them that of the rich" (Tocqueville, op. cit.: 137).

Tocqueville was discovering a society that was, for his time, remarkably fluid, middle-class, and also democratic. The average American was surrounded by almost infinite chances for rising and falling in fortune. The result: a restlessness in the midst of prosperity. Says Tocqueville, "In America I saw the freest and most enlightened men placed in the happiest circumstances that the world affords; [yet] it seemed to me as if a cloud habitually hung upon their brow, and I thought them serious and almost sad, even in their pleasures" (Tocqueville, op. cit.: 144).

After exploring a variety of possible explanations—hurry, envy, fear of missing the shortcut to happiness—he continues

> To these causes must be attributed that strange melancholy which often haunts the inhabitants of democratic countries in the midst of their abundance and that disgust at life which sometimes seizes upon them in the midst of calm and easy circumstances. . . . In America, suicide is rare, but insanity is said to be more common there than anywhere else. These are all different symptoms of the same disease . . . In democratic times enjoyments are more intense than in the ages of aristocracy, and the number of those who partake in them is vastly larger; but, on the other hand, it must be admitted that man's hopes and desires are oftener blasted, the soul is more stricken and perturbed, and care itself more keen (Tocqueville, op. cit.: 147).

The reader will recognize in this the seeds of Emile Durkheim's classic analysis of suicide due to *anomie*, published sixty years later. (We shall discuss anomie further in the concluding chapter of this book.)

What Tocqueville had recognized is that America is a restless country, where the temptation of future pleasures tends to cast a pall on present ones. It is also a fluid country of new things, names, and places: it is constantly in the process of inventing itself. This idea is nicely captured in historian Daniel Boorstin's (1973) portrait of American life since the Civil War, which begins

> Americans reached out to one another. A new civilization found new ways of holding men together—less and less by creed or belief, by tradition or by place, more and more by common effort and common experience, by the apparatus of everyday life, by their ways of thinking about themselves. Americans were now held together less by their hopes than by their wants, by what they made and what they bought, and by how they learned about

everything. They were held together by the new names they gave to the things they wanted, to the things they owned, and to themselves. These everywhere communities floated over time and space, they could include anyone without his effort, and sometimes without his knowing (Boorstin, 1973: 1).

Private and Public Lives   In American history from the Civil War onward, we see the natural unfolding or evolution of that passion for physical well-being Tocqueville had noted earlier. We also see the groundwork set for PRIZM and Claritas's discovery that 40 statistical communities (or neighborhoods) exist in America. (In fact, Boorstin devotes nine chapters to the rise of "statistical communities" in American society since 1865.)

What has proved an enduring conflict in American society is the split between private lives and public lives, or, as C. Wright Mills would have put it, between personal troubles and public issues. Tocqueville noted long ago that prosperous democracy has made it possible for Americans of every class to profitably pursue a course of "self-interest rightly understood." It was clear to Tocqueville that this *best* kind of self-interest would lead Americans to form free associations which would advance collective or communal, not merely personal, interests. Ever since, sociologists have remarked on the remarkable willingness of Americans to join and support such associations.

This should have produced a vigorous, healthy public life, one that engaged all Americans in the lives of all other Americans, and in the great public issues of the day. Yet this has not always happened. Rather, social scientists have continued to note a conflict between public and private spheres, and a progressive impoverishment of public life in America.

Writers on this topic differ in their analyses of the problem, and we risk oversimplifying their complex arguments with a few simple sentences. Yet two points of view are particularly compelling—those of historian Richard Sennett and sociologist Robert Bellah.

Sennett (1978) takes the conflict between private and public spheres as inevitable. We are all apt to value our own ideas, goals, and loved ones more highly than anyone else's. For a successful balance of public and private lives, there must be a compelling argument on the other side, a strong case for public involvement. Sennett sees this possibility being progressively eroded by the "fall of public man," through the systematic attack on the boundary between private and public.

To deal effectively with public issues, we must be able to distance ourselves from them psychologically—to see them as objects of rational study and debate. Yet, systematically, public life has been recast in the imagery of private life. We are invited—even forced by the media—to know all about the personal lives and loves of politicians, artists, and tycoons. As a result, we end up discussing their personal foibles, rather than the art, ideas, or policies they have been responsible for. We judge the people, not what they have done, and ultimately vote on whether we like them or not as people.

To recast public issues as the personal troubles of celebrities, as mass journalism does today, is to trivialize public discourse. What's more, it drives people away from participation in public life, which grows more and more similar to a popularity contest or Miss America pageant. It opens up what Sennett calls the "tyrannies of intimacy," by proceeding from the wrong assumption that impersonality is a bad thing. Under many circumstances, Sennett argues, impersonality is appropriate and necessary for civic virtue.

Robert Bellah (Bellah et al., 1985) views the problem slightly differently, proceeding as he does in a direct line of thinking from Tocqueville through Durkheim. The problem he sees is a conflict between individualism and commitment in American life, the same conflict Tocqueville remarked on a century and a half ago. On the one hand, liberal democracy offers more opportunity for personal freedom and self-fulfillment than any system yet devised. On the other hand, it creates a sense of normlessness, fluidity, and detachment from others that makes social cohesion difficult.

To what should a person commit him or herself in such a fluid society of infinite possibilities? How much of one's own time, money, and affection should a person contribute to the general good? And through what means should this investment of personal freedom be made—as taxpayer, concerned citizen, professional activist, or otherwise? Finally, what values will justify this involvement in public life and make it seem worthwhile? Is there a value system that all Americans could share that would motivate their commitment to the society?

If these questions seem large and vague, consider them in relation to a particular community. What do people owe their neighbors, and why do they owe it? What will they gain from involving themselves in the lives of these people, or lose by failing to do so? That is, how is good-neighboring and public responsibility still—as a century and a half ago—"the principle of self-interest rightly understood"? Can we show that people are most satisfied with life when their neighbors are also satisfied?

Evidence suggests that personal well-being is, indeed, tied up with communal well-being. Of all neighborhood characteristics, the things that people feel most satisfied about—their neighbors and other homes and buildings in the neighborhood—are the most highly and significantly correlated with neighborhood satisfaction. Campbell finds that "satisfaction with neighborhood is most strongly determined by the individual's perception of the condition of the neighborhood housing, of the friendliness of its residents, of its security from criminals, and of the convenience to work and shopping" (Campbell, 1980: 156–57).

Neighborliness is important to neighborhood satisfaction. Neighborhood satisfaction is lowest in large cities, because people move in and out too quickly to become neighborly.

If you want to be satisfied with your neighborhood, you should choose a place where you are likely to be satisfied with your neighbors. Choose neighbors who are socially and culturally like you and a neighborhood that is relatively stable, where you can get to know them. Not only are people who live near others like themselves more satisfied with their neighborhood, they are more satisfied with life overall.

People are slightly less satisfied with their house or apartment than they are with their neighborhood as a whole. Homeowners are generally more satisfied with their dwelling than home-renters. And *young* home-owners are especially satisfied with their dwelling. Owning rather than renting your home is especially gratifying when you are young. "Whether it is pride of ownership, sense of security, feeling of status, or some other psychological need that is fulfilled by the fact of owning one's home, there is no doubt that owners are more satisfied than renters, both in this country and elsewhere" (Campbell, 1980: 158).

All these location satisfactions—city, neighborhood, and dwelling—are significantly correlated with overall life satisfaction. But neighborhood satisfaction affects life satisfaction twice as strongly as dwelling satisfaction and city satisfaction do. The advice these data suggest? Buy a modest house in a neighborhood you love, rather than renting (or buying) a fancier place in a neighborhood or city you hate; and do it when you are young enough to enjoy it.

Why are people so satisfied with their locations and accompanying lifestyles? Few people want to live in high-rise apartments. Yet even apartment-dwelling families are satisfied because they expect to move eventually. Their difficulties are only temporary and, therefore, can be tolerated; people know they will make changes in the future (Michelson, 1977).

Locational expectations *are* eventually fulfilled, and most people end up getting more or less what they expected. People accommodate to temporary difficulties, while waiting for a future that is likely to arrive. Many life satisfactions are like that, which explains why so many people are satisfied with life.

CONCLUDING REMARKS

In choosing where to live, people probably come a lot closer to getting what they wanted than in many other areas of life. It is easier to continue changing locations over the life course than to continue changing educations, careers, marriages, or parental statuses.

Of course, many factors influence where you choose to live. They include where your work is located, where your spouse wants to live, what you can afford, and a variety of social and cultural barriers (for example, incomplete information and involuntary segregation). Campbell (1980) remarks, "We have a remarkable ability to adapt to the peculiarities of our environment and . . . most of us can learn to live with the situation we find ourselves in. We not only live with it, we can be satisfied with it" (p. 159).

But many people do not have to permanently adjust to where they live. They keep moving so that, gradually, they come as close as they ever can to the "good life" they dream about. Modern people use their time and money to create satisfactory lifestyles in idiosyncratic ways. As opportunity and variety increase, so does the possibility for a unique, personal combination of living conditions. Where and how you live are perhaps the most tailor-made of all your major life choices.

Do people get what they want out of location and lifestyle? To a large degree they do. People change locations and lifestyles quite frequently during their lives and express satisfaction with the results of their movements. Often these moves—for example, from a downtown apartment to a suburban single-family home—are motivated by a life-cycle change and the expectations people have of the kind of life they will be able to lead in a new location. But "What satisfies families in high-rise apartments in the short run is not what would satisfy them in the long run, nor in the short run either if they could not move elsewhere in the long run" (Michelson, 1977: 365). People are pulled forward by dreams.

Yet people's dreams and desires are also shaped by their experiences. So, for example, people who have stayed in or drifted back to high-rise apartments, after expressing an earlier desire for a suburban move, have now come to desire remaining downtown (Michelson, 1977: 335). People's actions are strongly influenced by factors only partly within their control (for example, aging and life-cycle changes) or well beyond their control (for example, social class, the availability of work and housing, and spouse's and children's desires). The consistently best predictors of residential mobility are macroeconomic changes in society—changes in the availability of jobs and housing. This explains Americans' continuing shift westward and toward the Sunbelt.

But people learn to want what they get. Many who were driven or lured to a new location by economic opportunity develop a fierce loyalty to that region, city, or neighborhood. People who have given up one thoroughly enjoyed lifestyle develop a strong liking for their new lifestyle. Lifestyles based in particular locations are often "subcultures," supplying people with a great deal of "meaning" as well as enjoyment.

The patterns of return migration by rural people, and by foreign-born migrants to their home country, suggest that economic opportunities and local lifestyles may not be enough to keep people where they have come to live. Others stay but hive themselves off from the local lifestyle through residential segregation. But these are the exceptions, not the rule. Most migrants do stay, and the longer they stay, the more they assimilate into the local lifestyle.

We now examine the problem of a gap between what you want and what you get, and draw some general conclusions from the findings presented in this book.

REFERENCES

ALLEN, J. P. & TURNER, E. J. (1988). Where to find the new immigrants. *American Demographics,* September, 22–27.

BELLAH, R., MADSEN, R., SULLIVAN, W. M., SWIDLER, A. & TIPTON, S. (1985). *Habits of the heart: Individualism and commitment in American life.* Berkeley: University of California Press.

BOORSTIN, D. (1973). *The Americans: The democratic experience.* New York: Random House.

CAMPBELL, A. (1980). *The sense of well-being in America: Recent patterns and trends.* New York: McGraw-Hill.

DAVIS, A., GARDNER, B. & GARDNER, M. (1941). *Deep south: A social anthropological study of caste and class.* Chicago: University of Chicago Press.

EWEN, S. (1976). *Captains of consciousness: Advertising and the social roots of the consumer culture.* New York: McGraw-Hill.

FUSSELL, P. (1983) *Class.* New York: Ballantine Books.

GARREAU, J. (1981). *The nine nations of North America.* New York: Avon Books.

JACKSON, G., MASNICK, G., BOULTON, R., BARTLETT, S. & PITKIN, J. (1981). *Regional diversity: Growth in the U.S., 1960–1990.* Joint Center for Urban Studies of the Massachusetts Institute of Technology and Harvard University.

JAHER, F. C. (1982). *The urban establishment: Upper strata in Boston, New York, Charleston, Chicago, and Los Angeles.* Urbana: University of Illinois.

MICHELSON, W. (1977). *Environmental choice, human behavior, and residential satisfaction.* New York: Oxford University Press.

————. (1985). *From sun to sun: Daily obligations and community structure in the lives of employed mothers and their families.* Totowa, N.J.: Rowman & Allanheld.

MITCHELL, A. (1983). *The nine American lifestyles: Who we are and where we are going.* New York: Warner Books.

RAINWATER, L., COLEMAN, R. P., & HANDEL, G. (1962). *Workingman's wife: Her personality, world, and life style.* New York: Macfadden-Bartell Books.

REED, P. (1976). *Life style as an element of social logic: Patterns of activity, social characteristics and residential choice.* Unpublished doctoral dissertation, University of Toronto, Department of Sociology.

RICHE, M. F. (1988). The post-marital society. *American Demographics,* November 23–26, 60.

ROBINSON, J. P. & CONVERSE, P. E. (1972). The impact of television on mass media usage: A cross-national comparison. In A. Szalai (Ed.), *The use of time: Daily activities of urban and suburban populations in twelve countries.* The Hague: Mouton.

ROBINSON, J. P., CONVERSE, P. E. & SZALAI, A. (1973). Everyday life in twelve countries. In A. Szalai (Ed.), *The use of time: Daily activities of urban and suburban populations in twelve countries* (pp. 113–144). The Hague: Mouton.

RUBIN, N. (1982). *The new suburban woman.* New York: Coward, McCann, and Geoghegan.

RUSSELL, C. & EXETER, T. G. (1986). America at mid-decade. *American Demographics,* January, 22–29.

————. (1989). All our children. *American Demographics,* May, 34–37.

SCHWARTZ, J. (1987). Family traditions. *American Demographics,* March, 58, 60.

SENNETT, R. (1978). *The fall of public man.* New York: Vintage Books.

SZALAI, A. (ED.). (1972). *The use of time: Daily activities of urban and suburban populations in twelve countries.* The Hague: Mouton.

TOCQUEVILLE, A. DE. (1945). *Democracy in America.* (2 Vols.) New York: Vintage Books. (Original work published in 1833.)

VARGA, K. (1972). Marital cohesion as reflected in time budgets. In A. Szalai (Ed.), *The use of time: Daily activities of urban and suburban populations in twelve countries* (pp. 357–76). The Hague: Mouton.

VEBLEN, T. (1934). *The theory of the leisure class.* New York: Modern Library.

VEENHOVEN, R. (1984). *Conditions of happiness.* Dordrecht, Holland: Reidel Publishing.

WARNER, L. W., MEEKER, M., & ELLS, K. (1960). *Social class in America.* New York: Harper Torchbooks.

WEISS, M. J. (1988). *The clustering of America.* New York: A Tilden Press Book, Harper and Row.

CHAPTER EIGHT

WHAT YOU WANT
AND GET:
Closing the Gap

RECAPITULATION

This book has argued that desires are patterned: different kinds of people want different things out of life. Life satisfaction is also patterned: some kinds of people are more satisfied than others. Further, satisfactions with particular domains are also patterned: some people get the most life satisfaction from their work, others from their marriage, and so on.

This patterning proves that social science has something to teach us about the conduct of everyday life. Without patterning, we could not hope to explain people's values, feelings, and behaviours. If explanation were impossible, the management of our feelings and behaviours would also be impossible. Then advice to choose in one way rather than another would be useless, since choice and change would not lie within our grasp.

But some choice and change *are* within our grasp, if we understand the forces that shape our lives, that make the patterns we observe. This book has discussed a variety of forces that shape our satisfaction with life in general and within particular life domains. Further, it has revealed two main problems people encounter in their search for satisfaction: downward accommodation, or the willingness to settle for a Fool's Paradise, and an inability to close the gap between what they want and what they get.

Fool's Paradise

Many people live in a Fool's Paradise. For these people, key elements in achieving satisfaction are conformity to the dominant cultural goals (that is, common or unextraordinary wants), limited information, low expectations, and having as much as the next person.

These people find conformity satisfying in itself. The less they know about the choices available to them, the higher their satisfaction rises. Other things being equal, their ignorance is blissful. The lower their aspirations (wants) fall, the less often a gap opens up between their aspirations and achievements. They know little about alternative possible lives, so they can be happy with their own lives.

It is easy to get into Fool's Paradise. For many, it is simply part of the "pragmatic acceptance" of inequality that we discussed earlier, in relation to "incapacitation" (Chapter 2). What we want out of life and get out of life is beyond our control, largely determined by our position in the class structure. Other factors, such as age, education, and gender also play a role. In general, everyday experiences make it likely we will know little, want little, get little. So we learn to value what we *do* get.

Social class is more influential in some areas of choice than others. Educational and career choices are obviously tied to class of origin. Marriage is less strongly tied to class of origin, but typically people marry within their own social class. Parenting behaviour is even more distantly related to social class of origin; but given the costs of bearing and raising children, the experience of parenthood will be very different for people of different social classes. Finally, where and how you live are also related to social class.

In each of these areas, what we get and what we want out of life are often well matched. Social class both limits what we are likely to get and prepares us for this by limiting what we are likely to want. As a result, most adults have limited—and in a sense, realistic—aspirations based on well-founded expectations about likely events and circumstances. When life disappoints them, people make small changes and lower their aspirations. They divert their attention from what they do not have to what they do. They find substitute satisfactions rather than fixate on what is missing.

Because of this fit between what they want and what they get, and the resulting "pragmatic acceptance," most people are unlikely to fight for major social changes that might give them more of what they had started out wanting. A lack of politicization is common even among the most deprived—the poor and unemployed, for example. This is another way in which the class structure perpetuates itself.

However, many people *are* aware of a gap between what they want and what they get. They are not in a Fool's Paradise, yet seem unable to do anything about it. They face the second of two problems we must discuss.

Inability to Close the Gap

Two kinds of dissatisfaction or unhappiness might be called Real Hell and Fool's Hell (Michalos, 1987: 45).

Fool's Hell is a state of dissatisfaction or unhappiness based on poorly founded information. Othello is miserable because he believes, incorrectly, that Desdemona has been unfaithful. "Joe" is miserable because he thinks his large nose is preventing him from getting dates with beautiful women. "Sally" is miserable because she thinks an off-colour story she told at work is going to hinder her chances for promotion. "Alfred" is miserable because he thinks he might have a serious medical problem but is afraid to see a doctor, to find out if he is right.

Each of these people in Fool's Hell is a little bit tragic and a little bit ridiculous. Each is unhappy but could be happier, even happy, by getting accurate information about some matter of vital importance. Instead, they remain unhappy and, worse, may take actions that end up making them even unhappier. The unwisdom of staying in Fool's Hell needs little further discussion.

Real Hell is a different kettle of fish. Consider the well-informed political radical who has spent a lifetime fighting injustice, yet sees that much injustice remains. That person has good reason to feel dissatisfied or unhappy with the state of the world and peoples' failure to improve it substantially. Yet there is also reason to feel satisfied for having fought to the limit of his/her capacities in a good cause. Will that person accept the seemingly inevitable and become satisfied with what has been accomplished, rather than remaining dissatisfied with what has *not* been accomplished? Or will that person fight on, in hopes of trading Real Hell for Real Paradise?

Many of the same class-based factors that limit what you get out of life—closure, incapacitation, and decoupling—limit your ability to close the gap between what you want and what you get. Closure denies the most deprived resources for an assault on the social order. The poorest in any society lack the money and organization to mobilize against the rich. Incapacitation denies the most deprived a sense of competence they need for the sustained attack on a more powerful foe. Decoupling denies them the channels of informal influence through which they might seek major changes more subtly than by frontal assault.

Thus, the very means by which the rich and powerful get what they want—by class closure, a sense of political competence and efficacy, and wide contacts with others in positions of power and authority—are least available to the poor in our own and other industrial societies.

Encompassing, sustaining, and reproducing this inequality is a world view, or ideology, that supports the way things are. The observed fit between what people want and what they get sustains a belief that people get what they want out of life. This liberal ideology blames the victims: it holds people responsible for what they do not get and treats the privileged as though they were rewarded for personal merit. By this reckoning, the deprived deserve their plight because they have failed to organize their lives properly—failed to get the right education, the right job, the right marriage, and so on.

Of course, many people *do* organize their lives badly and suffer for it. Yet many rich people who organize their lives badly are less likely to suffer for it. Further, even the most effective personal organization is only a temporary solution to the problem of unequal opportunity in our society. Much more important than personal organization in determining life outcomes is unequal opportunity. As we have seen, this results from a class structure that starts people at vastly different levels of competitiveness. Thus, in the long run, the solution to dissatisfaction and hardship must be sought through changes to the class structure, not better personal organization.

So this book does not argue for accommodation to a Fool's Paradise, nor for strenuous individual solutions which, in the long run, cannot solve the problem most of us face. It argues instead for a Real Paradise. You will remember that, in a Real Paradise, people seek the best information about what is possible, push the possible to its limit, and try to live with the result. This book supports the old maxim that "Man (sic) is the measure of all things," which means that people should idealize what is possible, not imaginary, then seek the ideal.

So far as we can tell, what is possible is what *is*, what *has been*, and what shows signs of *becoming*. A systematic understanding of the past and present is key to understanding and acting upon the future. Our understanding of what is possible will undoubtedly change with time and new evidence. But present evidence, though incomplete and imperfect, is better than ignorance.

Before considering the more effective collective solutions, we shall examine individual solutions to a gap between what people want and what people get.

Individual Solutions

In chapter after chapter, we have found no simple answer to the question, Do people get what they want, or do they learn to want what they get? In most cases, the answer is mixed. Generally people get some of what they wanted, and what they wanted is shaped by social structure—hence, by what they were likely to get anyway. In that sense, choice is illusory.

But it is not just an illusion. People do make many important choices in life—what kind of career to pursue, whether and whom to marry, whether to have children, where and how to live, and so on. Even in so restricted a domain as education, choice exists. Socioeconomic status, gender, and residence are powerful determinants of educational attainment. But even if half of the education a person actually gets is statistically explained by these powerful forces, another half is not.

Many other factors shape educational choice, each exerting a very small influence. Beyond that, an area of uncertainty and idiosyncrasy remains. Sociologist Christopher Jencks calls this region "luck," for lack of a better word. Some people are lucky enough to get profitable, satisfying, or good outcomes, however we want to measure them.

At present, we cannot say that people generally get what they want or generally do not. We must study the issue domain by domain, issue by issue. Likewise, we cannot validly generalize about whether people typically learn to want what they get. Previous chapters have shown that sometimes people learn to want what they get—the love people feel for a mate, child, or place of residence illustrates this—and sometimes they do not—job dissatisfaction and divorce illustrate that. In every realm, people accommodate as they get older; but even this is only a tendency, not a certainty.

Other factors also affect the ways people adapt. For example, some people have less opportunity to change situations, rather than accommodate. A woman with several young children and few job skills will find it harder to leave a bad marriage than adapt to it, for example, though neither solution is highly satisfying. Further, some personalities will prove more adaptable than others. People with a strong sense of mastery and control over their environment will find it easier to adapt to a situation *or* change it than people who feel powerless, alienated, and without choice. Again, we are far from knowing all of the factors that influence people's ability to want what they get, or to change it.

But on one matter the evidence is less ambiguous. Most people are only moderately satisfied with their lives, in whole or in part: they are not in a Paradise of any kind. Either they have not gotten all they wanted, or have not learned to want all they have gotten. If we were to examine an average person's life cycle, we would surely find periods of nonaccommodation. Probably most people fall out of accommodation at some times in their lives. And some people—strong political conservatives or radicals, for example—are likely to go through all of their adult lives in a state of nonaccommodation, or Real Hell. What do these unaccommodated do about it?

Proposal One: Merton's Contribution   American sociologist Robert Merton (1957a) redefined Durkheim's (1893, 1897) concept of *anomie* to analyse the consequences of a gap, or disjuncture, between what people want and what they can get by legitimate means. Considering anomie a result of the disjuncture between "culture goals" and "institutionalized means," Merton examined the variety of "modes of individual adaptation" to this problem.

Merton argued that Americans are faced with the demand that they accept society's culture goals, especially the goal of material success. People are raised to value success very highly and to evaluate themselves and others in terms of the material success they achieve in life. And for some, the conforming or "institutionalized" roads to success—a higher education and a job or career, chief among them—are open for travel and lead to suitable rewards.

For others—the one in nine who descended from black slaves or the one in two who could not vote until two decades into this century, to name two—equal opportunity in the competition for material success has been slow in coming. Job discrimination and unequal access to higher education persist today, in the United States as in Canada. How do people adapt to the inadequacy of "institutionalized means"?

Logically, only so many adaptations are possible. People might continue to accept both the culture goals and institutionalized means—to conform to social expectations even if they are not paying off. Or they might retain a belief in the culture goals while rejecting the institutionalized means: Merton called these adaptors "innovators." Instead, they might reject the culture goals but retain a belief in the institutionalized means: if so, they are "ritualists." Further, they might reject both the culture goals *and* institutionalized means, becoming "retreatists." Finally, they might replace both the culture goals and institutionalized means with substitute goals and means—doing so made them "rebels," in Merton's terms.

Merton's often-cited analysis documents each type of adaptation and its various forms—for example, the innovator as robber baron and racketeer, the ritualist as bureaucrat, the retreatist as tramp and drug addict, the rebel as political activist.

Merton (1957: 220–24) recognizes that multiple goals exist within a given individual, significant subcultures exist within the population as a whole, and multiple legitimate or nearly legitimate ways of "making it" are accepted in American society. It is this very complexity, and the lack of

CHART 8.1 Merton's Typology of Adaptations to Anomie (Source: Merton, 1957a.)

Modes of Adaptation	Culture Goals	Institutionalized Means
I. Conformity	+	+
II. Innovation	+	−
III. Ritualism	−	+
IV. Retreatism	−	−
V. Rebellion	±	±

theory about how some goals prevail over others, that leads Merton to focus on material goals. Regrettably, many users of his theory have misinterpreted Merton's subtlety, with unfortunate results.

This problem was demonstrated most dramatically when American social scientists Richard Cloward and Lloyd Ohlin (1960), building on Merton's theory, suggested dealing with youth crime by offering poor young people more access to legitimate means of upward mobility. Put into practice by a series of social programs in the 1960s, their interpretation was invalidated by the evidence that many poor young people did not seem to want the lives being offered them. Other goals—excitement, pleasure, risk-taking—beckoned; other means of getting by were more appealing than a nine-to-five job.

This and other research on subcultures has suggested that people are motivated by a variety of goals, not merely material success by means of an Anglo-Saxon middle-class lifestyle. Even in the United States, material success is not everything to everyone. Many people prefer family, romance, and community life. Emphasizing American culture's tendency to "place a high premium on economic affluence and social ascent for all its members" (Merton, 1957: 221) makes it harder for us to understand rebellion, conflict, and change, except as responses to limited opportunity for material advancement.

Many would claim that the popular movements of the last thirty years—the civil rights marchers, black city burners, antiwar protestors, women's liberationists, gay rights activists, native peoples, environmentalists, and others—were actually concerned with justice, human dignity, and the future of humanity. Too narrow an understanding of "anomie" gives us nothing to explain why these things happened, or when they did, or how they did, or who participated—often, white middle-class college students, with a stake in conformity—and with what result for the individuals involved or for society.

A single-minded focus on material goals also produces a moral equivalence between robber barons and alcoholics, racketeers and civil rights marchers. Saints and mass murderers are "the same" because they are both deviant, both adaptors to anomie. This viewpoint completely misses the hidden dynamic—the reason one person becomes a saint and the other a mass murderer. And it fails to explain how Martin Luther King's "adaptation to anomie" helped to change American society but Charles Manson's did not.

In short, it fails to distinguish between *nonconformers*, who "are trying to make justice a social reality" and *aberrants*, who secretly violate norms they consider legitimate, in order to advance their own interests (Merton, 1966: 810).

Finally, social life today—whether conformist, ritualist, retreatist, innovative, or rebellious—is increasingly collective life. The chief actors in a large, modern society—the actors-out of anomie and seekers of remedies—are organized groups. Merton even hints at this when he observes that nonconformists "have at least the prospect of obtaining the assent of other members of society whose ambivalence toward the current structure can be drawn upon for support" (Merton, 1966: 810).

Proposal Two: Westhues's Contribution   A recent formulation by Canadian sociologist Kenneth Westhues (1982) deals with many of the flaws by standing Merton's theory on its head. Unlike Merton, Westhues sees conformity, not deviance, as the problem that needs solving. Merton sees people as needing better chances for reward through conformity; and for Merton, a more stable society is the goal. Westhues believes people need more chances for nonconformity. Seeing "vice in conformity, virtue in deviance," more social justice is Westhues's goal. Thus Westhues equates deviance with "liberation," implying that our society is enslaved and conformity is the shape of that slavery.

At first glance, this reformulation of Merton's theory is just as easily dismissed. Surely, deviance per se is no better than conformity per se, and change is no better than persistence. To argue otherwise is to imply that there is nothing worth preserving in our society, just as to hold Merton's position is to imply that there is nothing wrong with it. Each extreme oversimplifies our picture of society.

Westhues does remedy some of the flaws in Merton's theory, though. First, his analysis is less focused on material success than Merton's. Second, his analysis is more complex. For example, Westhues's typology of "generic forms of liberation, or deviance" contains eight types of nonconformity, not four as in Merton's model. It distinguishes between types of liberation that (1) retreat from expectations or attack them; (2) individuals or groups try to carry out; and (3) deviate mildly or severely from conformity.

The basic condition for conformity, innovation, deviation, or liberation—all equated by Westhues—is a gap between previous learning and present experience. Old ideas, expectations, and practices fail to serve people well in the new situation. Ten secondary conditions evidently contribute to or create this gap: migration, membership in a deprived class, class mobility, intermarriage, social dislocation, Jewish identity, liberal schooling, intellectual occupations, a diverse environment, and catastrophe.

CHART 8.2 Westhues's Typology of Forms of Liberation, or Deviance (Source: Westhues, 1981.)

Degree	Withdrawal		Attack	
	Individual	*Collective*	*Individual*	*Collective*
Mild	Sleeping on the job	Escapist entertainment	Personal twists and new wrinkles in the performance of conventional roles	Fads, crazes
	Daydreams, fantasies	Sectarian religion		Under capitalism, marginally new products of private companies
	Loafing	Cults		
	Media opiates		"I'll do it my way"	Reformist social movements
	Occasional drunkenness		Minor innovations	
	Marijuana smoking			
	Many illnesses			
Severe	Refusing to settle down	Countercultural movements	Invention in science and technology	Under capitalism, major new products of private companies
	A hermit's life	Utopian communities	Boldly original art	
	Habitual drunkenness		New philosophic work	Revolutionary social movements
	Narcotic addiction		New forms of human organization	Mass migrations
	Psychosis		Religious prophecy	
	Suicide			

The outlets people choose for expressing discontent are conditioned by three main principles in Westhues's scheme: (1) people withdraw when they cannot attack; (2) signs of weakening invite attack; and (3) the available tools condition how people misbehave.

Westhues points to one central strain in our system—the value placed on creativity (a cultural goal) and the limited, diminished, and diminishing opportunity for innovation (Westhues, 1982: 463). We gear our children up to create, then capitalism denies most of them the legitimate opportunity to do so. No wonder they go to shopping malls and get into trouble, Westhues laments. Evidently, Westhues has taken Merton's framework and substituted "creativity" for "material success" as the chief motivating force, the goal everyone wants to maximize. (Class structure remains the central factor limiting access to legitimate means of attaining the culture goal.)

In making this transition, Westhues's work assumes two of the problems discussed earlier: the assumed uniformity of goals and the moral equivalence of wonderful innovating acts (for example, polio vaccine) and horrible innovating acts (for example, deathcamps). Perhaps creativity (read also, deviance and innovation) really is a more elevated goal than material success. Still, the research we reviewed earlier shows that neither is a prime determinant—a major life concern—of adult Americans.

But Westhues has taken us further, nonetheless. First, he has extended our understanding of the conditions that promote (or free up) nonconforming behaviour, specifying the groups and situations in society that are particularly likely to spawn nonconformity. We still lack knowledge of the social–psychological process that makes one person innovate, while another in the same situation conforms.

More important, Westhues emphasizes the difference between individual and collective acts of nonconformity. Collective mobilization is not only a condition under which individuals can each act with greater effect, it enables different kinds of nonconforming behaviour. Social movements, cults, and experimental communities are qualitatively different from individual adaptations to anomie; and they also carry a greater potential for changing society.

However, Westhues ultimately fails because he focuses on a single goal he assumes people are trying to attain. This makes his analysis less than completely helpful for people whose goal is not deviance and creativity in its own right.

Proposal Three: Various Individual Solutions Chapter 2 introduced four concepts—closure, incapacitation, decoupling, and scarcity—to explain the limits on people's opportunity. Remedies for these limitations fall into two categories, individual and collective, as we have seen. These remedies can be applied to closing any gap between wants and achievements you may be encountering. They do not presuppose a particular want, as Merton's and Westhues's analyses have done. However, limited space does not permit a full discussion of the way each remedy applies to each problem of dissatisfaction. You will have to translate these solutions to your own problems yourself. What follows are merely examples.

As an individual, you do best to solve the problem of *closure* by getting whatever credentials allow entry into the group you hope to spend your life in. Chapter 3 showed that higher education is the single best investment you can make, if your goals are material, and perhaps even if they are creative.

However, Chapter 2 showed that racial and ethnic discrimination continues to limit people's opportunity to gain entry into many lines of activity. For example, members of discriminated-against groups may not do as well in work settings controlled by other ethnic groups as they would by remaining within their own ethnic community, even with less education. The decision to be made here, a complex one, depends on several factors: (1) the actual extent of discrimination against your ethnic or racial group; (2) the probability of a significant reduction in that discrimination during your lifetime; (3) the range of attractive occupational opportunities within your own racial or ethnic community; and (4) the probability of a significant increase in occupational opportunities within your group during your lifetime.

Alone, you can do little to influence any of these factors. As an individual you can only choose between getting a higher education (and possibly cutting yourself off from your ethnic community), or getting less education (and cultivating the ties to your ethnic community). The first choice risks discrimination outside the community; the second, more limited opportunities for career selection and advancement within the community. Your contribution to a collective solution, to be discussed shortly, will be much more important.

You can solve the problem of personal *incapacitation* by changing the way you think about yourself—not an easy task, but one that a great many people manage to accomplish. This is partly what the major social movements of our times—women's liberation, native rights, and gay rights among others—are all about. Learn more about the history of your incapacitation as the member of a despised or belittled group. Discuss this condition with others, find mentors, and seek role models—people who are otherwise just like you (women or native peoples, or gays, say) who have done what others lead you to believe you cannot do. Most important of all, reject the victim-blaming ideology that you may be whipping yourself with. You have enough problems without being your own worst enemy.

Again, individual solutions are less likely to succeed than collective ones. For people to see that women, for example, can succeed in activities previously believed to be outside their competence requires that women be given a chance. Forcing open new opportunities often requires collective mobilization by the excluded group. Again, personally contributing to a collective solution may be the most important thing you can do, though admittedly results may take a long time in coming.

You solve the problem of *decoupling* by cultivating and making use of your social networks. This is the way people find good jobs (Chapter 2) and sometimes also mates (Chapter 5). To improve the size and heterogeneity of your network, you need to acquaint yourself with people who have larger and "better" networks—people who are themselves mobile and widely acquainted, are (typically) higher status, or operate within institutions that encourage interpersonal contact.

Social institutions that break down traditional gender, class, and ethnic barriers to interpersonal contact include institutions of higher education and government. Thus, higher education and involvement in civic affairs are doubly beneficial, they allow both self-improvement and increased connection with others. Unfortunately, both higher education and civic involvement sometimes run counter to the goals of participation in your own little community, especially if that community is institutionally complete. Here wrong individual choices are potentially most costly. Try being a "cosmopolitan" member of your community, with feet in both camps (Merton, 1957b). This connects both you and your community into the larger, outside networks of influence and opportunity.

Finally, you cope individually with real *scarcity* by helping to produce more of what people need; adjusting your thinking downward from the imaginary to the possible; and creatively seeking alternatives to scarce goods. It is the human ability to do this that has kept our species alive for a million years.

The danger here lies in confusing scarcity with maldistribution, considering scarcity beyond remedy, or lowering our heads rather than raising the bridge. The French demographer Alfred Sauvy (1969: 391) has called this excessively accommodative approach the "Malthusian Spirit . . . a state of mind characterized by the fear of excess—faced with two quantities that need adjusting, it tends to lower the highest instead of boosting the lowest. It is the opposite of courage and generosity." The "Malthusian" is a person who, facing a dinner party with too little food for the guests, wants to get rid of guests rather than get more food.

If apparent scarcity is really maldistribution, or a temporary shortage that could be remedied through innovation and higher productivity, collective remedies are called for. But such collective remedies will call for individual commitments to collective solutions and a patient acceptance of the effects these solutions will have on individual lives.

Collective Solutions

We have repeatedly claimed the superiority of collective solutions to individual solutions. An ideal collective solution will have two main characteristics: (1) It will operate within the realm of the truly possible; and (2) It will tie the advancement of collective well-being to the advancement of individual well-being.

As we have stressed repeatedly, only the realm of the possible is of interest to sociology. One of the earliest social scientists, Thomas Malthus, states my position in the following way: "A writer may tell me that he thinks man will ultimately become an ostrich. I cannot properly contradict him . . . (but) till the probability of so wonderful a conversion can be shown, it is surely lost time and lost eloquence to expatiate on the happiness of man in such a state" (Malthus, 1798). And so it is with all solutions social science might propose: we must leave poetry to the poets, fantasy to the dreamers, and consider only what seems truly possible.

As to the second criterion, we should give greatest emphasis to solutions that simultaneously serve both individual actors and the collectivity. Only solutions that serve the collective interest are likely to endure, but only solutions that promise to increase individual well-being are likely to motivate strong individual effort over the long haul. Ideally, then, solutions that serve both will produce the most change, the most benefit, and will survive.

Let us now consider some proposals for collectively solving the problems raised in this book.

Proposal One: Marx's Contribution   Most religions teach that humble aspirations (goals) are the best way of dealing with life in this world: greater rewards will come in the next life. Such humility allows the most religious people in our society to get the most satisfaction out of life (*Quality of Life*, 1981). But this kind of accommodation to inequality led Karl Marx to call religion the "opiate of the masses." An opiate dulls the pain of living; and under certain hopeless conditions, taking opiates is the only sensible course of action.

Marx held that religious opiates are not really necessary—indeed, are counterproductive—because hopelessness about the future is unwarranted. He argued that all history is the record of struggles that overturned the ruling classes or ruined the contenders in the process. Better the brief pain associated with revolution—something like the pain of giving birth—than the drawn-out pain of living in an unjust, alienating society, he argued.

Marx (1955) held that a revolution that eliminates ruling classes forever by eliminating private property—by putting the means of production in the hands of the State—would bring better conditions for all. With the eventual "withering away of the State," Communism would end history as we have known it, for it would end social classes and class conflict.

There are two problems with his formulation—one logical, the other empirical. First, a reading of history that shows that every society of any size has had a class structure and ruling class would *not* lead sociologists to the confident conclusion that a society with no class structure and no ruling class is truly possible. Rather, it would lead in the opposite direction—in the direction perhaps most often associated with the name of Robert Michels (1962) who enunciated the "iron law of oligarchy."

This principle, based on a socialist's study of the German socialist party—a sympathetic observer studying a radically democratic organization—holds that in every social grouping a dominant group will struggle to perpetuate its power, whatever its original ideology. That is, inequality is inevitable in human groupings, whatever their size or the members' ideology.

Empirically, Michels's "iron law" has not proved quite unbreakable. For example, a sociological study of the International Typographers Union, a democratic printer's union in the United States, has revealed some of the conditions under which oligarchy can be prevented or minimized (Lipset, Trow, & Coleman, 1963). So not every organization or society need be oligarchic. Yet the oligarchic organizations in our own society and elsewhere far outnumber the democratic ones. At best, we can only allow the chance that Marx was right about the possibility of a fully democratic society. It remains far from a foregone conclusion.

Second, the premise that history can end with a democratic class-free society is also thrown into doubt by a lack of evidence that communist revolutions have actually succeeded in bringing such a society about. In the century since Marx's *Communist Manifesto*, a number of groups have experimented with communism. Some attempts have been utopian or anarchistic, based in a small community or region (cf. Kanter, 1972; Hobsbawn, 1959). Except for Israeli kibbutzim and Hutterite communities, they have all failed or been overturned after varying periods of time, for a variety of reasons—an insufficient material base, inadequate planning, demographic pressures within, and attacks from outside, among them. Even the relatively successful kibbutzim and Hutterite communities have suffered serious losses of population, due to defections by native borns.

Other attempts have been more thorough. But contrary to Marx's expectation that revolutions would bring equality, they have produced new kinds of inequality. Whether the new inequalities are wider or narrower, more or less benevolent, than those they replaced must be studied case by case—in the Soviet Union, China, Albania, Cuba, Viet Nam, and so on. In every case, however, rule based on ownership of the means of production has been replaced by political and bureaucratic control.

In many cases, communism has greatly reduced material inequality and the worst effects of such inequality. The inequality that remains—

rule by a political elite, or "vanguard of the proletariat" as Lenin called it—may only be temporary. It may end when the people have fully accepted socialist goals and no longer seek to subvert communism. Moreover, the tight control government exercises in such societies may be a response to efforts made by capitalist nations to overthrow communism.

The communist alternative has proved more attractive in some parts of the world than in others. In particular, the potential benefits of capitalism and liberalism have meant little to most twentieth-century Third World peoples. They consider European nations unsuitable models to emulate, since they carry the stigma of colonialism. Further, "free enterprise" seems less likely to succeed quickly and painlessly in the Third World than large-scale economic planning. "One of the outstanding attractions of communism to Asian and African eyes was that it offered the underdeveloped peoples a blueprint for development" (Barraclough, 1967: 223).

On the other hand, some would argue that material inequality can be significantly reduced without communism, as it has been in the democratic socialist countries of Scandinavia, and, to a smaller degree, within certain advanced capitalist countries. Moreover, many people in the industrial capitalist countries—and not simply the very rich and powerful—may not want to give up private property in favour of communism. Values justifying acquisitiveness and "free enterprise" seem to appear whenever and wherever personal acquisition becomes possible. People offered the chance for personal acquisition and upward mobility appear, almost without fail, to seize that opportunity.

Finally, many believe the excesses of control under communism are not just temporary. They may be due to an overcentralization of planning and too few countervailing forces within the country. Supporters of liberal democracy argue that an open competition of ideas and interests produces solutions most satisfactory to the largest number.

Political participation by a large middle class and large, highly mobilized interest groups—political parties, consumer groups, women's and native rights groups, and other such associations—prevents uncontested rule in Western countries. Communist societies tend to lack a large middle class and large interest groups that can freely express their opinions. This absence allows political leaders to make potentially dangerous and harmful decisions almost unopposed.

This book has devoted chapter after chapter to showing that liberal democracy does not give people an equal chance to get what they want out of life. So it would be satisfying to believe that communism could do so. However, the current evidence on this question is ambiguous at best. Attaining more satisfaction for more people may be truly possible in American society; and communism may be the best means of doing it. But equally, it may not be. Moreover, the costs in human life of a wrong guess are enormous. People get killed in revolutions. We need much more supporting evidence before we can vote for revolution.

We have been unable to demonstrate that Marx's proposed solutions lie within the realm of the possible, or that they satisfactorily link the advancement of collective and individual interests. But that is not to say that socialist solutions would also fail to meet our needs. Indeed, any solutions that will help to equalize income and power may be beneficial. Let us turn, then, to some truly possible solutions and see whether they meet our requirements.

Proposal Two: Various Collective Solutions In every instance of limited opportunity, wholly individual solutions are available but they are "quick fixes" with temporary effects. Though the process may be difficult and slow, in the long run your ability to get more opportunity is greater as part of a collectivity. But if we rule out the revolutionary option, what remains? Again, what follows is merely schematic. It would be impossible, given the space available, to apply all of these proposed remedies to all of people's varied dissatisfactions.

Two collective solutions to *closure* are truly possible. One is legislation and social action that would make discrimination against people like you more difficult. To bring this about requires banding together with others who are discriminated against, joining forces across social barriers of ethnicity, class, gender, and region where necessary. The result will be a more assimilated, less discriminatory society.

A second solution is to mobilize within your own group—whether class, ethnic, religious, regional and so on—to increase institutional completeness. This has the effect of establishing closure in your own favour to counter the closure that is used against you. It is discrimination on your behalf. Many American groups and regions are using this tactic today.

Not the least of these are class-based political parties, unions, lobbies, and associations. The New Democratic Party, for example, has enjoyed considerable success in promoting legislation that protects workers, consumers, and other relatively powerless groups in society.

Group mobilization that is *not* based on social class is somewhat more problematic. First, it merely escalates the level of intergroup conflict without eliminating the underlying conditions that gave rise to it. Second, it narrows people's field of vision and makes them less available to solve problems that cut across groups—international problems of peace and scarcity, national problems of cultural unity and political or economic independence, and problems of class and gender inequality, among others. By elimination, the first solution—a frontal collective assault on privilege—is the only one that will benefit everyone in the long run.

Incapacitation can be eliminated by education and reeducation; the schools and mass media are key vehicles for such a change. As already noted, the strengthening of individual identities is best done collectively, since nothing changes people's minds more than the evidence that change is possible. The benefits of slow, incremental change are seriously limited (Kanter, 1977). For example, a sole woman given the opportunity to "model" executive capabilities in a large organization is under unusual pressures to succeed "on behalf of all women" and she will be judged by criteria quite unlike those applied to men. Confusion will arise between the unique characteristics of the individual and the characteristics of the "type" she represents.

For this reason, we really do not learn what historically excluded groups can do until we see large numbers of them performing in commonplace, emotionally neutral situations. Achieving this requires legislation that ensures the inclusion of as many of a social "type" as may seek it. Laws against discrimination not only break down traditional structures of closure but also reduce incapacitation and decoupling. Again, such laws will not be passed and enforced without collective mobilization.

Decoupling can be remedied by building bridges among social collectivities that currently have little connection—between racial, ethnic, regional, and occupational groups, for example. Typically, increased communication between the leaders of these collectivities has been the key to success. But anyone can increase connections by participating in broad-based activities and organizations.

Finally, material *scarcity* can be reduced by producing more of what people want and need, which means an international commitment to economic growth and redistribution. In turn, this may mean first breaking the monopolies that restrict productivity as well as sharing.

These proposals for dealing with dissatisfaction are collective (not individual) and firmly rooted in the realm of the truly possible. However, they do not systematically address the question of how people might link the advancement of their own interests with those of society as a whole. Such an approach would be ideal, if we agree with C. Wright Mills that the flip-side of personal troubles are public issues; or, stated otherwise, that personal troubles are shared and socially structured. It is to that question of linkage that we now turn.

Proposal Three: Linking Individual and Collective Solutions Both Merton and Westhues discuss why gaps arise between what people want and what they get. But each discussion ultimately fails because it seeks the single goal people are attempting to attain or, just as bad, each appears to do so. In any event, neither theory helps us understand how, amidst multiple competing goals, a single one will be selected.

Let us consider a different approach that takes satisfaction as the goal to be attained. By its nature, satisfaction is attainable in many ways—individual and collective, short-term and long-term—and in many life domains. All people seek satisfaction but people do not all seek the same satisfactions, much less seek satisfaction in the same ways.

Throughout the book we have discovered gaps between what people want and what they get: call this anomie (following Merton), or a discrepancy between aspirations and achievements (following Michalos). Such gaps produce dissatisfaction which people try to reduce. People seek greater satisfaction by lowering their expectations or raising their achievements, or both; moreover, they can do this individually or collectively.

In some cases accommodation is almost inevitable. No alternative is truly possible, at least at present. For example, we have no means of prolonging human life indefinitely. It would be foolish to remain perpetually dissatisfied over this state of affairs, however distraught we may feel about the expected or experienced death of a loved one. Life must go on. So here the reduction of dissatisfaction through accommodation would be justified, sensible, and moral.

In other cases, nonaccommodating solutions are truly possible. Imagine that your loved one is going to die because you cannot afford costly nursing care and medical treatment. Such care and treatment might prolong life for another ten, twenty, or thirty years; other people's lives *are* being prolonged by such a treatment. Should you accommodate to that situation, in order to reduce your dissatisfaction? If another solution to the problem is truly possible, you should not. Instead you should pursue both individual and collective strategies for changing the situation, not accommodating to it.

Moreover, in some circumstances increasing your satisfaction harms no one else and may even help others. For example, your enjoyment of a sunny day is not diminished by our enjoyment of it. We may even enhance each other's enjoyment. And, your opportunity to find satisfaction as a composer of opera music is not imperilled by our desire to write stories or lyrics, in fact, we can make operas together. In this case, our satisfaction is complementary or symbiotic. In some circumstances, then, individual solutions to the gap between wants and achievements are independent; in others, they are interdependent, maximized through collective effort or cooperation.

But in a great many cases, one person's satisfaction is dependent on someone else's dissatisfaction; this situation is sometimes called a zero-sum game. For every winner there is at least one loser. So, for example, Calabresi (1978) speaks of "tragic choices" in which no solution is equally satisfying for everyone, whatever choice is made. He gives as examples the allocation of scarce medical technology (for example, kidney dialysis machines) to equally needy patients, or the drafting of soldiers into a wartime army.

Since in this circumstance creating a winner means also creating a loser, people engaged in tragic choosing are constantly searching for new, more generally accepted principles of allocation. No principle can succeed in appearing just for long. Yet certain principles are more obviously unjust than others. Almost everyone would agree that allocating scarce life-prolonging equipment, or exempting young people from the military draft, on the basis of income would be unjust. It would amount to a market in lives: the rich live, the poor die. In fact, under conditions of pay-as-you-go medical care and draft exemptions for college students—both of which have obtained in the United States in recent times—such an injustice has prevailed. Not surprisingly, people have sought alternatives.

Obviously it is desirable to find solutions that give the most people the most satisfaction possible, even in zero-sum situations. But can it be done? Imagine the following scenario. You are faced with a dissatisfying gap between what you want and what you are getting. Closing that gap is truly possible. Many strategies for doing so, both individual and collective, are available. Further, imagine that your actions might affect other people's well-being adversely. To improve your well-being unilaterally, you must worsen someone else's well-being. To avoid doing so requires the cooperative search for a solution.

Chart 8.3 displays the logically possible solutions, following Merton's paradigm (see Chart 8.1) in format. But unlike Merton, we are concerned with the possible combinations of individual and collective well-being that various strategies might further.

CHART 8.3 Adaptations to a Gap Between What You Want and Get

	Your strategy furthers . . .	
Adaptation	*Individual Well-being*	*Collective Well-being*
Cooperate	+	+
Sacrifice	−	+
Self-indulge	+	−
Accommodate	−	−
Mythologize	—	—

You may choose to *accommodate*: do nothing—either individually or collectively—about your dissatisfaction. Simply lower your aspirations and get used to wanting what you have gotten.

Another solution is to *mythologize*: lower your aspirations, and maybe even urge others to lower theirs. But do not simply accommodate. Make up elaborate explanations, for yourself and others, about why the current situation is better than any other. Mythologizers do this by denying the importance of well-being in principle, saying "Suffering is good for people." They mystify the character of accommodation, saying "People don't know when they are really well off." And they utter paradoxes to distract attention from the problem at hand, saying things like "Less is really more," "Bad is really good," "The universe is inside you," or "Life is only a dream; reality lies elsewhere."

A third solution is to pursue personal goals at the expense of others; that is to *self-indulge*. This strategy achieves more individual satisfaction but not more, and possibly less, collective satisfaction. There are the same number of winners and losers as before, but now you are a winner and someone else is a loser. More important is the fact that this solution allows the original problem of unequal satisfaction—whether due to scarcity or maldistribution—to remain unchallenged. Someone else will have to challenge and change it, or others will continue to suffer from it.

In fact, we can distinguish two kinds of self-indulgence that we might call "parasitic" and "productive," respectively. Parasitic self-indulgence merely takes what you have and gives it to me. No more is created in the transaction, and the range of inequality may even be widened. Productive self-indulgence uses the system to produce more for me, while leaving you what you already have; here too, the range of inequality may be widened.

Indeed, the purpose of self-indulgence is self-advancement at the expense of other groups and individuals. This is not to be confused with cooperative redistribution, whose purpose is a broadbased equalization of rewards. We shall consider that option (as "cooperation") shortly.

Another solution, the exact opposite of self-indulgence, is *sacrifice*. Here, no effort is made to maximize individual well-being and every effort is aimed at maximizing collective well-being through collective strategies. However, here too we can distinguish between "productive" and "unproductive" sacrifice. Unproductive sacrifice gives you some of what I have, reducing the inequality between us; but no more is created. Productive sacrifice uses the system to produce more than before, and the new product is used to reduce the inequality between us.

A final adaptation might be called *cooperation*. The good citizen combines individual and collective strategies to pursue individual and collective goals. He/she seeks to gain greater satisfaction without hurting anyone else and, if possible, while helping someone else. This is done by cooperating with others in the search for a solution.

An example will help to understand how this works. Recall from Chapter 6 that parents of young children are very short of free time, and mothers are more deprived than fathers. Imagine that in the Jones family, Mr. Jones is dissatisfied because he only has three hours a day to relax. Mrs. Jones is also dissatisfied, and she only has one hour a day to relax. Mr. Jones wants to close the gap between what he has and what he wants.

He can accommodate, by simply shutting his eyes to the situation, by waiting for the children to grow up and leave home. Or he can mythologize about the nobility of hard work and how, in years to come, he will be rewarded for his unstinting efforts on his children's behalf. He may even tell his wife that she is a "real woman" and he thinks he will keep her. In both scenarios, Mr. Jones retains three hours of rest and Mrs. Jones one hour.

On the other hand, Mr. Jones may reduce his own dissatisfaction by exploiting his wife: he may pass on a few of his chores, so that he now has four hours of rest a day and she has none. This is the "unproductive" form of exploitation. Or, Mr. Jones may figure out a way of reducing the household workload through better planning, so that he has two more hours of rest a day. Now, he has five hours and his wife still has one: the domestic inequality has widened to 5-to-1 from an original 3-to-1 ratio. This is productive exploitation, "productive" in the sense that it has improved the domestic system (but "exploitation" in the sense that inequality has widened as a result).

Or, Mr. Jones may reduce his own dissatisfaction by reducing the household workload through better planning, and pass on some of the benefit to his wife. Imagine that his plan has freed up two hours a day. If he takes one free hour and Mrs. Jones takes the other, each will have gained more rest and the level of domestic inequality will also have narrowed to 2-to-1 from an original 3-to-1. This cooperative adaptation does not produce equality but it increases the well-being of both spouses, that is, the collective well-being.

Finally, Mr. Jones may choose to sacrifice his own immediate well-being in the interests of his wife's greater well-being, domestic equality and, thereby, collective well-being. He may value this on principle or because he believes it will lead to greater marital harmony. In either case, he may sacrifice unproductively (giving up one free hour a day to Mrs. Jones) or productively (keeping his three hours and "finding" two more for Mrs. Jones through better planning). Both strategies create an equality of free time in the household.

As we have seen in this example, sacrifice and cooperation are potentially system-changing adaptations, while accommodation, mythologizing, and exploitation are system-preserving ones. System-changing adaptations require collective action and attention to collective well-being. Thus, the most effective individual strategies are linked to collective strategies, and they are bound to change the system of inequality in society or in a household.

To use these strategies we must be alert to the ways individual problems and collective problems are related. Second, we must be aware of what is truly possible, and seek satisfaction in that realm. On the other hand, we can allow ourselves to feel satisfied with accommodation when faced with the truly impossible. If given the opportunity to make "truly possible" changes, satisfaction is warranted when we have actively sought to make them through cooperation or sacrifice. By this scheme of thinking, "exploitation" never justifies satisfaction, since it preserves and even worsens the problem many people are facing.

Following the same reasoning, you should not feel dissatisfied if you have fought the good fight—cooperated or sacrificed. Under these conditions, you are not to blame for failing to achieve the truly possible, nor for giving in to existing circumstances. More likely than not, you have enjoyed the fight; and you may want to fight on. What, generally, should people do to close the gap between what they have and what they want, particularly when this gap is the result of structured social inequality? How should they think about the problem?

Steps to Real Paradise

Prescribing lives for other people is risky, even foolhardy. This book will not tell you what the Good Life is, nor specifically how to find it. But implied in all that has come before is a method for thinking about your own life if you want to make it more satisfying. Though we recognize its many faults, we cannot think of a better method, so we offer it for your consideration. Use it if it seems useful.

First, analyse your own state of mind and present course of action. What do you want and are you getting it, or likely to get it, by the course you are presently following? Do people customarily get that outcome when they do what you are doing? Are you so different from the rest that you can expect a different outcome? Are there other outcomes, offered by other courses of action, that might prove even more satisfying? How likely are you to change your mind about what you want, but find yourself locked in by the decisions you are taking now? Can you think of a plan that would work toward your present goal but leave the door open for changes if you change your mind?

Second, analyse the relationship between your present course of action and the outcome you desire. If the desired outcome is unlikely, is that because of a personal deficiency or a structured inequality in society, a private trouble or a public issue? Are you prevented from taking another course of action that is likelier to produce the results you want? If so, is that because of a personal deficiency or structured inequality?

Third, analyse the contours of "the possible." Would it be harder to change your present course of action to one that will likely produce the desired outcome; or change the likelihood that your present course of action will yield the desired outcome? Which change is most possible in general? That is, which change are people already making most successfully? Which change is becoming more likely to succeed?

Fourth, analyse the strategies that are available, where change is demonstrably possible. *How* are people making the changes that are already succeeding, or increasingly likely to succeed? Is it through individual actions or collective actions; and what kinds of actions are they? Are they occurring in places (and times) similar to our own, or very different ones? How does this similarity (or difference) reflect on their usefulness in our own society today?

Fifth, analyse your ability and willingness to undertake these strategies. Given the possibility of their success, are you—the person you are today—able to use these strategies? If not, how would you have to change yourself to be able to use them in the future? Would you, for example, have to shift your concerns from a focus on short-term goals to a focus on long-term goals? Or from a preference for individual solutions to an acceptance of collective solutions? How would such shifts affect your social relations, or your attainment of other goals that may also attract you? Can you tolerate the consequences of these shifts?

Sixth, analyse the steps you must take to actually carry out these changes. Given your ability to shift to new, more successful strategies, what should you do first? Is there a group to join? A credential to gain? A commitment to make? Do you need more money or free time to make these changes, and if so, how can you get them? Are you able and willing to wait until you have the information, contacts, time, or money you need to carry out this new strategy?

Seventh, analyse the alternative, do-nothing strategy. If you cannot demonstrate to your own satisfaction that change is possible; or if possible in general, that it is possible for a person like you; or if possible for a person like you, that it is possible through a means you can accept; or if possible through a means you can accept, that it is possible given your personal resources—if you cannot accept these possibilities—then you are voting for resignation or accommodation. Can you imagine living with it in future, or will you regret having done nothing? If accommodation means that from now on, you will have to want what you can get, and what you will get is not what you currently want, can you see yourself accepting that state of affairs? If not, go back to Step Number Two.

CONCLUDING REMARKS

The Preface indicated that this book would be about one of social science's classic concerns: namely, the relationship between consciousness and social structure. We have aimed to discuss this complicated issue in relatively simple terms. Accordingly, we have translated issues of consciousness—values, perceptions, aspirations, and expectations, among others—into questions of "what you want"; and questions of social structure—limits on your ability to choose freely among desired alternatives—into questions of "what you get." Thus, the book has been, on the surface, about the relationship between what you want and what you get.

We have noted the congruence, for most people at most ages, between what they want and what they get. Two alternative explanations of this congruence are possible. One is the liberal (ideological) explanation, which argues that people generally get what they want if they approach the matter correctly. The other, a sociological explanation, argues that people are more likely to bring their desires into conformity with what is possible while preserving the illusion of choice. We have noted that, in fact, most people do both. As well, they consider and often carry through strategies for closing the gap.

In a modern society, people want choice and the knowledge they have choices to make. Life without choice is demoralizing, deadening. People who think they have no choices fail to make choices when they are truly available, or make bad choices when several possibilities are offered. In fact we all have some choices to make in life and have to practice making them well. This book has urged you to choose wisely, carefully, and with awareness.

This is *not* to argue that your choice is unlimited; in fact, it argues the opposite. If choice were unlimited, wrong choices would have no important consequences; you could always make a right choice that remedied the wrong one you had made earlier. But in fact, your present choices are limited by past choices as well as by the choices other people are making and by factors such as the class structure which are not, in any real sense, chosen by most of us at all.

Without the possibility of choice, however constrained, morality has no meaning. Morality means taking responsibility for your actions. People are not always responsible for the direction their life has taken, for they are not always in control. When they are, sometimes they are not aware of choosing, or their range of choices may be so small as to offer no real choice at all. Still, if we want to preserve the framework of a moral society, we must preserve the responsibility, and opportunity, of individuals to choose as freely and wisely as they possibly can.

All choice is constrained or limited, and we typically act to satisfy, not optimize, our desires. No other type of action makes sense. Yet even well-informed people vary in what they believe to be possible. This book has not aimed to make you set your sights lower, to get you to make the easiest or most popular choices. Rather it has aimed to make you aware of choosing and the limits placed on your choosing; and to make you ask whether our society might be better—freer, fairer, more moral—than it is today.

In the first chapter, we learned that a Real Paradise has two elements: moral sensibility and a knowledge of the possible. Moral sensibility demands an awareness of what a "worthwhile life" and a "good society" might look like. Few people besides philosophers are encouraged to think about these questions; many think they are nonscientific and therefore merely speculative or idiosyncratic concerns.

Yet making a good society and a worthwhile life presupposes planning, both individual and collective, which in turn presupposes conceiving of the goal. Whether the desired goal should be "the greatest satisfaction for the greatest number" or something else is beyond the competence of this present book. But the question should not be dismissed from consideration because it challenges the tools of analysis currently at our disposal.

"Good information" is something we *can* do something about more readily. We know a lot about the forces that limit the information people have at their disposal. According to the multiple discrepancy theory (discussed in Chapter 1), people set low goals for themselves because they make modest comparisons, comparisons with others like themselves. They judge the possible from their own history and the life histories of others just like them. More and better information about the attainability of other lives might lead to behavioural change—both individual and collective—that would make people's desires a reality.

We all need to seek better information about what is truly possible. Sociology is, in one sense, the study of the possible, since it is the study of what already is—lives that certain individuals, groups, or societies are already living. We are less readily manipulated into downward accommodation when we know that alternatives are possible, even if they are difficult and require collective, long-term thinking.

In closing, then, this book carries no simple message. It is not intended to make you accept your life *or* reject it, but to make you question it. Question your life more systematically, with information and awareness. Above all, recognize that as human beings we all make choices, however constrained. The future we shall choose, individually and collectively, and the best means for achieving that future, are yet to be determined. How well you construct your own future will demonstrate whether you have understood the purpose of this book.

REFERENCES

BARRACLOUGH, G. (1967). *An introduction to contemporary history.* Harmondsworth: Penguin.

CLOWARD, R. & OHLIN, L. (1960). *Delinquency and opportunity.* New York: Free Press.

DURKHEIM, E. (1965 [1983]). *The division of labor in society.* New York: Free Press.

———. *Suicide: A study of sociology.* J. Spaulding and G. Simpson, Trans. New York: Free Press.

HIRSCHI, T. (1969). *Causes of delinquency.* Berkeley: University of California Press.

HOBSBAWM, E. J. (1959). *Primitive rebels: Studies in archaic forms of social movement in the 19th and 20th centuries.* New York: Norton.

HOMANS, G. C. (1974). *Social behavior: Its elementary forms.* (rev. ed.) New York: Harcourt Brace Jovanovich.

KANTER, R. M. (1972). *Commitment and community: Communes and utopias in sociological perspective.* Cambridge: Harvard University Press.

————. (1977). *Men and women of the corporation.* New York: Basic Books.

LIPSET, S. M., TROW, M., & COLEMAN, J. (1963). *Union democracy: The internal politics of the international typographical union.* Garden City, N.Y.: Anchor Books, Doubleday.

MARX, K. (1955). *The communist manifesto.* S. H. Beer (Ed.). New York: Appleton Century-Crofts.

MERTON, R. K. (1957a). Social structure and anomie. In *Social theory and social structure* (pp. 131–60). (rev. ed.) New York: Free Press.

————. (1957b). Patterns of influence: Local and cosmopolitan influentials. In *Social Theory and Social Structure* (pp. 387–420).

————. (1966). Social problems and sociological theory. In R. K. Merton & R. A. Nisbet (Eds.), *Contemporary social problems* (pp. 775–823). (2nd ed.). New York: Harcourt, Brace and World.

MICHELS, R. (1962). *Political parties.* New York: Free Press.

RECKLESS, W. C. (1961). A new theory of delinquency and crime. *Federal Probation, 25,* 42–46.

INDEX